Shembe, Ancestors, *and* Christ

American Society of Missiology Monograph Series

THE ASM MONOGRAPH SERIES provides a forum for publishing quality dissertations and studies in the field of missiology. Collaborating with Pickwick Publications—a division of Wipf and Stock Publishers of Eugene, Oregon—the American Society of Missiology selects high quality dissertations and other monographic studies that offer research materials in mission studies for scholars, mission and church leaders, and the academic community at large. The ASM seeks scholarly work for publication in the Series that throws light on issues confronting Christian world mission in its cultural, social, historical, biblical, and theological dimensions.

Missiology is an academic field that brings together scholars whose professional training ranges from doctoral-level preparation in areas such as scripture, history and sociology of religions, anthropology, theology, international relations, interreligious interchange, mission history, inculturation, and church law. The American Society of Missiology, which sponsors this series, is an ecumenical body drawing members from Independent and Ecumenical Protestant, Catholic, Orthodox, and other traditions. Members of the ASM are united by their commitment to reflect on and do scholarly work relating to both mission history and the present-day mission of the church. The ASM Monograph Series aims to publish works of exceptional merit on specialized topics, with particular attention given to work by younger scholars, the dissemination and publication of which is difficult under the economic pressures of standard publishing models.

Persons seeking information about the ASM or the guidelines for having their dissertations considered for publication in the ASM Monograph Series should consult the Society's website—www.asmweb.org.

Members of the ASM Monograph Committee who approved this book are:

Gary B. McGee
Assemblies of God Theological Seminary, Springfield, Missouri

Anthony Gittins
Catholic Theological Union, Chicago

Dana Lee Robert
Boston University School of Theology

Shembe, Ancestors, *and* Christ

*A Christological Inquiry
with Missiological Implications*

EDLEY J. MOODLEY

American Society of Missiology
Monograph Series

2

PICKWICK *Publications* · Eugene, Oregon

SHEMBE, ANCESTORS, AND CHRIST
A Christological Inquiry with Missiological Implications

American Society of Missiology Monograph Series 2

Copyright © 2008 by Edley J. Moodley
All rights reserved. No part of this publication may be reproduced or transmitted in any form, electronic or mechanical, or stored on any information storage and retrieval system without prior permission in writing from the publishers. For permissions write to Wipf & Stock Publishers, 199 W. 8th Avenue, Suite 3, Eugene OR 97401.

Pickwick Publications
A Division of Wipf and Stock Publishers
199 W. 8th Ave., Suite 3
Eugene, OR 97401

Unless otherwise indicated, scripture quotations are taken from the Holy Bible, *New International Version*®. Copyright © 1973, 1978, 1984 by International Bible Society. Used by permission of Zondervan Publishing House. All rights reserved.

Scripture quotations marked NKJV are taken from the *New King James Version*. Copyright © 1979, 1980, 1982, 1990, 1995, Thomas Nelson, Inc., Publishers.

Scripture quotations marked KJV are from the King James Version.

Scriptures marked NRSV are taken from the *New Revised Standard Version* of the Bible. Copyright © 1989 by the Division of Christian Education of the National Council of the Churches of Christ in the USA. Used by permission.

ISBN 13: 978-1-55635-880-7

Cataloguing-In-Publication data:

Moodley, Edley J.

Shembe, ancestors, and Christ : a christological inquiry with missiological implications / Edley J. Moodley

American Society of Missiology Monograph Series 2

xx + 252 p. ; 23 cm. Includes bibliographical references.

ISBN 13: 978-1-55635-880-7

1. South Africa—Church history. 2. Shembe Church. 3. Ancestor worship—Africa. 4. Religion and culture—Africa. I. Title. II. Series.

Manufactured in the United States of America

Books published in the American Society of Missiology Scholarly monograph series are chosen on the basis of their academic quality as responsible contributions to debate and dialogue about issues in mission studies. The opinions expressed in the book are those of the authors and are not represented to be those of the American Society of Missiology or its members.

Contents

List of Figures ✦ *vi*
List of Tables ✦ *vii*
Foreword by Howard A. Snyder ✦ *ix*
Preface ✦ *xi*
Acknowledgements ✦ *xiii*
Introduction by Eunice Irwin ✦ *xv*

1. The Genesis of a Journey of Discovery ✦ 1
2. African and Zulu Traditional Religions: Views on God, Spirits, Ancestors, Traditional Leaders, and Healing ✦ 31
3. The African Initiated Churches: History, Beliefs, and Practices ✦ 58
4. The Religious and Cultural Worldview of the amaNazaretha Church ✦ 87
5. Recounting Stories (Research Findings) ✦ 101
6. Participant Observation in the amaNazaretha Church and an Interview with Vimbeni Shembe ✦ 145
7. Theology and Christology in the amaNazaretha Church ✦ 163
8. Conclusions, Missiological Implications, and Suggestions for Further Study ✦ 189

Epilogue ✦ *211*
Appendix: Statistical Data of Interviewees ✦ *213*
Bibliography ✦ *217*
Index ✦ *243*

Figures

1. A Typology of Sets ✦ 12
2. Four-Part Classification of African Independent Churches ✦ 13
3. The Basis for a Typology of African Prayer: Formal and Experiential Prayer ✦ 19
4. The Centrality of Religion in African Life ✦ 32
5. Facets that Make Up African Religion ✦ 33
6. Hierarchical Structure of the Spirit World ✦ 38
7. African Initiated Churches: A Typology ✦ 62
8. Symmetrical Mediation ✦ 166
9. One Form, Multiple Meanings ✦ 182
10. Several Forms, Same Meaning ✦ 182
11. A Revision of Turner's Four-Part Classification of New Religious Movements that Accommodates the Category of Post-Christian Groups ✦ 203

Tables

1. Theoretical Framework ✦ 9
2. Data from Sermon Extrapolation ✦ 152

Foreword

CHRISTOLOGY AND ECCLESIOLOGY—THE MEANING of Jesus Christ and his body, the church—are perennial issues in Christian theology, and both are especially crucial today. This important volume touches on both as it investigates the Shembe movement in the dynamic context of Christianity in contemporary Africa.

Most non-African Christians have probably heard of the so-called African Independent Churches (AICs), more accurately designated African Initiated Churches, but may know little about them. The label covers a range of diverse movements, and Moodley helpfully distinguishes between the varieties of movements and explains what we need to know about them. This discussion, together with his delineation of the character of African traditional religion, provides very helpful background for his in-depth study of Shembe and his movement.

This study has many strengths. I point to three in particular. First, the author's own location as a South African Pentecostal gives him empathy and insight that lend depth to the description and analysis. Moodley strives to understand the Shembe movement on its own terms.

Second, Moodley was able to gain unusual access to members and leaders of the movement, including a very significant interview with Shembe, the current leader and grandson of the founder. Through sensitivity and persistence over a period of years, the author was able to conduct very effective participant-observation research.

A third strength of this study is its theological, anthropological, and missiological depth. By focusing especially on Christology and the question of mediatorship—in other words, ultimately the question of the basis of salvation, from a Christian standpoint—Moodley delineates a set of findings that have considerable relevance beyond the immediate African context.

This book significantly deepens our understanding of an influential movement and the issues it raises for the practice of faithful Christian mission today.

Howard A. Snyder, PhD
Professor Emeritus, History and Theology of Mission
E. Stanley Jones School of World Mission and Evangelism
Asbury Theological Seminary

Preface

EARLY MISSIONARY ENDEAVORS HAVE certainly contributed to the spreading of the gospel across the continent of Africa to the point that today the center of gravity for the Christian movement has shifted southward and Africa is becoming the most Christian continent in the world. Nevertheless, the missionary enterprise was never intended to be merely a head count of persons joining a Christian church. At the heart of the Christian gospel is the incarnated Christ, whose words and works penetrate cultures across the world, drawing men and women to himself. In the words of Paul, "God was [and is] in Christ reconciling the world to Himself" (2 Cor 5:19). In living out their Christianity through the idiom of their own language and culture, the African Initiated Churches (AICs) claim to be such an expression of Christianity on the continent of Africa.

Isaiah Shembe (1867-1935), who received his catechetical instruction in a Wesleyan church and later joined the African Baptist Church, became an itinerant preacher in South Africa in the early 1900s. Through his charismatic gifting of healing and exorcisms, Shembe soon commanded a following. The amaNazaretha Church of Isaiah Shembe was formed in 1911. The church has grown tremendously to approximately two million members and has experienced three leadership changes since its founding in 1911. The current leader is Vimbeni Shembe, a grandson of the founder. From my study of the literature, I discovered that most scholars of the movement (such as Oosthuizen, Hexham, and Becken, *inter alia*) concluded that even by the time of his death in 1935, Isaiah Shembe was already deified by his ardent followers.

The question pursued in this study is whether Jesus Christ is still central in the lives of the amaNazaretha adherents after almost one hundred years of the church's existence. Hence the purpose of this study was to discover if the amaNazaretha Church today is a Christward movement. A Christward movement is defined as one that affirms that "Jesus is Lord," where people acknowledge and receive the person and works of Christ on the basis of the past (his work of atonement), present (his mediatorial role and intercession on our behalf), and future (his second coming in glory as the Christian hope). Three critical areas are the focus in the study: the role of Shembe, the role of ancestors, and the role of Jesus Christ as expressed in the life-world of the amaNazaretha adherents. If Shembe and ancestors still serve in mediatorial roles for the amaNazaretha members, then what role does Jesus Christ have in the lives of these people?

The study begins with an overview of African Traditional Religions and proceeds specifically to Zulu Traditional Religion, as the amaNazaretha membership are predominately Zulu speakers. It is argued that traditional aspects of Zulu religion and culture are carried over into their new religious belief system. I then offer a brief study of an African Initiated Church, namely the Zion Christian Church in South Africa, as one expression of African indigenous Christianity and show how this church contrasts with the amaNazaretha Church. Research was conducted over a period of thirteen months between January 2000 and January 2003, and included an interview with the current leader, Vimbeni Shembe. The study concludes with an evaluation of the amaNazaretha Church in the light of the status and role of Shembe, the ancestor, and Jesus Christ. The conclusion is that the amaNazaretha Church is not a Christward movement and that the role of Christ has been replaced by ancestors and Shembe. The study concludes with implications for missiology that emanate from this study, and further areas for research are proposed.

Acknowledgements

THIS STUDY, THE CULMINATION of a seven-year journey, is a revision of my PhD dissertation completed in March 2004. It was my good fortune to be brought into contact with significant people whose contributions to this project were indeed immeasurable.

In this regard, I have had the unique privilege of working with two gifted mentors. First, I offer my sincere thanks to Dr. Eunice Irwin, a constructive critic and friend, who taught me the art of critical thinking. Unfortunately her sabbatical prevented her from guiding my study project through to completion. Second, I wish to express my gratitude to Dr. Darrell Whiteman, who in the absence of Eunice Irwin, graciously offered to mentor me in the most critical phase of my writing, and also helped me through my dissertation defense. His selfless generosity and judicious observations helped me bring this project to a successful conclusion.

I wish also to thank the members of my dissertation committee, Dr. Howard Snyder and Dr. Terry Muck, for their helpful comments throughout this project, especially from their respective disciplines of theology and religious studies. My thanks also go to Dr. Dale Walker who read my manuscript. In the same breath, I wish to thank the whole faculty and staff of the E. Stanley Jones School of World Mission and Evangelism for nurturing an environment where integrity, spirituality, and a passion for kingdom work coalesce so beautifully.

I am also indebted to the staff of the B. L. Fisher Library for accommodating my numerous requests for library items not available in our library, some of them not even in the United States. My thanks and appreciation go to Dr. William Faupel, Dorothy James, and Jeff Hiatt.

I wish to record my sincere gratitude to my research assistant, Joseph Mhlongo, who assisted me with translations and also helped me navigate my way through the sociocultural and religious life-world of the amaNazaretha movement. Several members of the amaNazaretha Church helped me network with potential interviewees during my field research. My thanks go to Ministers Ngidi, Gcwenza, and Mpanza, and Evangelist Mpanza. Bishop Vimbeni Shembe graciously allowed me to conduct my research at the church's center, Ebuhleni, and also granted me an inter-

Acknowledgements

view. Professor Pippin Oosthuizen, a leading authority in South Africa on the AICs, encouraged me and offered me invaluable leads during the research in South Africa.

I owe a special debt of gratitude to Dr. Paul Conn, president of Lee University, whose generous summer grants afforded me the opportunity to travel to South Africa to complete my field research. My thanks and appreciation also go to Dr. Carolyn Dirksen, vice president for Academic Affairs, Lee University, for graciously granting me the space and time to complete my writing. I also wish to thank Dr. Jerome Boone, chair of the Christian Ministries Department, for his encouragement and support throughout the project. For friendship, counsel, and encouragement, I extend my sincere thanks to my colleagues, Dr. Emerson Powery, Dr. Michael Fuller, Dr. Rolando Cuellar, and Dr. Rob Debelak.

Finally, I wish to acknowledge my debt of gratitude to my family. To my wife, Flora, who assumed the dual role of homemaker and breadwinner, and who supported me with understanding and encouragement, I offer my thanks. To my daughters, Deborah and Eleanor, my granddaughter, Kjeersten, and my son-in-law, Jason, who all graciously and with understanding accommodated my long and frequent absences from home and family functions, I offer my sincere thanks.

Introduction

THE STORY OF THIS book can be traced to the summer of 1997 when faculty of the School of World Mission and Evangelism entertained prospective student Edley Moodley during a campus visit to Asbury Theological Seminary. A central question surfaced early in the interview: In doing PhD research, could a dissertation be written on the Ibandla lamaNazaretha, the large and well-established religious movement founded in 1911 by Isaiah Shembe in KwaZulu-Natal, South Africa? The Shembe headquarters was in his region, and he had some knowledge of their beliefs from prior readings.

Convenience, as it turned out, was not the real attraction. As a child living in Durban, South Africa, Edley became intrigued by the vibrant worship of the new movements. A women's prayer group from a nearby African Independent Church gathered regularly in the dining room of his grandmother's rented cottage. The origin of this book rightly belongs to those years of watching and wondering about the spirituality of the dynamic African movements, when his curiosity first framed questions about the faith that sustained indigenous prayer practices.

It is my honor to introduce the book you will read. It is the fruit of a colleague's industrious work in mission studies and prompted by his quest for answers. It is his discovery of how African spirituality encountered Christianity in the life of a remarkable Zulu prophet, and how the message he brought has been appropriated by the prophet's successors and members of his community.

Theology of Christ

The study of Isaiah Shembe and the amaNazaretha done by Edley Moodley marks a new attempt at theological inquiry into African Christology. Without relying exclusively on the movement's written materials or formal statements of belief, he constructed a research methodology adequate to identify, measure, and judge members' actual dependence on Jesus Christ. His approach was to locate phenomena of worship and prayer within the movement, then to construct provisional theological interpretation of their meaning. Finally, he drew conclusions through corroboration and

Introduction

verification. To his credit, although he applied Christian standards to his data, he did not impose foreign interpretations upon his findings or in ways unfaithful to members' self-representations.

Moodley investigated liturgies, celebrations, services, and daily religious practices in order to establish the presence of implicit theological understandings of Christ in the Shembe movement. He then noted whether the views of Christ were compatible with Christological norms articulated in the Western tradition of Christianity. To uncover faith components in everyday life, he elicited from members and leaders understandings of blessing, power, prayer, healing, destiny, and community—finding that ideas originated within and beyond the boundaries of circulating texts, written or verbal, Christian or Nazarite. The research surfaced a complex mix of messianic and biblical themes, having vague and peripheral reference to Christ but primary reference to founder Isaiah Shembe. He concluded that the Shembe movement in practice and intention is incompatible with any normative Christian standard or faith posture. These matters were evident: lack of desire for personal relatedness to Jesus Christ and absence of commitment to rely on the sole mediation of Christ in worship, intercessory prayer, or as the one hope of life after death.

Broad sampling of members was central to the research process. Persons from several levels of the amaNazaretha group were chosen as contributors in order to test consistency of religious understandings and patterns of faith. Participant observations and interviews of members were conducted at local "churches" in urban and rural areas. This generated new information, fresh articulations, about existential points of faith—the "substance of [their] things not seen"—which had not been conveyed in doctrines. To verify findings, Edley initiated specific dialogues with Shembe and his close leaders, and with his own research assistant, Joseph Mhlongo, who had years of experience in the religion. The conclusion was that Ibandla lamaNazaretha identity was not "Christian" nor was it "Christward"—that is, moving toward greater acceptance of Christ.

The study's findings do contribute toward clearer understanding of how the acts of prayer and worship in the encounter with God also involve recognition and honor given to the founder of their community. This adds to comprehension of important cultural factors limiting the view of Christ within theological systems of African Independent Churches as well as other new religious movements. Learning where to refocus theological and cultural discussion of Christ may reveal real yet provisional stepping-stones on the path to further refining of the movement's theology.

Introduction

The study makes a contribution by introducing phenomenological research as a method for gathering important empirical data for theology. This meets an essential need for firsthand research on new movements. Articulations captured provide new "texts" for theological discussion.

What It Is and What It Is Not

Edley Moodley's research demonstrates that the Shembe movement is not "Christward." That does close a first door of entry into conversation with Western Christianity's orthodoxy. But today it leads to a second door, opened widely now, where indigenous Christian theologians and historians (Bediako, Sanneh, Oborji, among others) are taking part in African Christianity's most urgent and definitive theological debates. What can be the relationship between Africa's prior knowledge of God found in its heritage (anchored in the ancestors and prophets) and its later knowledge of God through the Western presentation of the gospel of Christ (estranged from African culture and requiring a foreign form of Christianity)? While discussion in this study occurs in the context of the first room (Western Christian orthodoxy), the data can be useful to discussions in the second room (formulation of African Christian theology). The desire for missional encounter remains present. A few strategies are suggested, including further exploration of amaNazaretha openness to dialogue with self-identified Christians.

This study draws new lines for engagement. Important points identified in the study would suggest a theological prolegomenon is essential to undergird future dialogue. The list of points to consider would include but not be limited to themes recurring in the amaNazaretha tradition of faith and in the Christian tradition, often found in borrowed or conflated patterns.

Theology of Revelation

Western Christianity's theology of revelation—often too linear, too distant, too narrowly focused, and too bound to literary tradition—will encounter a local theologizing of Africans where discerning authoritative persons and "scriptures" is done through dramatic revelatory portrayals, in ways that make religious knowledge very present, very tangible, and very much remembered via rich orality. This may shift strategies for dialogue concerning the movement's several operative testaments—African religious heritage, the Old Testament, the New Testament, Shembe's life and contributions, and Christ's teachings, to name the obvious sources.

Introduction

Narrative theologizing will challenge yet broaden ways of discerning the revelation of God.

Western Christianity and amaNazaretha tradition affirm God's revelation in two testaments: Creation and Christ. Yet, why is the additional "testament of Shembe" so vital to Nazarite spirituality? Readers of the Creation testament (revelation to all peoples and to Israel) from Western perspective must allow for the possibility of significant interpretive inferences when humanity, in whatever situations, is found desiring relationship with God via wisdom given their human leaders. God "divinely appointed" such leaders to guide communities. Extraordinary spiritual powers are given to prophets on behalf of their communities to bless them, preserve them, and create a peaceful and strong life. Symbolic titles like "healer," "mediator," and "divine ruler" are thus indigenous anticipatory prefigurements that were meant to typify and dramatize recognitions of God's ultimate choice, Christ. Thus, as humans they must remain within a culture's collective memory and be "relatable" to historical events.

Isaiah Shembe's role, at the very least, testifies of God's faithfulness to raise the honor of the Zulu people, when during a time of spiritual and cultural extremity, a messiah was sent. His role evokes memory today through participation in ritual and celebration, causing the amaNazaretha to experience past awareness of the human-mediated revelatory presence of God among them. The role remains consistent with African religious history. This could open up theological "narratives" of Shembe's and Christ's messianic roles. The Gospels follow the crisis of interpreting Christ's role; both Jewish leaders and Jesus' disciples were required to determine Christ's self-claims to divine status on behalf of the nation's welfare. Such texts in conversation anticipate a fuller Christology.

Theology of Message and Messengers

Isaiah Shembe himself studied and interpreted the gospel in terms of African culture. His message was comprehensive, covering all areas of life. He provided the pattern by embodying it and making it available to followers wherever he went. Dialogue should consider the impossibility of an absolute separation between the message and the messenger as it would come in African context. This speaks, too, of a radical renewal of the apostolic ministry of Christ's church.

Theology of the Holy Spirit and the Trinity

The study adds to the growing evidence that the triune God is at work in and through the cultures of the earth, preparing and present in the new religious conversations, and drawing Africans to faith in Jesus Christ. The thesis of the Holy Spirit's activities prior to the arrival of the gospel is unquestioned. What is seen is the theological tension between recognition of the Spirit's work through black "messiah" figures and the recognition of the Spirit as it came in the flesh of God in Christ. Such encounter is found in the biblical story of John the Baptist and his role. Spirit-empowered to revive authentic faith in God in Israel, he glimpses and trusts in the Christ as God's Messiah. Isaiah Shembe is a similar paradoxical figure to John the Baptist. This comparison could start productive inquiry into Christology.

This leads to the necessity for theological discussion of canonical unfolding of Christian faith with reference to the Bible's use. Old Testament law, prophetic offices, and messianic forerunners precede New Testament narratives of Jesus' moral teachings. The connection between the two testaments can be seen. They had to converge in a person whose identity was not limited to Israel or to white Christians, but who had vital connections with the suffering servant of Isaiah; the lawgiver Moses; the healer Elijah; the father of the nation of Israel, Abraham; and the common ancestor and progenitor, Adam. This person is Jesus Christ. Every person in the Old Testament through whom spiritual understanding and ritual came has been mentioned in the New Testament accounts of the story of Jesus.

Isaiah Shembe in his own personhood does not make those claims. Rather, his role is decidedly related to prophetic and messianic offices on behalf of one nation. He role is seen as partial and related to the Zulu nation.

Theology of Spiritual Connectedness

The founder's roles as prophet, healer, messiah, and elevated ancestor have overtones of Christian theology. Dialogue should raise issues regarding the need for ongoing representation through his successors' earthly presence and actions on behalf of the nation. If the "spirit of Shembe" is divine, why does its presence require a human person's flesh in order to become operative? Issues of lineage and African destiny must be raised as well as issues regarding physical versus spiritual discipleship.

Theology of a Shared Ethnic Identity Having Divine Destiny— Life, Death, and Future Hope in the Community

The research highlighted discovery of religious relationships equally as much as collection and categorization of religious concepts. Moodley's research methods sought to preserve the spiritual integrity of the religious acts within the group settings, valuing corporate identity as a possible constructive location from which to build meta-cultural and meta-theological bridges so that Zulu Christians could theologize in the presence of their Nazarite kinfolk.

Isaiah Shembe's efforts restored spiritual life and brought physical survival to the Zulu nation through laws, teachings, and reinstitution of cultural customs. Their future destiny, however, remained at risk until they had enthroned Shembe as a special mediator on behalf of their lineage. How culturally fixed lineage needs do and do not encounter conflicts with the claims of Christ, whose promise is of eternal life shared with people from every tongue and tribe and nation (also fulfilling his own lineage through Israel), is an important point for discussion.

What the Movement Has Become and What It Will Be

Study of the new movements in Africa is not a new endeavor. Currently, African scholars participate in this, along with a few senior missiologists. Together they are leading the way to a new comprehension of religious groups, beyond the mission and independent church divide and the use of Western narrowly defined and less useful categories of theology. Their efforts will bring African Christians from the independence of nations to the independence of theology. Where are we in seeing this happen?

It is important to set an agenda that encourages the articulation of faith and fulfillment of spiritual aspirations. This will not bypass Christian doctrine but locate it within stories and histories of God's revelation and Christian presence. Edley Moodley has added to this agenda through his own writing. He is a valuable and capable researcher of new religious movements. As African-born and having observed the struggle between the old and the new, he understands the theological urgency for identity. His cultural roots and continuing connections to South Africa will keep him involved in extending this academic project and taking on new ones like it in the future.

Eunice Irwin, Ph.D.
Associate Professor of Christian Mission and Contextual Theology
E. Stanley Jones School of World Mission and Evangelism
Asbury Theological Seminary

I

The Genesis of a Journey of Discovery

IN MY CHILDHOOD DAYS, I recall observing a woman's group of the African Zion Church conducting their worship services in the dining room of our rented cottage in Durban, South Africa. I looked forward to Wednesday afternoons when this group of women, some thirty in number, would gather for their weekly meeting. Keen in my memory are the beating of the drums, women singing beautifully in heavenly harmony, exorcisms and healing practices, and the intense yet passionate worship to their God, *Unkulunkulu*. All this fascinated me, yet the meetings struck me as odd and quite different from our "Christian" way of worship. The manner in which they invoked the Spirit, *Umoya*, seemed rather bizarre. At the tender age of seven or eight, I thought that perhaps if they attended *our* church they might learn to have church the "correct" way, and the "correct" way was *our* way. These contextual "oddities" and other unique cultural expressions of the Christian faith have not been discerned clearly by people outside of the African Independent Churches (AICs), and there has been a rush to judgment on African Christian beliefs and practices.

My interest in and appreciation of African Christianity, though submerged in the intervening years, was to surface via my theological studies at the University of South Africa (UNISA) in an undergraduate course on the *African Independent Churches*, taught by M. L. Daneel, who worked among the Shona in Zimbabwe for several decades.

Following my initial exposure to African forms of worship, my studies at UNISA, further reading in my graduate and doctoral programs, and my work among Africans in South Africa and neighboring countries, I have become acutely aware of the diverse, rich, and varied expressions of the Christian faith, especially among the AICs.

In the era of apartheid, research on the AICs done by missionaries and anthropologists was not intended for reconciliation among the churches. Rather, the research focused more on the causes for dissension and secession, and it often emphasized syncretistic practices in the fledgling indigenous churches.[1] Today, with the advent of democracy and the abolition of apartheid, researchers may now study, live, and work among Africans without government restrictions. In this era of a new democratic South Africa, a researcher has the opportunity to become better acquainted with the AICs and gain an insider's perspective on their culture and religious beliefs. With segregation abolished, people are more open to each other, irrespective of their racial, cultural, and linguistic identities.

However, uninformed observers of the African Initiated Churches believe that these movements are still outside the mainstream of orthodox Christianity. Although this belief is not explicitly stated, one of the reasons for such a posture is the perception that the AIC members *worship* ancestors. For example, on one of my visits to South Africa, a senior official of our church inquired about my research interest. When he learned that I was studying the amaNazaretha Church, his reaction in the form of a question was "These people worship ancestors and are not Christian, are they?" These perceptions, whether implied or stated, have distanced, if not polarized, the African Independent Churches in South Africa from other white, Indian, and coloured denominations,[2] and also from other African mission and historic churches in the country.

Although many evangelical Christians live in proximity to members of the amaNazaretha Church, both by design (government restrictions) and misperceptions regarding their religious beliefs, Christians have been separated and polarized for too long. Thus, my study of the amaNazaretha Church seeks to offer an informed and sympathetic understanding of the

---

1. See for example, Barrett, *Schism and Renewal in Africa*; Sundkler, *Bantu Prophets in South Africa*; Sundkler, *Zulu Zion and Some Swazi Zionists*.

2. The architects of apartheid in South Africa developed a framework that classified hierarchically the various race groups in the country. The white race in South Africa began with the arrival of the Dutch in 1652, followed by the British in 1820. Indians came to South Africa in 1860, upon the invitation of the British, to work as indentured laborers in the sugar and tea plantations with the option of settling in South Africa at the end of their contract. Indentured laborers continued to arrive in South Africa at regular intervals in the period between 1860 and 1911, when Indian immigration ended. The third event, a compound of several factors, was the emergence of a heterogeneous group of people called the *Coloured*, also known as *Bruinmense* in Afrikaans. This indigenous group of people is the result of the process of miscegenation between the immigrant white colonists, the local Khoisan tribe, and other imported slaves from East and West Africa, Madagascar, Malaya and other islands off the coast of East Africa. They formed what Gavin Lewis called the "impoverished rural proletariat" (*Between the Wire and the Wall*, 8), who worked as slaves in white households and farms. The apartheid structure placed whites at the top of the sociopolitical ladder with the most privileges, followed by coloureds, Indians, and then blacks at the lowest rung of the ladder.

movement and, thereby, encourages evangelical Christians to study these churches as vibrant expressions of an indigenous form of Christianity and thus as fellow sojourners en route to the eschatological kingdom of God. At the same time, where my research uncovered practices and rituals that are different from and appear to be contrary to orthodox Christianity, I believe I still have the opportunity to initiate dialogue and discussion between the AICs and other churches, hopefully leading to a greater understanding of what form Christian discipleship could take among them.

The amaNazaretha Church

Isaiah Shembe (1867–1935) founded the amaNazaretha Church in 1911, when he claimed to have received visions to "preach, heal, and drive out demons."[3] According to his son, Johannes Galilee "J. G." Shembe, Isaiah first joined a Wesleyan church where he received catechetical instruction. When denied baptism by immersion in the Wesleyan church, Isaiah found his home in a Baptist church where he felt welcomed. Shembe strictly followed the Old Testament Jewish laws and rituals, such as removing shoes during worship, leaving hair uncut, and avoiding certain foods. The Baptist pastor William Leshega could not identify with Shembe's strict adherence of Old Testament Jewish rituals. Thus, after working with Leshega for approximately three years, Shembe seceded from the Baptist Church and began an itinerant ministry.[4] He saw parallels between the Jewish Nazarite sect[5] and the African people—both were dispossessed of their land, enduring foreign (white) domination—so he launched on the quest for (African) emancipation.

Upon Isaiah Shembe's death in 1935, his son, J. G. Shembe, assumed leadership. Upon the death of J. G. Shembe in 1975, however, a leadership struggle ensued, leading to secessions and minor skirmishes.[6] J. G. Shembe's son, Londa Shembe, claimed the right of leadership on the basis of ancestral succession, and in court papers he argued that "the applicant [Amos Shembe] contends for a democratic type church whereas I contend

---

3. Oosthuizen, *Post-Christianity in Africa*, 35.

4. Becken, "The Nazareth Baptist Church of Isaiah Shembe," 101–14.

5. See Walther Eichrodt, *Theology of the Old Testament*, 303–6. The Nazarites were characterized by their extreme asceticism, and, among other things, they were distinguished by their long locks. Oosthuizen states that "the significance of the Nazarites lay in their contribution to the strengthening of the sense of nationhood and of the religious basis on which it was built" (*Post-Christianity*, 36).

6. Hexham and Oosthuizen, *The Story of Isaiah Shembe: The Continuing Story of the Sun and the Moon*, xvi.

the Church is a Chief and tribe type of Church."[7] As a result of the leadership dispute, Londa Shembe usurped control of the village Ekuphakameni with a small number of the members. Unknown assailants, however, murdered him in 1989.[8] The majority of the members with their elected leader, Amos Shembe, the younger son of Isaiah Shembe, relocated to a new center, Ebuhleni. After the death of Amos Shembe in 1996, his son, Vimbeni Shembe, was elected leader and continues to function in that capacity today, leading a group of approximately two million adherents.[9] Londa Shembe's group today numbers some one thousand members.

Oosthuizen claims that Isaiah Shembe endeavored to bring together two religions: Zulu traditions and customs and the Nazarite Old Testament tradition. Oosthuizen treated the coalescence of these two systems with some reservation.[10] He came to the conclusion that the movement is post-Christian and Isaiah Shembe had become a Zulu messiah, adding, "The movement of Shembe—the outcome of the meeting of two cultures and two religions—has developed doctrinally into a syncretistic post-Christian movement . . . ."[11]

The Zulu socioreligious system, with its demands "for a living mediator acting on the inspiration of the spirits of the chiefs and royal ancestors," brings to the forefront the question of the status and role that the amaNazaretha Church accords to Jesus Christ.[12]

Charles Nyamiti's work *Christ as our Ancestor* (1984) brings one to a stark realization that ancestors are an integral part of the religiocultural ethos of Africans. Nyamiti does not debate the fact of the status and role of

---

7. Ibid., xvii.

8. Goody has shown that succession is never axiomatic. He adds, "Even in those systems we speak of as hereditary, some element of choice is always present, the extent of option varies greatly from next-in-line succession to 'dynastic election' " (*Succession to High Office*, 13). Rynkiewich, from his case studies conducted in Micronesia, elicits what he calls "five variables" that one may encounter in leadership succession. Three of the five variables seem to be consistent with the amaNazaretha Church: (1) "There was enough ambiguity in the rules to permit several candidates to interpret that they were the rightful successor to the deceased paramount chief; (2) In addition to the formal rules, succession depended on who could gain enough support to win the initial struggle, and leadership depended on the maintenance of support for the chief to exercise the prerogatives of office; (3) There were a variety of strategies for elimination of candidates and the usurpation of office, including assassination and warfare" ("The Ossification of Local Politics," 144–65).

9. It is difficult to quantify the church, and some officials within the movement claim that the church has some four million adherents.

10. Oosthuizen, *Post-Christianity*, 36.

11. Ibid.

12. Ibid.

ancestors in the African worldview; instead, he endeavors to show how the person and work of Christ may be incorporated into the African worldview without denying the African belief in ancestors. For Nyamiti, Christ becomes the ultimate or highest in the hierarchy of ancestors.

Scholars such as Cece Kolie of Guinea, Africa, and G. C. Oosthuizen[13] emphasize that Africans attribute any illness to a disturbance of the balance between people and spiritual forces. Thus the aim of healing is to restore the equilibrium.[14] If ancestors (the spirits of the departed) were indeed mediators of healing, the Christological question would be, "What role does Christ play in mediating healing in the African hierarchy of divinities?" To answer that question, among others, it became expedient that I first study African Traditional Religions (ATRs) to understand the historical development of the ancestor cult, especially with regard to mediation in prayer and healing. Second, it was necessary to discern any shift that takes place in the worldview of Africans who are converting from ATRs to AICs and whether they move in any way toward a Christocentric position when they take on the Christian faith, and if so, what is the nature of their Christology. Since the majority of Shembe adherents belongs to the Zulu nation, a brief survey of Zulu history, religion, and culture follows in chapter 3.

The Main Contours of the Study

The purpose of this study is to discover if the amaNazaretha Church is a Christward movement. A Christward movement is one that recognizes that "Jesus is Lord." The amaNazaretha Church could be considered a Christward movement *if* it affirms "Jesus is Lord" in the sense that adherents of the Christian faith acknowledge and receive the person and work of Christ on the basis of the past (his work of atonement), present (his mediatorial role and intercession on our behalf), and future (his second coming in glory as our hope).

In Jesus Christ we encounter the one unique mediator between God and humankind. This role is so because Jesus is both God and human in one incarnate person, and it is through him that reconciliation is effected. His mediatorial role is seen in his work of atonement (death and resurrection), healing, and intercession in prayers.

---

13. See Kolie, "Jesus as Healer," 128–50; and Oosthuizen, "Baptism in the Context of the African Independent Churches," 137–88.

14. Buhrmann, "Religion and Healing," 30.

First, Christians' confidence in the atoning work of Christ becomes a reality when they discover that Jesus Christ *is* the Son of God incarnate and one with the very Being of God. Thus forgiveness and reconciliation become possible for humankind through the atonement: "God was in Christ reconciling the world to Himself" (2 Cor 5:19 NKJV).

Second, when Christians pray, Jesus acts on their behalf both as representative and in a substitutionary way. This action is possible because he is both the one who offers and the offering on the Christians' behalf. Thus, in all Christian praying, public and private, formal and informal, they come before God only through Jesus Christ, and it is he who stands in the Christians' place and prays on their behalf: "We don't know what we should pray for. But the Spirit himself prays for us. He prays with groans too deep for words" (see Rom 8:26).

Third, that healing is mediated through Jesus is evident in both the Old and New Testaments. In Isaiah's prophecy the writer states, "He was wounded for our transgressions, He was bruised for our iniquities; the chastisement for our peace was upon Him, and by His stripes we are healed" (Isa 53:5). In Hebrews the writer speaks of Jesus' high priestly role thus: "For we do not have a High Priest who cannot sympathize with our weaknesses, but was in all points tempted as we are, yet without sin" (4:15).

In order to discover what kind of Christology is held in the amaNazaretha Church, this study considers to what extent ancestors, the leader, and Jesus Christ mediate between people and God. These questions were examined primarily through field research and participant observation, with interviews in the context of the amaNazaretha Church of Isaiah Shembe as this movement continues today in Durban, South Africa. I studied the larger of the two groups, whose headquarters is at Ebuhleni. The group is led today by Vimbeni Shembe, the son of Amos Shembe and grandson of the founder, Isaiah Shembe.

There were three areas that I researched in order to determine if the amaNazaretha Church is a Christward movement: the role of Shembe, the role of ancestors, and the role of Jesus Christ. The main questions that permeate this study are the following:

1. In what way does Shembe mediate on behalf of the people?
2. What roles do ancestors play in the religiocultural ethos of the amaNazaretha Church, and what status do they hold?

3. If ancestors and the leader, Vimbeni Shembe, function as mediators, what place does Jesus Christ and the Triune God occupy in their daily practices and beliefs?
4. What is the relationship between the founding leader, Isaiah Shembe, and the Triune God?
5. How does the current leader, Vimbeni Shembe, relate to the Triune God?

Definition of Terms
Ancestor Worship and Veneration

I do not dwell much on the discussion of whether Africans worship and venerate ancestors in this study for two reasons. First, from my own research of the literature on the subject and also my field research, I come to the conclusion that this point is moot and not a major point of dissension among Africans. Second, the debate on this question has been a Western one, or a non-African one, more than an African problem. However, African writers have addressed the issue only in response to non-African views on the subject, as my research will show. Still, I offer a brief discussion of the terms below to show the complexity of imposing Western categories on African religious and cultural practices.

Worship is universal, and all cultures of the world respond in veneration to a supreme or transcendent being. Veneration, on the other hand, is "the highest degree of respect and reverence; respect mingled with awe, excited by dignity, wisdom, or superiority, of a person."[15] It is with this understanding that I find Idowu's discussion on the distinction between deity, divinities, and ancestors helpful. He states thus:

> Deity and the divinities are distinctly, out-and-out, of the super-sensible world, while the ancestors are of the living persons' kith and kin. The ancestors are related to the living community in a way that cannot be claimed for deity or the divinities who are definitely of a different order.[16]

The above distinction sheds some light as to the manner and intent with which Africans approach ancestors. Although he does not define worship and veneration, on the question as to whether Africans worship ancestors, Idowu adds the following:

15. Woolf, *Webster's New Collegiate Dictionary*, 1297.
16. Idowu, *African Traditional Religion*, 184.

> Worship and veneration ... are psychologically closer than next door to each other: the emotional indicator is always trembling between the two, swinging to the one or the other in accordance with the emotional pressure or the spiritual climate of the moment.[17]

Idowu's comments raise the question as to what traditional Africans are doing when they approach ancestors. An African spiritual Ifa priest, speaking of ancestor worship, says, "[It] is our connection to the past and our road map to a better future."[18] This comment by the African priest highlights the pivotal role ancestors hold in their respective societies. Maulana Karenga claims that Africans do not worship ancestors but God only; however, his description of the honoring of ancestors closely resembles that of ancestor worship.[19] He adds thus:

> [Africans'] profound respect for ancestors, which admittedly has a spiritual dimension, is best called veneration. The ancestors are venerated because they are a source and symbol of lineage; models of ethical life, service and social achievement; and they are spiritual intercessors between humans and the Creator.[20]

The question of ancestor worship or veneration, or both, has received arguments for both positions in the literature without much consensus. In this work I show that Zulus in the amaNazaretha Church claim that they talk (*tetha*) with their ancestors and do not worship them.

Zulu Terms:[21]

Baba—the term used to address Shembe
Mfundisi—minister in the amaNazaretha Church
Mvangeli—an evangelist in the church who is lower in rank than a minister
Mshumayeli—a preacher who serves in a local temple and is lower in rank than the minister and evangelist
Mkhokheli—a woman's leader in the church
Ifortini—the married women's group's monthly meeting for all-night prayer
Ebuhleni—the church's present epicenter meaning "a place of splendor"

---

17. Ibid., 182.
18. Neimark, *The Way of Orisa*, 26.
19. Karenga, *A Celebration of Family*, 21.
20. Ibid., 21.
21. Other Zulu terms are embedded in the text of this study.

Ekuphakameni—the church's original epicenter, meaning "the elevated place"
Isangoma—a traditional healer
Isihlabelelo—the amaNazaretha hymnal

Theoretical Framework

The interpretation of data is always informed by theories relevant to the research question and sub-questions. These theories serve as interpretive grids for solving the research question, namely, "Is the amaNazaretha Church a Christward movement?" The secondary questions are under the three subsections: Ancestors, Shembe, and Christ. (See Table 1: Theoretical Framework below.)

TABLE 1: THEORETICAL FRAMEWORK

Problem	Data Needed and Methodology for Data Collection	Research Instrument	Theories

Is the amaNazaretha Church a Christward Movement?	A. Library Research	Literature on Shembe, Ancestors, and Jesus Christ as Mediator	1. Hiebert: Centered and Bounded Sets
			2. H. W. Turner: New Religious Movements Typology
			3. N. T. Wright: Caesar and Christ
			  a. (Phil 2:5–11)
			  b. (Eph 1:20–21)

	B. Participant Observation	Spradley: "Doing Participant Observation"	
	C. Interviews	Stewart/Cash: "Interviewing Principles and Practices"	

Sub-problems:	Data Needed and Methodology for Data Collection	Research Instrument	Theories
1. Role of Shembe	A. Library Research	Literature on Shembe and Succeeding Generations of Leaders	
	B. Participant Observation and Interviews Generating Stories	1. Interview Schedule 2. Interview Questions for Shembe 3. Field Notes 4. Tape Recordings	
	1. Sabbath Services		
	a. Sermons	Interview Schedule	1. Oosthuizen: "Isaiah Shembe and the Zulu Worldview" 2. Loubser: "The Oral Christ of Shembe: Believing in Jesus in Oral and Literate Societies"
	b. Hymns	Interview Schedule	3. Shembe Liturgical Song Book: Izihlabelelo Zamanazarehta. 4. Oosthuizen: The Theology of a South African Messiah: An Analysis of the Hymnal of The Church of the Nazarites.
	c. Prayers	Interview Schedule	5. Hexham: "The Scriptures of the amaNazaretha of EkuphaKameni" 6. Shorter: Prayer in the Religious Traditions of Africa

The Genesis of a Journey of Discovery

Sub-problems:	Data Needed and Methodology for Data Collection	Research Instrument	Theories
	2. Healing Services		
	a. Actions of Shembe b. Testimonies of Members c. Biblical Story by Researcher	Interview Schedule	1. Oosthuizen: "Isaiah Shembe and the Zulu Worldview" 2. Biblical: John 9:1–41 (Healing of the Blind Man)
	3. Funeral Services	Interview Schedule	1. Oosthuizen: Theology of a South African Messiah 2. Ephesians 1:20—2:6
	C. Interview with Shembe	1. Interview Schedule 2. Questions for Shembe	1. Oosthuizen: "Isaiah Shembe and the Zulu Worldview" 2. 1 Timothy 2:5 (Christ as Mediator)
2. Role of Ancestors	A. Library Research B. Participant Observation and Interviews Generating Stories	Literature on Ancestors in the Zulu Tradition and in the amaNazaretha Church	1. Oosthuizen: "Isaiah Shembe and the Zulu Worldview" 2. Boot: "Religious Pluralism in a Zulu Chiefdom"
3. Role of Jesus Christ	A. Library Research B. Participant Observation and Interviews Generating Stories	Literature on the Views of Christ in the amaNazaretha Church	1. Nyamiti: Christ as Our Ancestor 2. Biblical: Philippians 2:5–11 (Jesus Is Lord)

Theories to Answer the Main Research Question

I have used three theories to interpret the research question, "Is the amaNazaretha Church a Christward movement?" First, from a behavioral science perspective, I use Hiebert's "Bounded and Centered Sets" model to determine whether the amaNazaretha Church is a Christward movement or not.[22]

The two categories that I consider from Hiebert's model are the "Intrinsic Bounded Set" and the "Extrinsic Centered Set" (see figure 1).

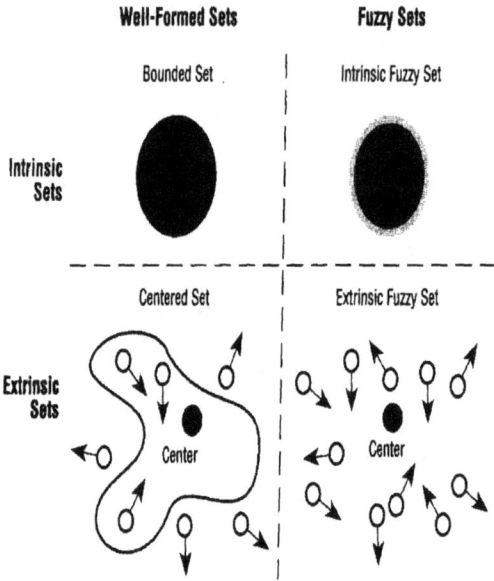

FIGURE 1. A Typology of Sets[23]

Intrinsic Bounded Sets, according to Hiebert, "are formed on the basis of the essential nature of the members themselves—on what they are in and of themselves.... They are all uniform in character."[24] According to Hiebert's diagram, the only change occurs when one moves from outside to inside the category, or alternatively, from the inside to the outside.[25] If Christianity is perceived as a Bounded Set, the boundary determines where the person is in terms of her or his Christian faith. The boundary separates a Christian from one who is *not* a Christian.

22. Hiebert, *Anthropological Reflections*, 107–36.
23. Ibid., 112.
24. Ibid., 110.
25. Ibid., 109.

The Genesis of a Journey of Discovery

The Extrinsic Centered Set, however, is defined by its center and the relationship of people to that center. Hiebert's idea in this model is that in the case of people who may or may not be considered Christian, the reference point is not the fixed boundary as in the Bounded Set, but movement toward the center or away from the center. In other words, "Distant members can move toward the center, and those near it can slide back while still headed toward it."[26] However, there is still the boundary—whether one is making a conscious effort to move in a Christward direction. The conversion experience orients one in the direction of the set though one may not be close to the center.

When I use Hiebert's "Bounded and Centered Sets" theory to interpret the data and answer the research question, "Is the amaNazaretha Church a Christward movement?," the main criterion for making that assessment will be to discern if Shembe members follow Christ and the Bible and whether they make Jesus Christ the center and Lord of their lives. According to Hiebert's diagram, the test will demonstrate whether the amaNazaretha Church is moving toward the center (Jesus Christ) or away from it.

The second theory is from a religious studies perspective. I use H. W. Turner's "Four-Part Classification" of New Religious Movements to help answer the research question as indicated in figure 2.[27]

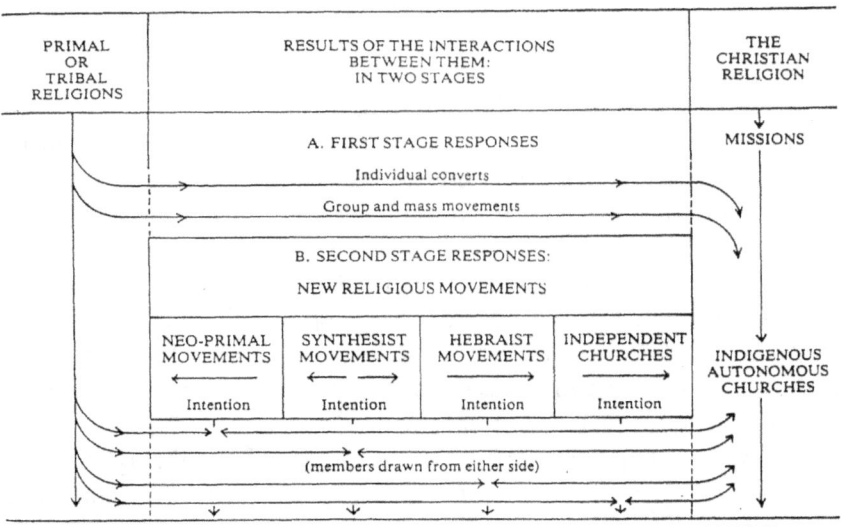

FIGURE 2. Four-Part Classification of African Independent Churches

26. Ibid., 124.
27. H. W. Turner, "Religious Movement," 49.

The terms these four categories represent are (a) Neo-primal, (b) Synthesist, (c) Hebraist, and (d) Independent Churches.[28]

Neo-primal movements are those that are near the primal religions but endeavor to rework and revitalize themselves with the influence of Christianity—some aspects of Christianity are borrowed; for example, the belief in one supreme God. The next grouping, Synthesists, do not identify with either the traditional primal religion or Christianity. They do, however, borrow from both, and the result is a new religious movement that is distinct from either the old primal religion or the Christian tradition. Hebraists, on the other hand, make a conscious move away from traditional religions to the world of the Bible. They place their emphasis, however, on the Old Testament, and consequently do not fully embrace New Testament teachings on the person and work of Christ. Finally, there are Independent Churches that have converted from traditional religions and now follow the teachings of the Bible. According to Turner,

> They use the Scriptures, they make something central of Jesus Christ and especially of the Holy Spirit. . . . They may be described as having been founded in Africa by Africans for Africans to worship God in African ways and to meet African needs as Africans feel them.[29]

Turner's "Four-Part Classification" together with Hiebert's "Bounded and Centered Sets" are helpful grids for me to evaluate whether the amaNazaretha Church is a Christward movement.

Even if the amaNazaretha Church is in some sense declaring Christ as the only way to God, what is the biblical and theological test for such a claim? Here my research design moves beyond phenomenological analysis, and I seek out Christian criteria to help interpret the data and offer a solution to the research problem.

For a theological/biblical interpretation and solution to the main research question, I use two chapters in N. T. Wright's *What Saint Paul Really Said*, titled "Herald of the King" and "Paul and Jesus."[30] I also use his article "Paul's Gospel and Caesar's Empire."[31] Wright offers an exposition of Philippians 2, where he juxtaposes the Greco-Roman slogan "Caesar is Lord" with Paul's proclamation that "Jesus is Lord." Wright argues that in Philippians 2:5–11, Paul not only exalts Jesus Christ as the risen Lord; he

28. I discuss Turner's classification later in ch. 4 in greater detail.
29. H. W. Turner, *Religious Movements in Primal Societies*, 10–11.
30. N. T. Wright, *What Saint Paul Really Said*, 39–62, 63–76.
31. N. T. Wright, "Paul's Gospel and Caesar's Empire," 1–13.

The Genesis of a Journey of Discovery

implicitly contradicts the claim of the political and religious lord of that day, namely, Caesar. For Wright, Caesar's empire, the colonial outpost at Philippi, is the parody, and Jesus' empire, the church at Philippi, is the reality. According to Wright,

> Caesar demanded worship as well as secular obedience; not just taxes, but sacrifices. He was well on the way to becoming the supreme divinity in the Graeco-Roman world, maintaining his vast empire not simply by force . . . but by the development of a flourishing religion that seemed to be trumping most others either by absorption or by greater attraction. Caesar, by being a servant of the state, had provided justice and peace to the whole world. He was therefore to be hailed as Lord, and trusted as Savior. This is the world in which Paul announced that Jesus, the Jewish Messiah, was Savior and Lord.[32]

The Philippians hymn, "Every knee shall bow and every tongue shall confess that Jesus is Lord, to the glory of God the Father" (see 2:10–11), that forms the centerpiece of Wright's interpretative scheme may help with some observations I made during my previous visits to the amaNazaretha Church. For example, at the commencement of the Sabbath service, members kneel and bow as Vimbeni Shembe comes into the worship center. Further, the bumper stickers "Shembe Is the Way" and "Shembe Is the Black Messiah" are slogans used by the members of the church. These observations and designations will need to be interpreted from a theological and biblical standpoint as well, and N. T. Wright's work assists me in answering the research question.

To interpret issues of the mediatorial roles and power of Shembe and the ancestors, I use the enthronement passage in Ephesians 1:20–21, which speaks of Christ seated at the right hand of God, "far above all rule and authority, power and dominion, and every title that can be given, not only in the present age but also in the one to come."

To get at the question of mediation, I consider the biblical passages that allude to Christ's role as mediator in salvation, healing, and prayers. The biblical passage that forms the basis for the Christian understanding that Jesus Christ is the sole mediator between humankind and God is 1 Timothy 2:5 ("There is one God and one Mediator between God and men, the Man Christ Jesus" [NKJV]). Regarding mediation in prayers, I consider passages in John's gospel (e.g., 14:13–14; 16:23) where Jesus

---

32. Ibid., 4.

encourages his hearers to "ask anything of the Father in my name," and "he will give it to you."

Scholarly Analyses Related to the Secondary Questions

The three secondary questions this study addresses are the role of Shembe, the role of ancestors, and the role of Jesus Christ in the amaNazaretha Church. Under each of the three secondary questions, I offer scholarly analyses for interpreting the observed phenomena: the Sabbath liturgical services and the healing services.

The Role of Shembe

According to Oosthuizen,[33] for the Zulu, God is not really known since he is all-powerful and so far away that people cannot approach him, or rarely do. Oosthuizen develops the theory that in the light of God's absence, other forces take precedence. He comes to the conclusion that "Shembe has . . . usurped the position of God, who is still somewhat distant in the sense of being difficult to approach. He [Isaiah] is himself the very first among the gods and messiahs preached by missionaries."[34] From the data I collected through my participant observation and my interview schedule, I tested Oosthuizen's statement (ch. 7) and discovered what members of the amaNazaretha Church believe about the leader, Vimbeni Shembe. To achieve this goal, I participated in the following activities.

The Sabbath Liturgical Services

At the Sabbath liturgical services, I collected data to interpret from sermons, hymns, and prayers to solve the research questions.

Sermons ☙

I heard and recorded several sermons preached by Vimbeni Shembe and also others to whom he delegated the preaching. To interpret the data collected, I use Loubser's work, "The Oral Christ of Shembe: Believing in Jesus in Oral and Literate Societies."[35] Loubser researched twenty-three sermons preached by Londa Shembe in the period from 1983 to 1986. These sermons, originally in Zulu, were recorded on audiocassette and transcribed and translated into English by research specialists at the institute for the study of New Religious Movements and Independent

---

33. Oosthuizen, "Isaiah Shembe and the Zulu Worldview," 1–30.
34. Ibid., 7–9.
35. Loubser, "The Oral Christ of Shembe," 70–80.

The Genesis of a Journey of Discovery

Churches (NERMIC) in KwaZulu-Natal, South Africa. Loubser says that one of the keys to understanding Shembe's "unorthodox Christology may be found in the theory of orality."[36] Here he appeals to the work of Walter Ong, stating, "Not only the speech conventions change when a society develops from an oral to a literate society, but the perception of reality itself is modified."[37] One aspect of orality that Loubser discusses is contextualization. He adds thus:

> Because oral communication . . . necessitates a direct contextual involvement of the speaker it requires that every narrative must be introduced uniquely into a unique situation. . . . The oral mind is uninterested in definitions. . . . The meaning of every word is thus controlled by the real-life situations in which the word is used here and now.[38]

Loubser thus comes to the conclusion that on the understanding of the theory of orality, the following becomes evident:

> The identification of Shembe becomes almost inevitable. . . . It is unavoidable that a hermeneutic process arises in which the real events in the life of Shembe are constantly communicated in terms reminiscent of Jesus. The focus is never on Jesus or God, but on Shembe as exponent of divinity.[39]

Loubser's theory of orality is helpful to me, first, for the interpretation of the data I collect from the sermons preached at the Sabbath services, bearing in mind that the amaNazaretha Church, like the Zulu nation in South Africa, is rapidly becoming urbanized and literate. Second, most of the literature on the amaNazaretha Church pertains to the founder, Isaiah, and his sons Galilee and Amos Shembe; consequently, my study tests Loubser's theory of orality to discern how significant a shift is evident in the members' beliefs regarding the role of Vimbeni Shembe and the ancestors as compared to the role of Christ.

---

36. Ibid., 73.
37. Ibid.
38. Ibid., 74. Hans-Jurgen Becken, in "Narrative Church History as Proclamation of the Gospel Message," affirms that "preaching by telling the story is different from sophisticated sermons in Western churches" (173). While narrative fits into the thought patterns of a script-less society and oral communication is still part of their culture, there is every sign that they are in the stage of transition, moving away from a culture that was entirely script-less. This is evident among the amaNazarites who read from their Bibles and sing from their hymnbooks.
39. Loubser, "The Oral Christ of Shembe," 74–75.

Songs ✧

The amaNazaretha Church uses its own liturgical songbook for the Sabbath services.[40] The book contains biblical passages and responsive readings along with hymns written by Isaiah Shembe and Galilee Shembe. To understand and translate the data, I use Oosthuizen's *The Theology of a South African Messiah: An Analysis of the Hymnal of "The Church of the Nazarites."* This work contains a complete translation and interpretation of all the hymns in the Shembe liturgical book. According to Oosthuizen, the theology implied in the hymnal shaped the theology of the amaNazaretha Church.[41] For example, Oosthuizen claims that Isaiah Shembe was not only mediator but Messiah to his followers.[42] He continues thus:

> The Messiah in the Izihlabelelo [hymns] is not Jesus Christ. Shembe is the mediator of the iBandla lamaNazaretha. In order to establish who the messianic figure actually is, one has to analyze the context in which certain concepts are being used.[43]

In light of the fact that Jesus is only mentioned in a "few hymns," and that Shembe features prominently, Oosthuizen concludes that "he [Shembe] himself has usurped the place of Jesus."[44] I test Oosthuizen's theory against the interpretation of the hymns offered by the interviewees to solve this subproblem.

Prayers ✧

On my previous visits to the amaNazaretha Church, I attended several Sabbath services. During the services members engaged in corporate prayer, and often I would hear people begin their prayers with the phrase *Nkulunkulu Ka Shembe*, meaning "God of Shembe." When I asked why this was so, one member said, "We approach God only through Shembe; he gets us through to God." In my analysis of prayers at the amaNazaretha Church, I raised this issue with my interviewees and elicited their response as to who mediates their prayers. I then tested their interpretations by using Irving Hexham's edited work, *The Scriptures of the amaNazaretha of EkuphaKameni*. Londa Shembe, grandson of Isaiah Shembe, interpreted the prayers in this volume shortly before his tragic death in 1989. According to Londa Shembe, "Isaiah Shembe was the mouthpiece and

---

40. Shembe, *Izihlabelelo ZamaNazaretha*.
41. Oosthuizen, *Theology of a South African Messiah*, ix.
42. Ibid., 4.
43. Ibid., 35.
44. Ibid., 36.

The Genesis of a Journey of Discovery

instrument of Jehova, whom he reflected among the people, to lead the Zulu nation out of bondage."[45]

I am familiar with Heiler's classic work, *Prayer: A Study in the History and Psychology of Religion*, especially his chapter on "Primitive Prayer."[46] I concur with Shorter, however, that this work is both dated and does not assist us in understanding mediation in prayers in the African context. I am also aware of John Mbiti's essay on prayers, *The Prayers of African Religion*, in which the author records and analyzes some three hundred prayers. His work, although valuable, does not address the question of mediation. Shorter's work, *Prayer in the Religious Traditions of Africa*, on the other hand, is more useful to this study. When observing prayers made by the members of the amaNazaretha Church, I got at the question of who mediates their prayers. Here Shorter offers a typology that I use as illustrated below.

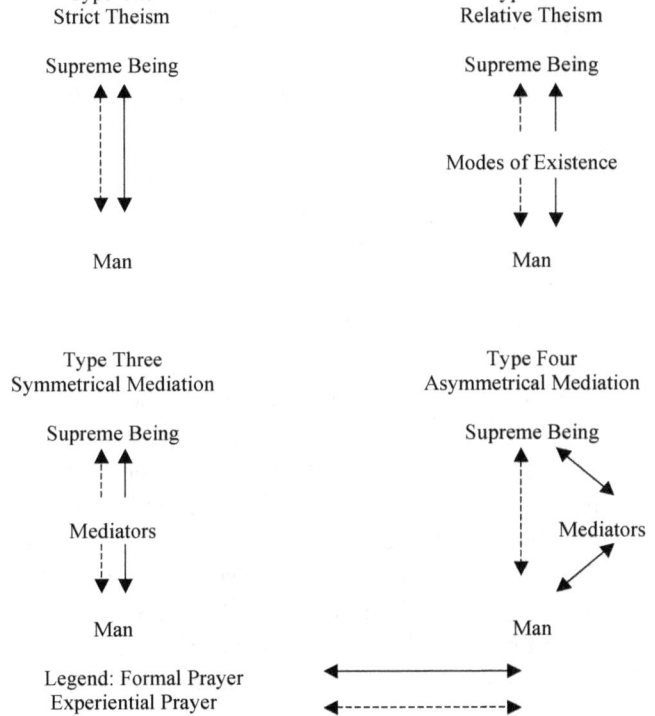

FIGURE 3. The Basis for a Typology of African Prayer: Formal and Experiential Prayer.[47]

45. Ibid., xxiv.
46. Heiler, *Prayer*, 1–64.
47. Shorter, *Prayer in the Religious Traditions of Africa*, 10–11.

The four types that he proposes are (1) *Strict Theism*: a supreme being is invoked directly, and ancestral spirits play no significant role in mediation; (2) *Relative Theism*: the supreme being is called upon through a variety of spirits and heavenly bodies; (3) *Symmetrical Mediation*: here ancestral spirits are called upon to mediate prayers and worship and also mediate reciprocally on behalf of the supreme being; and (4) *Asymmetrical Mediation*: mediators act mainly as channels of prayers and worship; however, the supreme being is still experienced directly by people.[48]

Healing Ceremonies

As is the case with any other African group in South Africa, healing in the amaNazaretha Church cannot be viewed only through a Western rational approach. African healing is rooted in a worldview that is more integrated and holistic. Oosthuizen offers one model for interpreting healing in the amaNazaretha Church. I use his work, "Isaiah Shembe and the Zulu Worldview,"[49] to interpret the data I collected in regard to healing. Oosthuizen quotes Galilee Shembe as saying, with regards to healing,

> The Zulus were once told of a God "who cannot see, who has neither love nor pity. But Isaiah Shembe showed you a God who walks on feet and heals with his hands, and who can be known by men, a God who loves and who has compassion."[50]

Oosthuizen theorizes that Isaiah Shembe (and consequently Galilee, Amos, and Vimbeni Shembe) follows in the tradition of the diviner (*isangoma*). Diviners are said to be mediums of supernatural power and are possessed by the spirits of ancestors. Their main function is to heal the sick, and the ancestors or the spirits of ancestors are the source of power to them. In ch. 7, I test Oosthuizen's theory to see to what extent Shembe mediates healing through the ancestors and what role Christ has in healing.

For a biblical theory or hermeneutic on healing, I use the story of Jesus' healing the blind man when he applied "spittle and clay" on the man's eyes and instructed him to wash in the pool of Siloam (John 9:1–41). John Marsh, in his commentary, *The Gospel of Saint John*,[51] offers a theological rationale for Jesus' use of spittle and clay. He says the following:

---

48. Ibid., 8–11.
49. Oosthuizen, "Isaiah Shembe and the Zulu Worldview," 1–30.
50. Ibid., 7.
51. Marsh, *The Gospel of Saint John*, 376–90.

> Much more is involved in healing one infirmity than the restoration of one function to a person; rather does Jesus' healing constitute the re-creation of the whole person. This is symbolically represented in the Johannine narrative by the introduction of the clay that is mixed with spittle, reminding the alert reader of the fact that in Genesis God had first made Adam out of the dust of the ground, when it had been softened by rain and mist (Genesis 2:5-7).[52]

I use this miracle to show that it has affinity with the methods of healing employed by the Shembe community. In interviews, I discussed the method and means of healing to get at the question of ultimately who heals.

Interview with Shembe

In order to interpret the responses to the interview questions I received from Vimbeni Shembe, I first use Oosthuizen's work, "Isaiah Shembe and the Zulu Worldview." Second, for a biblical perspective as an interpretive grid to analyze the responses I received from Vimbeni Shembe, I use 1 Timothy 2:5: "For there is one God and one Mediator between God and men, the Man Christ Jesus" (NKJV). The theological assumption that Jesus Christ is the mediator between God and humankind is explicit in scripture. The Greek word *mesites* (mediator) also appears in the book of Hebrews (8:6; 9:15; 12:24), referring to the role of Christ and the different dimensions of his mediatorial work.[53] By way of example, we may look at Christ as mediator of our prayers. The Christian's prayer is mediated by Christ. We are encouraged by Christ himself to pray in his name (John 16:23–34). Praying in Jesus' name becomes possible because of his ministry as mediator from the heavenly realms. We are told in Hebrews 4:15 that Jesus, our mediator, is one who sympathizes with our weaknesses. These biblical citations all corroborate what Paul says in 1 Timothy 2:5, and thus they are helpful in interpreting the data I collected through my interview with Vimbeni Shembe.

THE ROLE OF ANCESTORS

Given the fact that ancestors have always played a role in the religiocultural practices of Africans, my study seeks to discover to what extent ancestors are important to the amaNazaretha Church. Oosthuizen claims that "ancestor worship stands at the center of the Zulu tradition"[54] and

---

52. Ibid., 378.
53. Nash, "The Notion of Mediator," 89.
54. Oosthuizen, "Isaiah Shembe and the Zulu Worldview," 3.

perhaps also in the amaNazaretha Church. In an interview with a close aide to Amos Shembe, Frans H. Boot raised the question about the role of ancestors in the amaNazaretha Church. The aide, Rev. Alex Mpanza, said the following:

> To say that in Zulu society there are those who have completely forgotten about it [ancestors] would not be fair to your question. Most of my colleagues and ministers I have questioned won't preach about the ancestors and educate their congregations. About a minister who preaches critically about the ancestors it is said: *azombulula amadlozi* he will be killed by the ancestors.[55]

I observed the Sabbath and healing services to discover to what extent ancestors are still active in the religious life of the amaNazaretha Church.

To interpret the data, I use the work "Religious Pluralism in a Zulu Chiefdom," by anthropologist Frans H. Boot. Boot did extensive fieldwork among Zulu people in Natal, the home of the majority of Shembe members, where he investigated the role of ancestors in the everyday life of Zulus and particularly of members of the amaNazaretha Church. Boot's field research and his conclusions assist me in interpreting the data I collected regarding the role ancestors have in the life of the amaNazaretha Church.

My main source, however, for interpreting the data is Oosthuizen's work, "Isaiah Shembe and the Zulu Worldview." He argues that in Isaiah Shembe's time no barrier existed between this present world and the next; the living and the dead constituted one community.[56] The result was that when one became a Christian, there was tension between the ancestor worldview and the new beliefs of the Christian faith. Oosthuizen's theory is that "Isaiah Shembe attempted to overcome this tension by making what is basic in the Zulu worldview the determining factor in religious living."[57] His conclusion is that Shembe's emphasis on the Zulu tradition with ancestor worship as central in his doctrine was attractive to his followers. Thus "Shembe's emphasis on the function of the ancestors was due to his concern for the well-being of the Zulu nation, which always depended on right relations with the ancestors."[58]

---

55. Mpanza, *The Biography of Isaiah Shembe*, 132.
56. Oosthuizen, "Isaiah Shembe and the Zulu Worldview," 4.
57. Ibid.
58. Ibid.

The Role of Jesus Christ

Here I use two interpretative grids to analyze the data I collected from my participant observation at Sabbath and healing services.

First, I had anticipated using Charles Nyamiti's work, *Christ as Our Ancestor*, where he demonstrates that an African teaching on the ancestors is preparatory for the Christian teaching on Christ as the chief ancestor. In his work Nyamiti shows how cultural values may be purified or modified and introduced into Christianity:

> For what does the African desire from his ancestors if not their supernatural power and mediation in his favor, together with material and spiritual benefits, contact with God and his dead relatives? But where could these values be found in a higher or better form than in Christ the God-man?[59]

Nyamiti's work is an attempt to develop an African Christology. The discussion moves on the lines that since Christ is the Father's Son, and we are the Father's children, Christ becomes our Brother-Ancestor;[60] it is he who will redeem us from death. Nyamiti goes on to claim that just as ancestors heal and serve as prophets, advisors, and priests, Christ serves in similar functions, except that he exceeds them all. Nyamiti dwells on the similarities between ancestors' functions and Christ's pastoral and redemptive function and thus draws his conclusions to demonstrate how superior Christ is to ancestors. While this work is helpful, I discovered that Nyamiti's work does not fit the profile of the amaNazaretha where their Christology does not appear to be consistent with orthodoxy.

Second, to better understand what Christ is doing for Africans in the African worldview, I use a post-Resurrection text, Philippians 2:5–11, to interpret theologically his role in the amaNazaretha Church. I have already discussed this passage in my discussion of the main research question above.

Below is a brief discussion of significant writers whose works are foundational to any study of the African Initiated Churches and African Traditional Religions.

---

59. Nyamiti, *Christ as our Ancestor*, 69.

60. Nyamiti defines *Brother-Ancestor* as "a relative of a person with whom he has a common parent, and of whom he is mediator to God, archetype of behavior and with whom—thanks to his supernatural status acquired through death—he is entitled to have regular sacred communion" (Ibid., 23).

General Background to the amaNazaretha Church

Given the proliferation of the African Independent Church movement in Africa and particularly in South Africa, it is no surprise that since Bengt Sundkler's *Bantu Prophets in South Africa*,[61] publications and scholarly articles have appeared unabated and with monotonous regularity.[62] However, I have identified some foundational works by scholars both prior to and after Sundkler. These works include John Dube's *Ushembe*, a biographical sketch of Isaiah Shembe, the founder.[63] This source is the earliest available in print in Zulu and was published shortly after the death of the founder in 1935.[64] Esther L. Roberts, an anthropological student, produced a biographical sketch including a firsthand account of the death and burial of Isaiah Shembe for her master's thesis, *Shembe: The Man and his Work*. Almost ten years passed before Zulu scholar Absolom Vilakazi produced his unpublished master's thesis, "Isonto LamaNazaretha: The Church of the Nazarites." It was not until 1986 that Vilakazi's revised version of his thesis was published under the title *Shembe: The Revitalization of African Society*. Then came the work of South African Afrikaans Reformed scholar G. C. Oosthuizen, who in 1967 published his *The Theology of a South African Messiah*. Oosthuizen attempted to elicit a theology of Shembe from the hymns that Shembe had written. Albeit a controversial work, Oosthuizen came to the conclusion that Shembe "[had] usurped the place of Jesus."[65] In 1976 Sundkler produced his second work, *Zulu Zion and Some Swazi Zionists*, in which he retracted some of his criticisms of the amaNazaretha

---

61. Sundkler was a Swedish Lutheran missiologist who served as missionary to the Zulus in South Africa in the mid-1950s.

62. Kitshoff notes that whereas in 1913 there were thirty-two known independent churches in South Africa, by 1980 the AICs had grown to include 3,270 denominations with a membership of nearly six million" (*African Independent Churches Today*, 97). See also Kitshoff, "African Independent Churches: A Mighty Movement," 97–103. Oosthuizen says, "In 1959, fully 75 to 80 percent of all Black South African Christians were members of the mainline churches; only 12–14 percent were members of the AICs. By 1980, the mainline share of Black Christian population had dropped to 52 percent, while the AICs had increased to 27 percent; by 1991, the figures were 41 percent and 36 percent" ("Indigenous Christianity and the Future of the Church in South Africa," 8).

63. Dube, *The Biography of Isaiah Shembe*.

64. John Dube was founding member and first president of what is now the African National Congress, the political party in power in South Africa. He was the pastor of the American Board Mission working at Lindley Mission, neighboring Shembe's Ekuphakameni village. Dube was also the editor of the newspaper *Ilange laseNatal*, a paper still published in Natal to this day.

65. Oosthuizen, *Theology of a South African Messiah*, 35.

The Genesis of a Journey of Discovery

Church.⁶⁶ In the interim, David Barrett produced his *Schism and Renewal in Africa*, in which he analyzed the causes of independence in some six thousand movements in Africa. Hans-Jurgen Becken, a Lutheran scholar from Germany, in the late 1970s and early 1980s produced some significant writings out of his empirical research among the Shembes; for example, his work "Ekuphakameni Revisited" is an attempt at delineating the various stages of development and growth of the movement. Becken, in all of his works, alludes to his judgment that the amaNazaretha Church is "Christian."⁶⁷ Other works of significance discussed in this review are those of Carroll Muller, Elizabeth Gunner, Mike Kitshoff, and G. C. Oosthuizen, the most prolific writers to date on the movement.

Robert C. Mitchell and Harold W. Turner compiled *A Comprehensive Bibliography of Modern African Religious Movements*, which was later edited by Harold Turner in *Bibliography of Modern African Religious Movements*, Supplement I (1968) and Supplement II (1971). This source is important because it is linked to the corresponding microfiche texts in *Turner Collection on Religious Movements Vol. 2: Africa* and is one of seven volumes. Stan Nussbaum edited Turner's work with a new index in 1993. The work, which is divided into two main sections, namely, a section on theory and a "general description" section, is important as there have been few significant works of this nature since this work was published.⁶⁸

Hans-Jurgen Becken, in his work "The Deeds of Shembe as Described by His Eyewitnesses" in *Afro-Christian Religion at the Grassroots in Southern Africa*,⁶⁹ recounts the life and times of the prophet Isaiah Shembe, a wandering ascetic, itinerating through the country preaching, teaching, and baptizing until he finds a haven to rest from his labors. This place becomes his settlement, with various ministries exercised for the well-being of the

---

66. In his earlier work, *Bantu Prophets*, Sundkler concluded after attending some of the Shembe worship services that the "Messianic Churches" firmly believed in a Black Messiah. Gleaning from the content in their hymnal and sermons, he believed that Isaiah Shembe had replaced Christ and thus became the mediator of the people (283). In his later work, *Zulu Zion* (1976), Sundkler states that in revisiting Shembe's hymns, he admits that his earlier conclusions were "too Western, too dogmatic" (309).

67. It should be noted that Becken conducted his research in the Johannes Galilee Shembe and Amos Shembe eras.

68. However, Josiah U. Young, professor of Systematic Theology at Wesley Theological Seminary in Washington, D.C., produced in 1993 his *African Theology: A Critical Analysis and Annotated Bibliography*, which covers a broad range of theological issues facing the African continent. It complements Turner's work produced more than ten years earlier, thus containing sources beyond Turner's time of publication.

69. Becken, "The Deeds of Shembe," 151–63.

members and adherents. The location becomes the center for yearly pilgrimages and celebrations, attracting the membership from distant places.

In his article "Ekuphakameni Revisited: Recent Developments within the Nazaretha Church in South Africa," Becken delineates the history of the amaNazaretha Church in three phases: The first period, from the establishment of the church in 1910 to the death of the founder prophet Isaiah Shembe in 1935, was shaped by his ascetic personality and may be called the *stage of formation*; the second period, from the installation of the founder's fourth son, Johannes Galilee Shembe, in 1936 to his death in 1976, was molded by this able chief-type leader of the second generation and may be called the *stage of consolidation*; the third period in the history of an AIC can be described as the *stage of institutionalization*.[70]

An early work that sets the context for secession and independency is Sundkler's *Bantu Prophets in South Africa*. Sundkler traces historically the beginnings of the African Independent Churches, citing the earliest recorded secessions in South Africa as occurring in 1884 (Tile) and 1892 by the Ethiopian church. He, however, records an even earlier attempt at emancipation from a mission church by the Basuto congregation named Hermon in 1872. In Sundkler's work, one encounters for the first time an attempt at a typology of the churches among the African Independent Churches.[71] Here Sundkler differentiates between two main types of churches: Ethiopian and Zionist.

While Sundkler devotes little space and discussion to the amaNazaretha Church in this volume, his second work, *Zulu Zion and Some Swazi Zionists*, gives the movement wide coverage beginning with the prophet Isaiah's early life and the events that led to the formation of the amaNazaretha Church. In this work, Sundkler calls attention to the writings of scholars such as Esther L. Roberts (1936), Absolom Vilakazi (1954), Katesa Schlosser (1958), G. C. Oosthuizen (1976), and Hans-Jurgen Becken (1972). Sundkler's works are characterized as the first attempt at a serious and comprehensive study of the African Independent Churches.

In addition to terminologies, writers have developed typologies to study the phenomena prevalent within the various churches. Establishing a common framework or grid becomes imperative if only for the sole purpose of distinguishing the essential features of the individual movements. Here Harold Turner's work *Religious Innovation in Africa: Collected Essays on New Religious Movements* has become the standard and the point of

---

70. Ibid., 162–63.
71. Sundkler, *Bantu Prophets in South Africa*, 38–64.

The Genesis of a Journey of Discovery

departure for scholars attempting a working typology[72] for the African religious phenomena. Turner's four-part categorization[73] of Neo-Primal, Synthesist, Hebraist, and Independent Churches[74] is still used by scholars today; for example, in M. L. Daneel's *Quest for Belonging*. This work points me to an essential feature in the amaNazaretha Church, namely that they are Sabbatarians, keeping rigorously the fourth commandment, and are closely tied to the Old Testament. Thus, researchers like Oosthuizen would refer to them as Hebraist and therefore not "Christian."

Oosthuizen has demonstrated through field research that AIC prophets and leaders are most likely to be called to their office by *ancestors* through dreams and visions. In *The Healer-Prophet in Afro-Christian Churches*, Oosthuizen cites the case of Isaiah Shembe and his calling by ancestors.[75] While Oosthuizen does cite additional ways that prophets are called (dreams, visions, and the Holy Spirit), Daneel, in *The Background and Rise of Southern Shona Independent Churches*,[76] demonstrates that among the Shona in Rhodesia (Zimbabwe), leaders received their call through dreams and primarily visions and possession by the Holy Spirit.[77] I use these sources as points of comparison in my study of Shembe and his understanding of ancestors and their role in Zulu religious life.

General Background to African Traditional Religions

To discover what Africans believe about God, Shembe, ancestors, and Christ in African Independent Churches, it was imperative that I first study African Traditional Religions.[78]

72. See also, Andrew Walls, *The Missionary Movement in Christian History*, especially the chapter "The Challenge of the African Independent Churches" (111–18) for a further discussion on terminology.

73. See also Harold Turner, "New Vistas: Missionary and Ecumenical: Religious Movements in Primal (or Tribal) Societies;" and "The Approach to Africa's Religious Movements."

74. Turner, *Religious Innovation in Africa*, 9.

75. Oosthuizen, *The Healer-Prophet*, 28. Oosthuizen quotes Shembe as saying, "I saw an angel opening its wings when I was asleep, but the voice of that angel was like the voice of my grandfather who said I should wake up. Immediately I saw many of my relatives . . . they were calling me to be a prophet."

76. This work appears under a different title: *Old and New in Southern Shona Independent Churches: Volume 1: Background and Rise of Major Movements*, 1971.

77. Daneel, *The Background and Rise*, 463.

78. Harold Turner, in *Living Tribal Religions*, would remind us that tribal people "differ very greatly in their beliefs and ways of life, and therefore their religious ideas and practices differ also and each should be studied in itself" (6). He, however, delineates the similarities and groups them together as the religions of tribal societies. Turner defines a New Religious

E. Bolaji Idowu, professor of religious studies and teacher of African Traditional Religions in Nigeria, in his book, *African Traditional Religion: A Definition*, outlines the history of African Traditional Religion before he goes on to describe its nature and structure. This study is helpful in that it treats systematically African belief in God, divinities, spirits, and ancestors.[79] Idowu's basic premise is that ancestors obtain blessings and favor from the Supreme Being and act as dispensers and mediators of such blessings and favor. My research questionnaire was designed to investigate this issue in the context of the amaNazaretha Church.

John Mbiti, in his work *Introduction to African Religion*, discusses the rituals and ceremonies of various African religions and was the first to coin the phrase *living-dead* to refer to ancestors. On the question of worship or veneration, he maintains the following:

> Although African peoples use . . . intermediaries [ancestors] in performing some of their acts of worship, they do not worship the intermediaries themselves as such. They simply use them as conveyor belts, as helpers or assistants.[80]

Mbiti's articulation of the role and status of ancestors in African Traditional Religions is important for this study because it helps us to discern the shifts in beliefs and practices on ancestor mediation when people move from African Traditional Religions to Christianity.[81]

John Pobee, in his work *Toward an African Theology*, reminds us that culture and religion are never static, and therefore he warns against "fossil culture" and "fossil religion."[82] This work brings an acute awareness that one system of belief is not pervasive in Africa due to the diversity found there. Hence, one may not speak only of "*an* African religion or *an* African worldview."[83]

Consequently, Pobee thus articulates the belief and practice of ancestors only in his own context, namely, the Akan society of Ghana.

Movement as "a historically new development arising in the interaction between a tribal society and its religion and one of the higher cultures and its major religion, involving some substantial departure from the classical religious traditions of both the cultures concerned, in order to find renewal by reworking the rejected traditions into a different religious system" ("The Way Forward," 697).

79. Idowu, *African Traditional Religion*, 135–203.

80. Mbiti, *Introduction to African Religion*, 64.

81. See also Mbiti, *Concepts of God in Africa*; and Mbiti, *African Religions and Philosophy*.

82. Pobee, *Toward an African Theology*, 44.

83. Ibid.

The Genesis of a Journey of Discovery

Somewhat different from Mbiti, Pobee, in his work "Aspects of African Traditional Religion," says the following of ancestors:

> We come to the old problem of whether it is ancestor-veneration or ancestor-worship.... It is more than veneration.... Since ancestors have a more direct and immediate interest in the affairs of the clan in the here and now, they are for all practical purposes the real forces in life, especially when their judgments are immediately manifested in disasters. Thus for all practical purposes they are worshipped and are the second pillar of Akan religion.[84]

I will refer to Pobee's works to show that ancestors are an integral part of African Traditional Religions, although acknowledged differently depending on the particular society.

Benezet Bujo, an African theologian and author of *African Theology in its Social Context*, suggests in an article, "Toward an African Ecclesiology," that the ancestors of earlier generations transfer power to ancestors that follow. Thus a chain is formed assuring unity throughout the generations to the present in a given community.[85] Bujo does not say how power is transferred from one generation to another. His thesis is that "a clanic community [gathers] around a founding ancestor from whom all members originate."[86] I will test Bujo's conclusions through a questionnaire on the status of the founding Shembe in the community.

Darrel M. Hostetter, a researcher of the Zion Swazis, surveys some representative views of ancestors among Swazi Christians and compares them with some Zulu Christians in South Africa. His work "Disarming the Emadloti: The Ancestors" helps us see a general pattern and corpus of beliefs emerging with regards to ancestors. Hostetter quotes from a survey conducted among Zulu people in South Africa, where a series of questions were posed: "Does an ancestral spirit accompany a person to protect him and bring him good fortune?" and "Was Jesus Christ who lived on the earth the Supreme Being?"[87] Sixty-nine percent of the respondents answered in the affirmative to the first question, and to the second, 59.8 percent. Hostetter concludes that Zulu Christians were more likely to turn to ancestors than to Christ for solutions to their problems.[88]

---

84. Pobee, "Aspects of African Traditional Religion," 9.
85. Bujo, "Toward an African Ecclesiology," 3.
86. Ibid.
87. Hostetter, "Disarming the Emadloti: The Ancestors," 356.
88. Ibid.

In Kwame Bediako's work *Christianity in Africa: The Renewal of a Non-Western Religion*, the author speaks of Christ as "Supreme Ancestor." He says, "Christ, by virtue of his incarnation, death, resurrection and ascension into the realm of spirit-power, can rightly be designated, in African terms, as Ancestor, indeed Supreme Ancestor."[89]

Summary

In this introduction, I have mapped out the main themes for this study and I have also apprised the reader of the literature foundational to the study of African Traditional Religions, Zulu Traditional religions, and the African Initiated Churches, specifically, the amaNazaretha Church.

In chapter 2, I specifically look at both the African and Zulu traditional religions and focus on their views on God, spirits, ancestors, traditional leaders, and healing as expressed in their beliefs and practices. In chapter 3, I offer an overview of the history, beliefs, and practices of the African Initiated Churches (AICs), which then leads into a study of the religious and cultural worldview of the amaNazaretha Church of Isaiah Shembe, in ch. 4. The following two chapters, 5 and 6, I devote to my research findings and participant observation respectively. I interpret my research findings in ch. 7, offering my conclusions and understanding of the amaNazaretha Church's theology and Christology they espouse in their beliefs and practices. Finally, in chapter 8, I offer some missiological principles elicited from my study that may be generalized for other missionary contexts.

---

89. Bediako, *Christianity in Africa*, 217. See also Bediako, "Biblical Christologies in the Context of African Traditional Religions," where he writes, "Once Jesus Christ comes, the ancestors are cut off as means of blessing and we lay our power-lines differently . . . from the standpoint of the Gospel, God's saving activity towards us is focused on Christ, mediated through the Holy Spirit" (35).

2

African and Zulu Traditional Religions: Views on God, Spirits, Ancestors, Traditional Leaders, and Healing

THIS CHAPTER WILL SHOW what aspects of African Traditional Religion are carried over when African traditionalists join the African Initiated Churches (AICs). After a general survey of ATRs' beliefs and practices, this chapter will delineate more specifically Zulu beliefs and practices, since the majority of adherents in the amaNazaretha Church belong to the Zulu nation.

African Traditional Religions

Africans live out their lives as religious people. They possess a set of rituals for every phase of life, beginning with conception, proceeding through the womb, then birth, infancy, puberty, initiation, marriage, and physical death to the "beyond" or afterlife.[1] Thus "the practical role that religion plays in African society can be seen in almost every sphere of life."[2] Scholars have attempted the study of religions from different approaches: sociological, philosophical, psychological, functional, and structural, to mention a few.[3] Nida goes on to suggest that religion

> constitutes a componential feature of all the basic motivations [that produce] meaning with supernatural sanctions . . . . When this meaning takes on supernatural character and provides a mechanism by which people may establish communicative links with the supernatural, this is religion.[4]

---

1. Stine and Wendland, *Bridging the Gap*, 20–21.

2. Turnbull, *Man in Africa*, 74. However, Turnbull also claims that generalizations made of African religion and culture can be tenuous and cautions against them. See also his *Lonely African*.

3. Nida, *Message and Mission*, 97–98.

4. Nida, "New Religions for Old," 244–45.

Anthropologist Clifford Geertz, in his work *The Interpretation of Cultures*, attempts to relate culture to religion through his study of the behavior of individual groups. He offers a definition of religion that is helpful in analyzing the ritualistic and symbolic phenomena inherent in the African religiocultural ethos. In this context the term *religiocultural ethos* is a reference to the specific characteristics that go to make up the religion and culture of African people. Geertz sees religion as

> [a] system of symbols which acts to establish powerful and long lasting moods and motivations in men by formulating conceptions of a general order of existence and clothing these conceptions with such aura of factuality that the moods and motivations seem uniquely realistic.[5]

A. H. Mathias Zahniser, complementing Geertz, says, "Religion falls within the broader category of 'symbol systems,'" adding that a system "is an interconnected network of meaningfully related components."[6] For the non-African, or one who approaches African religions from an emic perspective,[7] the internal logic of an otherwise complicated socioreligious system becomes intelligible when individual symbols and rites are seen as integral components of the larger whole. Wendland illustrates this integrated wholeness of traditional African life, belief, and practices through the seven stages of the life cycle, with religion at the center, thus:

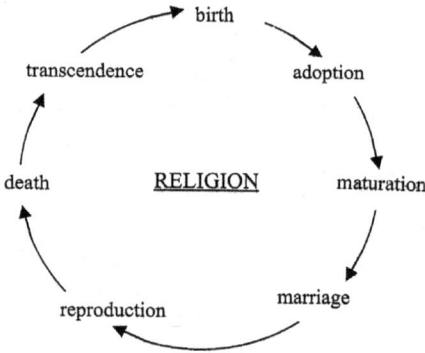

Figure 4. The Centrality of Religion in African Life.[8]

5. Geertz, *The Interpretation of Cultures*, 90.

6. Zahniser, *Symbol and Ceremony*, 30.

7. I use the term *emic perspective* in the context of one studying a specific culture from within the group or people so that one may accurately describe or narrate beliefs and practices one observes phenomenologically.

8. Stine and Wendland, *Bridging the Gap*, 20.

To the serious observer, African religion may be evidenced in peoples' history, their "migrations, calamities, wars, invasions, hunting, fishing, food-gathering, domestication of animals, farming, mining, metal work, and settlement in villages and cities."[9] Religion shapes African life in its totality—people's culture, social and political activities, and economic well-being. Mbiti, who claims that "Africans are notoriously religious,"[10] articulates their religiosity thusly:

> Wherever the African is, there is his religion: he carries it to the fields where he is sowing or harvesting a new crop; he takes it with him to the beer party or to attend a funeral ceremony; and if he is educated, he takes religion with him to the examination room at school or in the university; if he is a politician he takes it to the house of parliament. Although many African languages do not have a word for religion as such, it nevertheless accompanies the individual from long before birth to long after his physical death.[11]

According to Wendland, African religion "is not an abstract philosophical system. . . . It involves a dynamic application of the worldview to human character and conduct in their totality."[12] In the following diagram, he illustrates his point that every aspect of life is laden with religious phenomena:

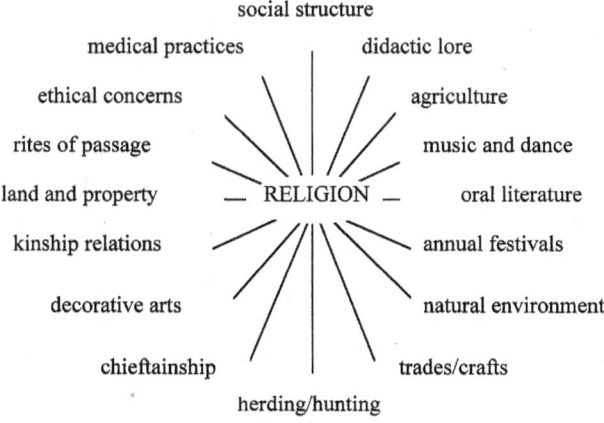

Figure 5. Facets that Make Up African Religion.[13]

9. Mbiti, *Introduction to African Religion*, 4–5.
10. Mbiti, *African Religions and Philosophy*, 2.
11. Ibid.
12. Wendland, "Traditional Central African Religion," 19–20.
13. Stine and Wendland, *Bridging the Gap*, 20.

The many facets that make up religion are analogous to the hub of a spoked wheel. Apart from its central position, it also directs the forward motion of the whole system.

According to Mbiti, African Traditional Religion is also "pragmatic and realistic."[14] Its dynamism and openness to new ideas is evidenced in response to life's situations and needs as they arise. While African religions may not possess a "holy book," the religion is a progression of historical events indelibly imprinted in the hearts and upon the minds of Africans.[15] Mbiti further asserts that "African religions have neither founders nor reformers. They may, however, incorporate national heroes, leaders, rulers, and other famous men and women into their body of beliefs and mythology."[16] Each individual in the African tradition is a religious carrier.

African religiosity is a paradox in that it displays both diversity and unity evident among the various traditions and cultures across the vast continent. Hence, there is the ongoing debate as to whether one should speak of "African Traditional Religion" in the singular or *religions* in the plural.[17] This problem becomes evident as we later study specifically Zulu Traditional Religion (ZTR). Given their three thousand ethno-linguistic groups, one can expect African Traditional Religion to be diversified in nature and scope, in that it signifies different things to different ethnic groups. Yet, it could also be a unity in that there are distinct strands that run through all the African traditions, irrespective of where on the continent people are situated. What follows is a general view of African traditional beliefs and practices.

Beliefs and Practices

Africans construe life as being holistic. It would appear that there is no solid demarcation between the sacred and secular. Therefore, there is the saying "Our world is like a drum; if you beat one part, everything vibrates."[18] I have earlier stressed that African religion pervades every aspect of African life, but it is a kind of "omnipresence" that easily eludes the

14. Mbiti, *Introduction to African Religion*, 15.
15. Ibid.
16. Mbiti, *African Religions and Philosophy*, 4.
17. Idowu, *African Traditional Religion*, 103. Idowu makes a case for African Traditional Religion in the singular: "There is a common Africanness about the total culture and religious beliefs and practices in Africa. This common factor may be due either to the fact of diffusion or to the fact that most Africans share common origins with regard to race and customs and religious practices."
18. Mugabe, "Christology in an African Context," 344.

casual observer, so much so that early Portuguese explorers to Africa claimed that Africans had no religion.[19] With intentionality and patient study, one may discover the "pervasive qualities" that "underlie specific beliefs, myths, symbols and rituals" of African culture.[20]

Some of the more relevant aspects of African Traditional Religion that will later have a bearing on a discussion of beliefs and practices in the amaNazaretha Church are as follows.

THE IDEA OF THE CREATOR GOD

Most Africans hold to some traditional image of God in their religious ethos. God is said to be the "Creator God," responsible for the primal origins of the world,[21] nature, and humanity. God is considered to be the ground of everything that exists, although God does not directly control everything. In this sense, Africans would view God more in the sense of transcendence rather than immanence. Therefore, the God of Africans is said to be detached from human affairs, and for want of better terminology, a *Deus otiosus* or *Deus remotus*.

In his study *The Primal Vision*, John V. Taylor, while conceding that the belief in a High God in African Traditional Religion is ambivalent, appeals to "the references [to the Creator God] everywhere in songs and proverbs and riddles, whose archaic grammatical forms attest their antiquity."[22]

In the absence of a spontaneous relationship with God, the African tends to turn to the more accessible spirit world. God is placed at the apex of the religious hierarchy, and consequently the only contact with God is through lesser gods and spirits.

The question of God being either transcendent or immanent in the everyday lives of Africans is critical to the understanding of when and how Africans approach God the Supreme Being. Taylor says, "The African

19. Booth, "An Approach to African Religions," 1.
20. Ibid., 6.
21. There are several myths concerning Creation and the role God plays in the African worldview. Benjamin Ray, like Mbiti and Idowu, among others, whose works have shaped theological discourse about African religions, offers several of these stories showing that God is always an integral part of the African religious and cultural worldview, albeit at times a distant entity. Recourse to God was through intermediaries. See Ray, *African Religions: Symbol, Ritual, and Community*.
22. Taylor, *Primal Vision*, 75. For example, Taylor quotes some ancient songs and poems that reveal the presence of a Supreme Being in African thought: "The cattle shelter under the same tree with God;" "Wherever the elands graze in herds, there is God;" "God is in the great trunk and in the low branches."

myth does not tell of men driven away from paradise, but of God disappearing from the world."[23] Consequently, "Man projects his inward sense of the lost Presence and fixes God in the sky. The pervasive Spirit becomes the remote and unknowable Creator, the First Cause, the Owner."[24]

In a more localized context, the Nupe of Northern Nigeria refer to God as *Soko lokpa*, meaning that "God is far away, yet in a more mystic sense he is present always and everywhere."[25]

To highlight the fact that we are dealing with an issue of immense complexity, as far as human interaction with God is concerned in African religiosity, a more recent scholar, Benjamin Ray, in *African Religions: Symbol, Ritual, and Community*, comes to the following conclusion:

> Having formed the immutable structures of sky and earth and the orderly human cycle of birth, life, and death, the Supreme Creator God remains in the background like a distant ruler or patriarch, occasionally intervening but generally leaving the fortunes and misfortunes of everyday life to lesser agents, the gods and spirits. Both types of divinity, the One Creator God and the many lesser powers are essential to the full range of traditional religious experience.[26]

Ray states that while Africans acknowledge the existence of a Supreme Being, the function and role of such a Being is understood differently across the continent. The question this statement raises regarding mediation in the African Christian context is "How are these beliefs and practices regarding the Supreme Being interpreted when Africans leave African Traditional Religions and cross over to Christianity?" In other words, if lesser gods, spirits, and ancestors mediate between people and God, is Christ's mediation mitigated or annulled?

Laurenti Magesa claims that in African Religion "the universe is a composite of divine, spirit, human, animate and inanimate elements, hierarchically perceived, but directly related, and always interacting with each other."[27] Magesa offers a convincing rationale for both God's reticence and familiarity with humankind in African religion. Magesa explains:

23. Ibid., 76.
24. Ibid.
25. Ibid., 78. Taylor offers several other examples of localized views of God. He says, "There are a few African tribes—the Ashanti, the Dogon, the Ambo and perhaps three or four more—in which the Supreme God was actively worshipped in the traditional religion with a cult and a priesthood; but in the great majority no shrines are raised to him and no sacrifices offered. People may pray to him still in moments of special need."
26. Ray, *African Religions*, 45.
27. Magesa, *African Religion*, 39.

> The rebelliousness of humanity against God [i]s the reason for God's consequent withdrawal from humanity. Yet . . . if God is not now immediately and directly involved with human ethical life, human beings are still ultimately accountable to the Divine in all aspects. Since the original fault of humanity, God requires and deserves respectful distance, but does not seek non-involvement in the ethical life of humanity.[28]

Among the Yoruba of Nigeria, the consequence of a rupture in the relationship between the Creator God Olodumare and one of his created gods, Odudua, caused Olodumare to withdraw to the sky. Yet, he rules the world through lesser gods known as *orisha*. It is said that Olodumare is "transcendent, all-knowing, and all-powerful."[29] For the Yoruba, Olodumare may still be invoked and praised, and people may bring to him their requests and needs.[30]

It would appear that in African Traditional Religion the existence of God is never doubted, though people are ambivalent in their understanding of God's transcendence and immanence. Yet it would be appropriate to suggest that God is both "ultimate and intimate"[31] in the everyday affairs of African people. More pointedly, if God is only transcendent or ultimate, the question of "Who are the intermediaries or mediators?" becomes crucial when an African changes his allegiance from African Traditional Religion to Christianity. This issue is raised in chapter 7.

DIVINITIES

Wendland, citing the Mulungu in Chewa and Lesa (Tonga) as examples, sketches the hierarchical order in African cosmology.[32] Divinities in the African context refer to spiritual beings that are the agents or representatives of the Supreme Being. In the African religious hierarchical structure of the spirit world, people place divinities immediately under the Supreme Being. Africans have some of the aspects sketched below, although their religious worldview is not totally confined to these aspects.

---

28. Ibid., 43.
29. Ray, *African Religions*, 10.
30. Ibid.
31. Zahniser, *Symbol and Ceremony*, 36–40. Mathias Zahniser uses these terms to help explain God's transcendence and immanence.
32. Wendland, "Traditional Central African Religion," 88. Wendland's hierarchy may not represent the religious worldview of all Africans. However, what is consistent is the understanding that between humans and the Supreme Being are lesser spirit beings.

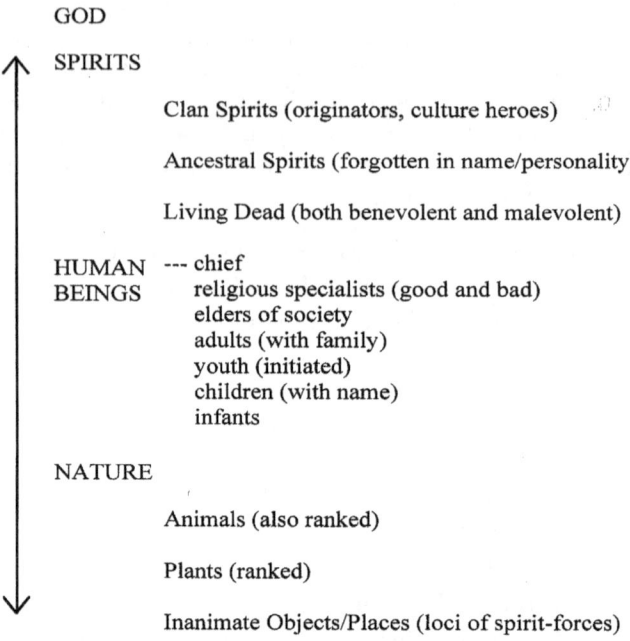

Figure 6. Hierarchical Structure of the Spirit World.[33]

Divinities are thought to be created by God. According to Mbiti, "They are associated with Him, and often stand for His activities or manifestations either as personifications or as the spiritual beings in charge of these major objects or phenomena of nature."[34] These "major objects of nature" may include the sun, mountains, seas, lakes, rivers, rocks, and boulders, objects both animate and inanimate.[35] Ray suggests that in some African religions, "God operates as a principle of ultimacy," bringing unity among the lesser deities. They are intermediaries of the one God.[36] For example, in the Yoruba culture people may be devotees of *Oshun*, the goddess who facilitates birth and promotes health and wealth, especially to women. In this instance the Supreme God Olodumare is relegated to the background but is always ever present.[37]

Another example of the role of divinities is evident among the Ashanti, who believe that God manifests God's presence through interme-

33. Stine and Wendland, *Bridging the Gap*, 88.
34. Mbiti, *African Religions and Philosophy*, 76.
35. Parrinder, *African Traditional Religion*, 43–52.
36. Ray, *African Religions*, 27.
37. Ibid.

diaries. These intermediaries are known as *abosom*. It is believed that God created the *abosom* to protect people. These divinities are departmentalized according to people's activities, experiences, and sociopolitical structures.[38] They may be divinities of war, of smallpox, of harvest, of health, and even of healing. The number of divinities will vary according to the needs of a particular community. Idowu maintains that some of the divinities are no more than ancestors who because of their "prowess during their lifetime earned deification."[39]

The question this aspect of African Traditional Religion raises is whether people from African religions and cultures coming to accept Christianity still gravitate to these spirit beings in times of calamity or when human needs are left unattended or unresolved.

Ancestors: The Living-Dead

The closest link African people have to the spirit-world is through their ancestors. Ancestors may be defined as "the spirits of the socially significant deceased members of family, lineage, clan, and tribal groupings."[40] In terms of lineage, Noah Dzobo asserts that an ancestor is "one from whom one is descended and who is usually more remote in the line of descent than a grandparent."[41]

Mbiti refers to ancestors as the "living-dead," a term now in common parlance in African literature. It is through the living-dead that the spirit-world becomes personal to African people. The living-dead are considered "people" who have not yet become spirits. They are said to visit their families from time to time, showing interest in intimate details of their families' everyday life. As guardians of the family's affairs, they communicate with the living head of the family. In some sense they act as mediators between their families and God. This role is intelligible to the African because the ancestor knows the family's needs; he was once a living member of that family. In addition, he has full access to communicating with God directly. Parrinder lends weight to this idea, saying, "In South Africa the ancestor spirits are the most intimate gods of the Bantu: they are part of the family or tribe and are considered and consulted on all important issues."[42]

---

38. Mbiti, *African Religions and Philosophy*, 76.
39. Idowu, *African Traditional Religion*, 172.
40. Kitshoff, *African Independent Churches Today*, 23.
41. Dzobo, "African Ancestor Cult," 333.
42. Parrinder, *Africa's Three Religions*, 57.

As for the specific activities of ancestors, Africans believe that they are not far away; they watch over their families "like a cloud of witnesses."[43] The health and fertility of the family are of utmost concern, since the ancestor will seek rebirth in the same family. It is believed that the family land is the property of the ancestor; when the property is to be leased to other people, the ancestor should be first consulted. In Kenya, for example, the ancestors are believed to fertilize the land and facilitate the growth of crops. At the time of harvesting, offerings, or the firstfruits of the land, are brought to them.

Ancestors are known to speak in dreams to their relatives. These dreams may be of an instructional nature. The relatives are then expected to act accordingly. If the spirit appears to be pleased or angry, appropriate action is necessary on the part of the person or family. When the dream is not clearly discernable, one has to consult a *medium*. The medium, for an agreed-upon price, unravels the dream and instructs the person as to the necessary steps to be taken.

The relationship between the living relatives and the ancestor is ambivalent. The living relatives revere the ancestor and take solace in the fact that the ancestor has power to protect them. Yet, the ancestor is also feared and, from time to time, has to be appeased with offerings through commemoration ceremonies. When evil or disaster befalls a family or tribe, it may be that the ancestor was either neglected or not consulted in some important matter. In this instance, the family or tribe coerce and placate the offended ancestor by means of sacrifices.[44]

In a more localized context, the Akan of Ghana believe that ancestors are those who have completed their role in the land of the living and have departed to the place of the dead, a spiritual waiting place called *Uumbwardo* (literally "God's house"). According to Pobee, not all the dead are elevated to this status. The person in life who was bankrupt does not qualify to be an ancestor; neither is the one who dies tragically or through some loathsome disease such as leprosy. The ancestor is one who lived in an exemplary manner to a ripe old age and who did much to enhance the prestige and well-being of his immediate family, clan, and tribe.[45]

In this Akan community, people believe that ancestors are believed to give children to the living so that there will be continuity of the ancestral name. Ancestors are also responsible for a good harvest—hence, the commemoration of ancestors during the harvest festivals. Moral life in

---

43. Ibid., 58.

44. Mbiti, *African Religions and Philosophy*, 85.

45. Pobee, "Aspects of African Traditional Religion," 8.

Akan society is said to be controlled by ancestors who provide the code of conduct. These codes are handed down from generation to generation, and offenders who abrogate the code are punished by sickness and even death. It is the responsibility of ancestors to provide a sense of cohesion and well-being in Akan society.[46]

Making libations is the main religious form of showing respect, honor, or recognition to the cult of ancestors, at least for the Akan people. Before eating and drinking, before and after travel, a libation is offered to the ancestor. This act signifies the Akans' dependency on the dead for their well-being. At the community or tribal level, "the cult of ancestors is mediated by a ritual specialist such as a chief, linguist or priest."[47]

Mediatorial Role of Ancestors Among the Shona

The nature and functions of ancestors among the Shona people are nuanced differently. Daneel[48] depicts the hierarchical structure where the ancestors, placed between the Supreme Being, *Mwari,* and the living, act in a mediatorial role. The ancestors represent Mwari, negotiate between the living relatives and Mwari, and carry out Mwari's instructions. Mediatorial functions of ancestors in the Shona tradition are dependent on certain activities carried out by the living relatives. To court the favor of ancestors, living relatives remember the dead by according honor to them. The dead relative becomes a mediator only when the living relatives carry out an initiatory rite called the *kugadzira,* the initiatory rite that elevates the dead to the status of ancestor. Therefore, "The mediatory function of the living with respect to the dead is thus a precondition for the eventual mediation of the dead with God on behalf of men [people]."[49] However, Daneel warns that one should not place too much emphasis on mediation, since ancestors also possess "great power." If the ancestors are correctly honored by the living relatives, ancestors are quite capable of meeting the needs of the living without the aid of Mwari.

The ancestors can serve positively and for the good of their society; however, there are also negative circumstances when ancestors can inflict harm on their relatives. As already noted, this fact occurs in other traditions. Here, sickness, death, and accidents are frequently attributed to the ancestors. Ancestors do not bring harm directly to their relatives, but

46. Ibid., 9.
47. Ibid., 10.
48. Daneel, "The Christian Gospel and the Ancestor Cult," 46–73.
49. Ibid., 48.

they can withhold their protective powers from the people, thereby leaving them exposed to the enemy and the powers of evil. This understanding is akin to Christian thinking that God has two wills—God's *perfect* will and God's *permissive* will. Perhaps the latter would account for the calamities in the African worldview.

As in other African cultures, the Shona keep regular contact with their ancestors. From the side of the ancestors, this contact is maintained through dreams, and sometimes ancestors communicate their wishes through a medium. The living relatives maintain contact with the ancestors through symbolic ways. They offer the ancestors food during meals in the form of libations. Sometimes they talk with the ancestor through a specially designated object or icon. In the case of the Shonas, this object may be a beer-pot or a blanket. In view of the Shonas' belief in ancestors, the convert to Christianity would need to reassess the role of an ancestor in light of the work of Christ as mediator. This discussion leads to a consideration of whether ancestors are worshipped, venerated, or both.

Ancestor Worship and Veneration

That ancestors are an integral part, albeit a controversial one, of the religio-cultural ethos of the African world is well established. To take away the ancestors from Africans is to strip them of their dignity, but much more, to destroy their roots. The question often raised is whether Africans worship or venerate ancestors. To this question there are a profusion of answers: many for worship and many for veneration. Still others have suggested that there is little or no difference between worship and veneration.[50]

In the Igbo culture of Southern Nigeria, life becomes meaningful for older people because they know the power and presence of ancestral spirits. Dickson says, "The father of the family begins his day by praying to them [ancestors], dedicating himself and his entire family to their protection, offering kola-nuts, and also palm wine when available."[51] It would appear that in this Igbo community, ancestors are worshipped and venerated, and libations are offered to them. Dickson also says that yearly feasts are held in honor of ancestors, and it is forbidden not to set out

---

50. The question of worship or veneration is not confined only to academic discussion among scholars, both African and non-African. Some of my interviewees, for example, brought up this issue even before I raised questions about the status of ancestors, insisting that they did not worship ancestors, but only honored them. See explanation of terms in chapter 1.

51. Dickson, *Biblical Revelation and African Beliefs*, 43.

some food for the ancestors during suppertime.⁵² It is an established fact that ancestors play a mediating role between the living and the Supreme Being in Igbo culture.

Jean-Marc Ela, however, argues against the use of the term *worship*. In reference to the terms *cult* and *worship*, he says the following:

> The words do not have the sense they have for many Christians. "Cult" and "worship" are terms inappropriate to the African context in which man expresses in a relationship of communion his respect for the founders of the tribe. A family relationship should not be given the title "cult" in the strict sense of the term. When people offer beer and food to the dead, they are very well aware they are not worshipping the dead, but are reliving a form of kinship with them, by actualizing it in an existential situation.⁵³

Ela claims that the above action is not religious but a "mode of symbolic expression."⁵⁴ It is evident, however, that more often than not the sacred and secular are not dichotomized in African culture.

Idowu holds to the belief that "communion and communication are possible between those who are alive on earth and the deceased and that the latter have the power to influence, help, or molest the former."⁵⁵ Idowu cites scholars such as Parrinder, Danquash, and Driberg on the question "Do Africans worship ancestors?" and concludes that those who too readily accept the affirmative are simply deluding themselves with "wishful thinking." However, those who categorically deny any form of worship accorded to ancestors, he believes, have forgotten the complexity of the "working of the human mind."⁵⁶ The following is his own conclusion:

> While technically Africans do not put their ancestors, as ancestors, on the same footing with Deity or the divinities, there is no doubt that the ancestors receive veneration that may become so intense as to verge on worship or even become worship.⁵⁷

Idowu, rather surprisingly, is emphatic that the cults of the ancestors do not rightly constitute African Traditional Religion and says, "It is a gross error to equate them with the religion."⁵⁸ He goes on to suggest that the

52. Ibid.
53. Ela, "Ancestors and the Christian Faith," 39–40.
54. Ibid., 40.
55. Idowu, *African Traditional Religion*, 179.
56. Ibid., 182.
57. Ibid., 186.
58. Ibid.

ancestor cult is made up of people who, although "dead," are still part of the family or community life by extension. The cult establishes a means of communion and communication between those who are living on earth and those who dwell in the spirit-world.[59]

Research has shown that Africans generally profess some connection with the ancestors. Sacrifices are often offered to ancestors at special stations along life's journey. Africans possess rites for every stage of life, beginning at conception and extending beyond the grave. In each of these phases, ancestors are remembered, venerated, worshipped (for want of better terminology), and even offered sacrifices. As Idowu earlier pointed out, "Worship and veneration . . . are psychologically closer than next door to each other: the emotional indicator is always trembling between the two, swinging to the one or the other in accordance with the emotional pressure or the spiritual climate of the moment."[60]

Healing

When a person becomes ill, Africans believe that the disorder is not only a physical matter but a spiritual one as well. Any illness implies that there is a fracture or imbalance between the metaphysical and the human world. For the illness to be eradicated, the cause of the imbalance or fracture needs to be established first. To achieve this end, the person afflicted with the illness approaches traditional healers or diviners. They are "directed by the ancestors and other spirits from whom they receive power, [and thus] utilizes this supernatural power for healing purposes."[61]

The ancestors or spirits are the ones who supply the diviners with power. Consequently, the diviners have to keep in contact regularly with the ancestors and spirits.[62] While diviners are somewhat different from herbalists and "medicine doctors," their work does overlap in that both endeavor to provide healing to the afflicted. However, the role of the diviner appears to be elevated, compared to that of the herbalist. Oosthuizen explains:

> The spiritual life of the tribe is the concern of the *Isangoma*. The continuous threat against the community by invisible negative, destructive forces of life makes the function of the *Isangoma* a necessity . . . . A main function is to heal the sick and in his contact

59. Ibid.
60. Idowu, *African Traditional Religion*, 182.
61. Oosthuizen, *Afro-Christian Religions*, 29.
62. Oosthuizen, "Isaiah Shembe and the Zulu Worldview," 14.

African and Zulu Traditional Religions

with the spirits through dreams and trance situations, which is a religious medical contact, his supernatural power is strengthened. He counteracts evil forces, especially those that cause disease, and he fights his way through the magical world and its dangers and attacks it right at the center.[63]

Summary of African Traditional Religions

African Traditional Religion has provided Africans with fundamental beliefs and practices through a well-defined hierarchical system of harmony, cementing relationships between humans on one hand and the Supreme Being on the other. What becomes clear as one studies African Traditional Religion is that at the center, at its core, is the consciousness of relationships. Thus, Mbiti's adage "I am because we are, and because we are I exist"[64] speaks eloquently to the issue of life in its continuity from conception to the afterlife.

There is an interconnectedness of individuals to each other and to forces higher than and below the individual. In this regard, the African believes that there is a force of divinity higher than the individual, namely, God. God is paradoxically both transcendent and immanent to people. God's transcendence is accepted as an inevitable fact, and because of God's power and might, ordinary humans are reticent to approach such a Supreme Being. However, Africans believe that God may be approached through intermediaries, such as ancestors.

Thus ancestors play an important role in the lives of the living. In Mbiti's terms, the "living-dead" are considered to be closer to the Supreme Being, and consequently they are in a position to carry the requests of their living relatives to God. In this capacity ancestors become mediators between the living and God. Given the strategic place that ancestors hold in the lives of traditional Africans, the ancestor cult, with all of its ritual and ceremony, becomes an integral part of the religiocultural life of Africans. The role of ancestors becomes an important consideration when traditional Africans accept the Christian faith. Now, the person and work of Christ have to be factored into their new consciousness. Do ancestors still mediate between God and the living? Closely tied to the issue of ancestors is the question of healing. How strategic a role do African diviners and herbalists play in the lives of people who have accepted the Christian faith? Who mediates healing for the converted traditionalists? These ques-

---

63. Ibid., 15.
64. Mbiti, *African Religions and Philosophy*, 106.

tions are pursued in chapter 7 below in the context of the amaNazaretha Church. Since the amaNazaretha adherents are predominately Zulu, a closer study of Zulu traditional culture and religion follows.

Zulu Worldview

In the province of KwaZulu-Natal, on the southeastern side of South Africa, live the Zulu people. According to Beck, South Africa, and more specifically the Eastern Cape and KwaZulu-Natal, were the home of the oldest known fossils of humankind, dating back some one hundred thousand years.[65] In 1999 a two-thousand-year-old mummified body, more than likely a Khoisan man, was discovered in the Eastern Cape.[66] The Khoisan are a collective group made up of the pastoralist Khoikhoi people and the hunting-gathering San people. At the beginning of the Christian era, they migrated from central Africa to the south, encountering the Zulu and Xhosa people en route.[67]

The Bantu speakers, a family of more than two hundred related languages, comprise four main cultural-linguistic groups: Nguni, Sotho, Venda, and Tsonga.[68] The Nguni is the dominant group further delineated into northern and southern parts. [69] The Zulus, part of the northern group that settled in KwaZulu Natal, acquired their name sometime in the seventeenth century from the chieftain of a small clan, numbering some fifteen hundred subjects. Shaka, a powerful young prince, who emerged as leader in the nineteenth century, welded together most of the Nguni tribes into the powerful Zulu nation, ruling from 1816 to 1828.[70] Dingane, Shaka's brother, assassinated him and usurped leadership, only

---

65. Beck, *The History of South Africa*, 9–10. The author argues for the existence of some form of ancient human life in the subcontinent of Africa by citing the discoveries of archaeologists such as Ron Clark, who in December 1998 discovered a skeleton and skull in a cave in Krugersdorp. This find was preceded by Raymond Dart's discovery of a small skull in the Northern Cape in 1924. Hence, the author's claim that southern Africa is the "possible cradle of humanity."

66. Ibid., 10.

67. Ibid., 15. See also Maylam, *A History of the African People of South Africa*, for a fuller discussion of the history and composition of South African peoples.

68. Beck, *The History of South Africa*, 17. See also Morris, *The Washing of the Spears*, 24.

69. The Nguni may be described as a broad-based linguistic family made up of Zulu and Swazi in the north and the Xhosa, Thembu, Mfengu, Mpondo and Mpondomise in the south.

70. Buthelezi, "The Early History," 19.

to be defeated by the Boers (Battle of Blood River, 1838) and the British (Battle of Isandhlwana, 1879).[71]

In 1910, Natal became part of the Union of South Africa. This political event together with the death of Dinzulu, the last of the Zulu monarchs, brought to a temporary halt the era of the Zulu monarchy.

Zulu religion is cohesive and relational—a relationship between the natural and supernatural, the living and the dead, and higher spiritual beings. At the top of the religiocultural hierarchy is the Supreme Deity. In the Zulu religious tradition, this Supreme Deity operates and manifests his presence through several intermediaries.[72]

Zulus approach the Supreme Being through the next level of beings, namely, spirits and ancestors, or the "living-dead."[73] As noted earlier, it is through the living-dead that the spirit-world becomes personal and accessible to African people. The living-dead are considered "people" who have not yet become spirits. They are said to visit their families from time to time, showing interest in the intimate details of their families' daily lives. In some sense they act as mediators between their families and God. This idea is credible to Africans because they believe the ancestors know the family's needs, since the ancestors were once living members of that family, and also because they have full access to communicating with God directly.[74] Parrinder, lending weight to this idea, says, "In South Africa the ancestor spirits are the most intimate gods of the Bantu: they are part of the family or tribe and are considered and consulted on all important issues." [75]

The Zulu family is patriarchal; men are heads of their families and the sole figures of authority. Marriage is exogamous. *Lobola*, bride-wealth, is still practiced by the traditional Zulu. Usually a gift of cattle is offered to the bride's family. In an urban environment, however, it is not unusual to offer money as *lobola*. Given South Africa's living conditions and the fact of urbanization, Zulus live in two worlds: an urban world where men work in the city and live in hostels away from their families, and a rural world where family members live in small homesteads or kraals with subsistence farming their chief means of survival. It is not uncommon today

---

71. Giles, *Peoples of Southern Africa*, 98.

72. Jafta, "One, the Other, the Divine, the Many," 79.

73. The term was first used by John S. Mbiti (*Introduction to African Religion*, 63) referring to people who died recently and are remembered for up to four or five generations by their families, friends, and relatives. The term *living-dead* distinguishes them from those who died long before that.

74. Nyamiti, *Christ as Our Ancestor*, 15–16.

75. Parrinder, *Africa's Three Religions*, 57.

to see younger Zulu women working and living in the cities of South Africa, having traded their traditional roles of tending farms and children for hectic city life.

The rural-urban paradox is very evident among Shembe members. In Sabbath services in the inner city, Shembe men come to the services dressed in Western attire (formal suits and ties), carrying attaché cases in one hand and umbrellas in the other. The attaché cases contain white religious dress, headband, and other vestments that are worn at these services. Within minutes the "Western executive" becomes the African religiocultural person, only to revert to the "Western" person again after the service. Today Zulus in the city dress no differently than other modern urbanites. However, Zulu cultural dress is worn at religious and cultural ceremonies such as weddings, funerals, dances, and commemorative holidays. The amaNazaretha Church is a typical example of those time-honored Zulu traditions that are retained and observed, especially in the annual dances held in January and July.[76]

The leader, Vimbeni Shembe, and ancestors do play a role in the spiritual life of the Shembe Church; however, to what extent, and how those roles relate to the person and work of Christ is unclear. This study endeavors to discern the Christology that is evident in the Shembe Church.

According to Berglund, Zulu prayer is seldom directed to God. One of this scholar's informants said, "We do not speak of him [God] as if he were our acquaintance. So we simply keep quiet and say nothing."[77] Zulus claim that their reticence to communicate with the Supreme Being is that they are intentional about safeguarding the integrity and honor of God. Some Zulus state that they did not pray directly to God, but that prayers were made via an intermediary, Shembe, or ancestors. Since ancestors mediate on behalf of the Zulus, their idea of Christian prayer becomes important. The ideas held by members of the Shembe Church on the relationship of Christ to God, and to the people, in the light of the views they have always held of their ancestors raise the question of whether the Shembe Church is a Christward movement.

John Pobee, while conceding that culture is never static, maintains that "Christianity, Islam, secularism, political change, and the whole drift of the present age have combined to undermine African cultures and traditional religions."[78] While culture is dynamic and always changing, though often in imperceptible ways, globalization and urbanization have

76. Becken, "On the Holy Mountain," 139–49.
77. Berglund, *Zulu Thought-Patterns*, 42.
78. Pobee, *Toward an African Theology*, 44.

of late also contributed to the erosion of traditional religion and culture in the continent of Africa. According to UNICEF's statistics,[79] 57 percent of the South African population now resides in urban areas. Zulus in South Africa occupy various economic sectors—some university professors, school principals and teachers, medical doctors and nurses, business administrators, and still many more as laborers doing menial chores to eke out a living in a struggling fledgling environment—in post-apartheid South Africa. Yet, the Zulus in South Africa have consciously endeavored to maintain fundamental aspects of their traditional religion and culture in their daily lives.

These aspects of traditional religion and culture are evident in the beliefs and practices in the amaNazaretha Church. Their implications are discussed in ch. 7. In what follows, I discuss some key aspects of tradition and culture that are pertinent to the study of amaNazaretha Church.

The Idea of God

Early travelers and missionaries observed that the Zulus acknowledged the existence of a Supreme Being whom they considered responsible for Creation.[80] Joseph Shooter, an early researcher in Natal (1857), discovered through interviews that Zulus believed in a Superior Being, a Creator-God, even before the first Western missionaries arrived. Shooter observed the following:

> The Kafirs of Natal and the Zulu-country have preserved the tradition of a Being whom they call the Great-Great and the First Appearer or Exister. He is presented as having made all things—men, cattle, water, fire, the mountains, and whatever else is seen.[81]

The Zulu name for God is *uNkulunkulu*, "Great-Great One." The "First Appearer or Exister" is another name for God, which in Zulu is *uMvelinqangi*. Henry Callaway,[82] who worked among the Zulus in the latter part of the nineteenth century, shows that Zulus believed in a Creator-God, but this God was unknown to them. Callaway's research

79. UNICEF (United Nation's Children's Fund) figures were compiled in 2001.
80. Shooter, *The Kafirs of Natal*, 159; cf. Thorpe, *African Traditional Religions*, 35.
81. Shooter, *The Kafirs of Natal*, 159.
82. Henry Callaway was a missionary doctor from England who worked among the Zulus in the former Natal Province (now KwaZulu-Natal) of South Africa beginning in 1854. He studied Zulu and was responsible for translating part of the Bible in Zulu. His definitive work is *The Religious System of the AmaZulu*, first published in 1870. For scholars today, Callaway's writings have become a standard reference on the beliefs of the Zulu people. The 1970 edition is a facsimile reprint of the original version.

shows that Zulus had two names for the Supreme God, *Unkulunkulu* and *Umvelinqangi*.[83] According to Callaway, missionaries added one other name, *Utikxo*.[84] Nonetheless, Callaway's conclusions are that none of these names accurately represent the Christian understanding of the Supreme Being, God. He says, "For there is no name, whether *Utikxo*, or *Morino*, or *Unkulunkulu*, which, without possessing any primary signification referring to divinity, has not much, both etymologically and traditionally, which is highly objectionable, and calculated to mislead the young convert."[85] Oosthuizen adds that "the Zulu creation myth leaves many questions unanswered with regard to the relationship between Unkulunkulu and Umvelingqangi."[86]

Berglund ascertained that just as in the Hebrew language, God is known by God's attributes (Jehovah Jireh, Jehovah Shalom, among others). Likewise, in the Zulu tradition, God has many names, and each name is representative of his attributes or functions. For example, the Zulu words *uSomandla* and *uMninimandla* signify that God is both almighty and powerful.[87] However, it is not clear whether Zulus believe in one Supreme Being with many functions or whether there are lesser beings who control the various aspects of creation, such as the weather and human beings. Among Zulus, prayer is not offered directly to the Supreme Being because of the awe, esteem, and respect they hold for such a being. Zulus follow a hierarchical line of communication that begins with the living elders and diviners and then channels via ancestors to the Supreme Being.[88] In Zulu Traditional Religion, *uMvelinqangi* is the name more often used than any other. My own field research among the amaNazaretha, however, shows that the name for God most often used is *Unkulunkulu*. Although the Supreme Being is seldom directly approached by people, he still occupies a significant place in the hierarchy of Zulu cosmology.[89]

Regarding the one who is worshipped, when Callaway asked the question one informant responded, "There are none [who pray to *Unkulunkulu*]. They pray to the *amatonga* [ancestral spirits]; they honor them that they may come and save them."[90] The informant continued,

83. Callaway, *The Religious System of the AmaZulu*, 1–104.
84. Ibid., 105
85. Ibid., 112–13.
86. Oosthuizen, "Isaiah Shembe," 2.
87. Berglund, *Zulu Thought-Patterns*, 36.
88. Thorpe, *African Traditional Religions*, 36.
89. Boot, "Religious Pluralism," 116.
90. Callaway, *The Religious System of the AmaZulu*, 42.

"In the process of time we have come to worship the *Amadhlozi* [another term for ancestral spirits] only because we know not what to say about *Unkulunkulu*; for we do not even know where we separated from him, nor from the word which he left with us."[91]

Ancestors

Zulus do believe in a Supreme Being; however, they also believe that this Being is inaccessible, remote, and withdrawn from being involved in human affairs.[92] Consequently, the distance between the Supreme Being and people is so vast that out of necessity they must approach lesser spiritual beings for guidance and assistance in the exigencies of life.

Although the idea of transcendence is evident in the Zulu understanding of God, it is not akin to the Deistic understanding that was theorized in eighteenth-century Europe, that God created the world and was then separated from the creation. According to Zulus, God is active in the daily existential lives of people. God's interaction with humankind is expressed through the hierarchical structure of Zulu cosmology.

Here the ancestors appear to occupy a critical role in the lives of the Zulus. The Zulu understanding of the role of ancestors is functionally similar to the perspectives on ancestors in other parts of Africa. Fortes stresses the integral place of ancestors in the life of Africans in general: "[W]henever it occurs, ancestor worship is rooted in domestic, kinship and descent relations, and institutions. It is described by some as an extension of these relations to the supernatural sphere, by others as a reflection of these relations, yet again as their ritual and symbolic expression."[93]

Pobee, from Ghana, offers another perspective that ancestors are "those who have gone before . . . . The family consists of the living, the dead, and the still unborn. It is not only the living. Consequently, these ancestors, though dead, are still believed to be concerned with and involved in the affairs of the living."[94] However, it is Mbiti who offers a general African perspective of ancestors, whom he refers to as the "living-dead." He describes such an individual as "a person who is physically dead but alive in the memory of those who knew him or her in life as well as being alive in the world of the spirits. So long as the living-dead is thus

---

91. Ibid., 44.
92. Thorpe, *African Traditional Religions*, 36.
93. Fortes, "Some Reflections," 122.
94. Pobee, "Aspects of African Traditional Religion," 8.

remembered, he or she is in the state of personal immortality."[95] Other scholars refer to ancestors as *shades* so as to distinguish those who affect daily lives from lineal relatives who upon death have no direct intervention in the lives of the living relatives.[96] Thorpe adds that older people in the Zulu community are considered ancestors as well, as they "are already on their way to ancestorhood and are accorded due respect."[97] The respect and honor paid to living elders and those recently dead are the same in Zulu culture. The difference is the method of approaching the elders who are now ancestors, since communication is one-way, or a monologue, and is less frequent than that which is conducted with respected elders who are still alive.[98]

Upon the death of a person, family members bring back the deceased person to his or her former home.[99] This "bringing back" is not a literal or physical event, but is ceremonial. The ceremony takes place approximately one year after the death of the individual. It is referred to as the *ukubuyisa idlozi* (bringing home of the spirit) ceremony.[100] Oosthuizen describes the ceremony thus: "At the *ukubuyisa* ceremony, the putting into office of the ancestor, a small piece of meat is burnt with *impepho* . . . as it is prepared for the shades."[101] The ancestor, upon installation, officially assumes responsibility for the well-being of the living relatives. The relationship between ancestors and the living relatives is ambivalent; it may be both punitive and benevolent. When ancestors are propitiated and sacrifices offered on

---

95. Mbiti, *African Religions and Philosophy*, 25.

96. For example, in Martin West's "The Shades Come to Town," he refers to the work of Monica Wilson where she differentiates between shades and ancestors in that "relatives who have died are ancestors, while the shades are more specifically dead people who are believed to affect the living directly" (185).

97. Thorpe, *African Traditional Religions*, 38.

98. Kopytoff, "Ancestors as Elders in Africa," 133

99. Congdon, "An Investigation into the Current Zulu Worldview," 296.

100. Frans H. Boot, anthropologist from University of the Western Cape, South Africa, recorded this response with a minister regarding the *ukubuyisa* ritual: "Even among Christians the ukubuyisa is performed so that the spirits of the deceased may be guardian angels to their children. If the living do something wrong the spirit reprimands them and orders them to stop it. When a person dies, the spirit remains at the home to look after the inhabitants of the kraal. This is true for both Christians and non-Christians. These spirits communicate with God and intercede on behalf of the living. They ask God to forgive the sins. They protect and punish" ("Religious Pluralism," 127). This response, from a Lutheran minister, accentuates the complexity of the ancestor cult and its implications for the everyday life of the Zulu. The status and role of Christ becomes the all-important question when one considers the cultural role ancestors have in the Zulu worldview.

101. Oosthuizen, "Isaiah Shembe," 21.

their behalf, it is believed that the ancestors give material blessings to their living relatives. On the other hand, if ancestors are neglected or forgotten, living relatives are punished.[102] The head of the household is subject to the ancestor and has the primary responsibility for cultic activities.

Jabulani Nxumalo, after conducting a funeral service for a Zulu child, recounted this piece of communication between the father of the dead child and the ancestors. The body of the child lay near the *emsamo* in the main hut of the kraal. The father, squatting next to the dead body, addressed the ancestors with these words: "You members of the lineage of N. N.[103] we beseech you to please kindly receive this child into your midst as we are about to accompany him bringing him to yourselves."[104] Just as ancestors are notified about the birth of children, ancestors are informed when people die.

Communication

Ancestors communicate with their living relatives in several ways. Zulus believe that the spirits of ancestors inhabit snakes and visit their living relatives.[105] When such a snake appears in their home, Zulus treat the snake with respect by offering it milk. When the creature leaves the home, the householders are content that they acknowledged the presence of the ancestor and that the ancestor was pleased with the hospitality and respect received.[106]

More frequent communication between ancestors and their living relatives occurs through dreams. Ancestors sometimes identify themselves by revealing their names and at other times through some characteristic known by the family member who has had the dream.[107] Anderson cites one example where an individual was killed in a motor accident and family members went to a diviner to ascertain the reason for the victim's death. The diviner informed them that the deceased person had failed to obey the "rules of the ancestors as revealed in a dream," hence the accident and subsequent death of the victim.[108]

---

102. Nxumalo, "Christ and Ancestors in the African World," 10.

103. N. N. are probably the initials of the interviewee, whose identity the author wanted to protect.

104. Nxumalo, "Christ and Ancestors in the African World," 12.

105. Makhathani, "Ancestors, Umoya, Angels," 156.

106. Congdon, "An Investigation into the Current Zulu Worldview," 297.

107. Anderson, *Tumelo*, 27.

108. Ibid., 28.

Guidance and Protection

Ancestors are also known to offer guidance and protection to living relatives. Ngubane, a Zulu researcher who wrote his master's thesis on the subject "The Role of the Amadlozi/Amathonga as Seen in the Writings of W. B. Vilakazi,"[109] cites a case where a woman, Nomanzi, had a dream in which her grandmother urged her to leave her village without delay. The woman and her two friends left the village. No sooner had they left than the village was surrounded by unknown assailants who massacred all the people in the village that same night. I was told a similar story where the ancestors appeared to a woman in a dream urging her to leave her home because her separated husband was on his way to murder her. The woman left her home in the thick of night and subsequently heard that her husband did indeed come to her lodging that night to harm her. It is clear from the above examples that Zulus believe their ancestors have the capacity to lead and guide them; however, at other times the ancestors allow danger to befall the living when the ancestors have been forgotten or ignored.

It is the traditional view among the Zulus that the ancestors are constant companions to their relatives and thus considered to be omnipresent. Hammond-Tooke speaks of this unique attribute of ancestors when he says, "Invisibility, and the ability to be in a number of places at once, feeds power into the state of ancestorhood."[110] Consequently, it would appear that the ancestors are always near their relatives and that they do not carry out their responsibilities from a distance.[111]

DEIFICATION

In Zulu culture prominent leaders, royalty, and chiefs are deified and remembered long after their death. Elders, chiefs, and royalty are not only remembered and respected long after death, but serve as maintainers of tradition and values that the living perpetuate and model in everyday life. Moral life in a given tribal society is sanctioned by the ancestors.[112] Zulus believe that "the deification of some of the 'dead' ancestors, especially

---

109. Benedict Wallet Vilakazi (1906-1947), a Zulu, was the first African to teach in the all-white University of the Witwatersrand, Johannesburg, in 1935, teaching Bantu languages. Ngubane elicits cultural Zulu traditions and anecdotes from the literary works penned by Vilakazi.

110. Hammond-Tooke, "Do the Southern Eastern Bantu," 137.

111. Ngubane, "The Role of Amadlozi/Amathongo," 62.

112. Pobee, "Aspects of African Traditional Religion," 9.

those in authority, is . . . a grasping back to the source of everything, a way of maintaining contact with the supernatural world."[113]

According to Dzobo, "A human being as a unique individual is less important than a human being as an individual link in the chain of generations."[114] Consequently, life's creative powers that have their source in God are not for the sole benefit of the individual, but rather pass through the person to others in the lineage. Therefore, when one participates in the ancestor cult, one knows that the creative power transcends the individual, yet one is still part of the creative power of life.[115]

Kings, chiefs, and diviners are said to be carriers of "life force" or power, and such power enables them to offer "benefits, protect, heal and even hurt" people.[116] The Zulu king or chief thus "forms an important link with the supernatural world.[117] In the Zulu religious system, the absence of priests brings to the fore the critical role of the family head in ceremonies important to the individual family. Where the community as a whole is concerned, the king or chief plays a prominent role in religious affairs. According to Krige (as quoted by Oosthuizen), "[The king or chief] is the highest symbol in the Zulu society of what is powerful: he is the personification of law, the representative of the royal ancestors, and thus the center of ritual . . . . Treason against the Chief is the same as treason against the whole people, for the Chief is the symbol of the unity of the tribe and as such sacred."[118] Even long after death such leaders are remembered, and their traditions, customs, and laws are revered and respected among the tribe and community. Their influence is the bedrock for the social and religious practices enacted in the daily life of the Zulu.

The role and status of Isaiah Shembe (1887–1935) become relevant when the influence and awe of the founder of the amaNazaretha Church are considered. The role and status of Vimbeni Shembe in the church today also comes into question in the light of the influence of Isaiah Shembe, the founder.

---

113. Oosthuizen, "Isaiah Shembe," 3.
114. Dzobo, "African Ancestor Cult," 335.
115. Ibid.
116. Oosthuizen, "Isaiah Shembe," 6–7.
117. Ibid., 10.
118. Ibid.

Healing

In the Zulu worldview, the concept of health transcends the physical. Healing is viewed holistically; thus good health means more than a healthy body.[119] Illness for the Zulu is more than just a physical or mental disorder; it is also a religious matter.[120] In Zulu thought, life is a gift from the Creator to enjoy; this life is not lived in isolation but in community. Therefore, illness experienced by one member of the community affects the whole community. In this regard Placide Temples suggests that the goal of life for the Zulu is to live well, and this kind of life is achieved through the acquisition of "vital force."[121] "Vital Force" or power to live well "is preserved and strengthened by prayers, sacrifices, and rituals, wisdom and proper conduct."[122]

Diviners

Identifying the cause of illness, the treatment, and the prognosis is the task of the diviner (*isangoma*). The diviners (male or female) do not attain their status by their own free will and choice. The potential diviner receives his or her calling through revelation from one's ancestral spirit, and such a call is irresistible.[123] Ancestors or spirits are sources of power for the diviner. According to Oosthuizen, the diviner "is a medicine man or woman whose medicine has magical rather than pharmaceutical value."[124]

The diviner's function in Zulu society cannot be underestimated, as he or she possesses power to identify and understand spiritual phenomena that are beyond the comprehension of ordinary people. Such power is obtained only from the ancestor.[125] Further, the diviner also holds a strategic position in Zulu society because he or she is concerned about the spiritual well-being of the community, always looking out for threats against the community from "invisible, negative and destructive forces."[126]

In the Zulu worldview people perceive Western medicine to be merely a means of treating symptoms. For Zulus, unless the cause of the illness is determined, any treatment is thought to be superficial. The cause is usually

---

119. Ngubane, *Body and Mind in Zulu Medicine*, 28.
120. Mbiti, *Introduction to African Religion*, 134.
121. Temples, *Bantu Philosophy*, 44.
122. Thorpe, *African Traditional Religions*, 112.
123. Callaway, *The Religious System of the AmaZulu*, 259.
124. Oosthuizen, "Isaiah Shembe," 14.
125. Bryant, "The Zulu Cult of the Dead," 143.
126. Oosthuizen, "Isaiah Shembe," 15.

attributed to the disruption of unity resulting in stress on the individual and the group.[127] Oosthuizen concludes the following:

> While Western medicine has become divorced from religion, and a split has taken place in treating the body, mind, and soul by the physician, psychiatrist, and priest, respectively, and the social worker has been concentrating on social problems, the diviner relates to all these issues as a trusted person in the community. Religion remains a major significance in healing procedures among . . . traditionalists [and] those from independent/indigenous churches.[128]

In Zulu culture the *isangoma* or diviner is not the only person responsible for administering healing to the afflicted. Medicine doctors and herbalists also engage in healing activities. While they also serve an important function in the life of the Zulu, this study is concerned with the influence Zulu Traditional Religion has in the amaNazaretha Church and especially the transference of the role of the diviner to Vimbeni Shembe and the founder, Isaiah Shembe.

Summary

In this chapter, I summarize the beliefs and practices of African traditionalists generally and, more specifically, those of the Zulu culture. As has been shown, African religion and daily life cannot be dichotomized. Therefore, to separate what is cultural from what is religious or to separate the sacred from the secular is impossible as all of life is sacred for the African. The missiological challenge is to find ways to contextualize Christian beliefs in Zulu culture and be faithful to Christian orthodoxy without demeaning the indigenous culture. To what extent this occurs in the AICs and more specifically the amaNazaretha Church (ch. 4) will become clear later.

---

127. Thorpe, *African Traditional Religions*, 111.
128. Oosthuizen et al., *Afro-Christian Religion*, 47.

3

The African Initiated Churches: History, Beliefs, and Practices

THE MOMENTOUS GROWTH OF African Initiated Churches is one response by Africans to the necessity of indigenizing the gospel so that it meets the felt needs of its adherents. Rather than repeat the historical traditions handed down to them, the African Initiated Churches today seek ways to give expression to the gospel in their own idiom while endeavoring to be faithful to the Christian gospel and the biblical text.

This chapter investigates the phenomenal rise of several of the African Initiated Churches in South Africa. This investigation sets the stage for our specific study on the amaNazaretha Church of Isaiah Shembe in ch. 4.

Phenomenal Growth

The growth of the church in Africa is surely one of the surprises of the past century; a review of some of the early literature attests to this fact, where the AICs are one example. Bengt Sundkler, the noted missionary observer, in his incisive work describing new indigenous Christian churches, *Bantu Prophets in South Africa*, could not envision the impact of the movement. He concluded, "The syncretistic sects were the bridge over which Africans are brought back to heathenism."[1] However, in his later book, *Zulu Zion and Some Swazi Zionists,* he acknowledged his error, saying, "From the point of view of those involved, Zion was not turned to the past, but to the future and was their future."[2] Rather than a steady retrogression to tribal and syncretistic practices, the surprise became evident in the sustained progression, even an avalanche of movement, toward Christianity. Yet, some AICs have moved away from orthodox Christian positions and thus would

---

1. Sundkler, *Bantu Prophets*, 297.
2. Sundkler, *Zulu Zion*, 305.

likely fall into the category of what Oosthuizen called "post-Christian,"[3] or in the terminology of Turner, "New Religious Movements."[4]

According to Daneel, there are more than seven thousand African Initiated Churches in Africa, with more than thirty million adherents.[5] In South Africa alone, there are some five thousand groups, the largest being the Zion City Church (ZCC). According to Barrett's 1995 statistics (published in 2001), there are some eight million adherents in the two largest and better-known churches in South Africa, the ZCC (seven million) and the amaNazaretha Church (approximately one million).[6]

Terminology

The problem of employing an adequate nomenclature that would be descriptive as well as consistent with the ethos of these churches has long been debated.[7] In times past, Sundkler, Barrett, Oosthuizen, Turner, and Daneel have all reflected on how best to characterize the AICs. Sundkler referred to the AICs as "Bantu Independent Churches" in his work *Bantu Prophets in South Africa*. He argued that the name "Native Separatist Churches," as used by the South African government was unacceptable to the indigenous African people. Sundkler claimed that the word *native* is pejorative and is despised by the local indigenous African people, while the term *separatist* could equally apply to white secessionists as much as it does to Africans.[8] He used the term *Bantu independent* "as referring to such religious organizations as, in their desire for independence from the Whites have seceded from mission churches."[9] He probably was influenced by the fact that D. Westermann had already also used the term *independent*.[10] While Sundkler argued for the use of the term *independent*, in the new chapter added to his

---

3. Oosthuizen, *Post-Christianity in Africa*.

4. Turner, *Religious Innovation in Africa*.

5. Daneel, *Quest for Belonging*, 25. Muzibuko claimed that in 1989 there were more than ten thousand such groups in Africa (*Missiology: Mission as African Initiative*). Philip Jenkins suggests a figure of thirty-five million adherents in the subcontinent (*The Next Christendom*, 57).

6. Barrett et al., *World Christian Encyclopedia*, 681.

7. Nya Kwiawon Taryor, from Liberia, West Africa, for one, offers a definition for terms that one would encounter in such a study as this one. He discusses terms such as Independency, Indigenous, Initiated Churches, Separatist, Prophetic Movements, Messianic Churches, and Mission Churches (*Impact of the African Tradition*, 262–70).

8. Sundkler, *Bantu Prophets*, 18.

9. Ibid.

10. See Westermann, *Africa and Christianity*.

1961 edition of his work *Bantu Prophets in South Africa*, he surprisingly gravitated to the use of the term *separatist*.

Barrett also argued for the term *independent* in his *Schism and Renewal in Africa*. He reasoned:

> The term is . . . a good description for the widespread phenomenon in which large numbers of former adherents of mission churches have seceded in order to assert their right to freedom from larger ecclesiastical control, and in which others have founded new movements and organizations independent of direct or indirect control from the Western world.[11]

After discounting terms such as *prophet churches, native churches, indigenous churches*, and *separatist churches*, Turner also concludes that the most appropriate and only alternative should be *independent churches*.[12] Admitting that the term *independent* is not the most precise, Turner argues that it "is devoid of offence and free from the confusions and the more patent inaccuracies associated with the other terms."[13] Turner defines this phenomenon as "[A] church which has been founded in Africa, by Africans, and primarily for Africans."[14] This definition encapsulates the essential features of the churches in the movement—that they are of African origin, were founded by Africans, and while not exclusivist, they are essentially adapted to meet the needs, worldview, and lifestyle of African people.

Daneel, who has done extensive research and written much on the Shona Zion Churches in Zimbabwe, also believes that the most appropriate term for these churches is *independent*. He claims, " 'Independent' is an apposite adjective, since in their organization and worship these groups are in fact independent of the Western mission churches that had initially imported the Christian message."[15] Daneel further describes this new phenomenon from a sociological perspective:

> An Independent Church is a new movement arising from the interaction between a tribal community and its religion on one hand, and a heterogeneous foreign culture intruding with its (Christian) religion on the other. In several respects the new movement deviates significantly from the classical religious traditions of both the

---

11. Barrett, *Schism and Renewal in Africa*, 49.
12. Turner, *Religious Innovation in Africa*, 91.
13. Ibid.
14. Turner, *African Independent Church*, xvi.
15. Daneel, *Quest for Belonging*, 31.

The African Initiated Churches

cultures involved. Elements of both traditions are renewed, modified and embodied in a new religious system.[16]

Field research indicates to what extent the amaNazaretha Church of Isaiah Shembe fits Daneel's taxonomy.

Another researcher and scholar of African Christianity who has incisively grasped the essence of these churches is Andrew Walls. He reworks Turner's definition of the African Independent Churches, calling them "[an] historically new development arising in the inter-action between a tribal society and its religion on one hand, and an invader culture and its religion on the other, involving a substantial departure from both and a reworking of rejected traditions into something new.[17] Walls argues that AICs are the expression of African Christianity that "may likely be a new religious movement reworking the old and the new . . . . The distinction between independent and older churches may be of decreasing value."[18]

In spite of the preference and arguments adduced for the use of the term *independent* by scholars of repute, in this work the acronym AIC will mean "African Initiated Churches," a designation that has become accepted to adherents of these churches. John Pobee and Gabriel Ositelu II, writing on the eve of the World Council of Churches' fiftieth anniversary conference held in Harare, Zimbabwe, in 1998, argued that while Turner's definition had its merits, the term *African Initiatives in Christianity* best describes the movement today.[19] Pobee states:

> While it is true that in earlier times the mission churches were colonial churches, today they are nearly all independent, even if they retain aspects of their origins. What is unique about AICs is their character as *African* Initiatives and, therefore, in accordance with the African genius and culture and ethos.[20]

---

16. Ibid., 32.
17. Walls, *The Missionary Movement in Christian History*, 113. Turner himself defined new religious movements as "a new development arising in the course of the interaction of a tribal or primal society and its religion with one of the more powerful and sophisticated cultures and its major religion, involving some substantial departure from the classical religious traditions of both the cultures concerned by reworking the contributing traditions into a different religious system" (Ibid., 14).
18. Ibid., 113.
19. Pobee and Ositelu, *African Initiatives in Christianity*, 4.
20. Ibid.

Nevertheless, it must be pointed out that the discussion on what designation best reflects the whole ethos of the AICs is still debated by both African and Western writers.

Typology

In many ways, Bengt Sundkler's work *Bantu Prophets in South Africa* was the catalyst for the avid interest in the AICs by scholars within the academy. Not least among them were Africans. The question of the best descriptive nomenclature of the AICs was debated then as it is in our day. There is consensus among missiologists such as Bengt Sundkler, David Barrett, Inus Daneel, and Harold Turner, among others, that there should be a taxonomy that would facilitate identification and study of the AICs.[21] Turner's typology is still considered the most definitive and widely used to this day. The chart below depicts the three most common types of New Religious Movements in sub-Saharan Africa (i.e., Ethiopian, Sprit-type, and Messianic) together with their subgroups.[22]

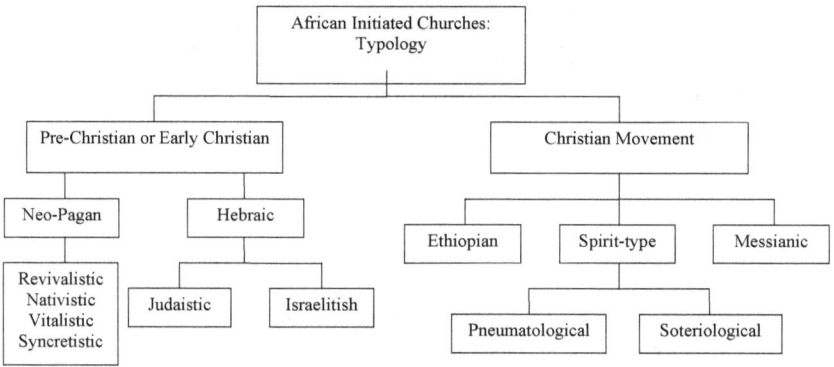

Figure 7. African Initiated Churches: A Typology

21. Sundkler's attempt at formulating a typology resulted in his distinguishing between the "Ethiopian" type and the "Zionist" type of churches in South Africa. Sundkler concentrated his energies mainly on the Zulus in the province of Natal (see Sundkler, *Bantu Prophets*, 53). David Barrett, undertaking a more general study of the AICs in the continent of Africa, surveyed some 850 tribes. After engaging the reader in a discussion on terms such as *prophetic, messianic, millennial, nativistic, syncretistic* and *separatist*, Barrett argues for the use of the term *Independency* (see Barrett, *Schism and Renewal*, 44–63). Daneel, on the other hand, relies extensively on Turner's typology (see Daneel, *Quest for Belonging*, 34–42).

22. Turner's typology used in this work was documented in two different sources, namely, "A Typology for African Religious Movements" in *Journal of Religion in Africa*, vol.1 (1–34) and *Religious Innovation in Africa* (80–108). Cf. also Daneel, *Quest for Belonging*, 34–42.

Scholars believe that there are two distinct groups within the movement: movements that are considered pre-Christian or early Christian and those that are Christian movements.

The former may be subdivided into two further groups: neo-pagan movements and Hebraic movements. The first group represents those who have overreacted to Western influences, which they believe impinged on their sociocultural practices. Consequently, these movements have attempted to revive and reshape the ancient cults. These neo-pagan movements are described as *revivalist, nativistic, vitalistic,* and *syncretistic.*[23] The Hebraic movements differ somewhat from the neo-pagan in that they are not considered pagan in any sense.[24] However, in moving away from paganism they have built their faith in one God around the Old Testament, thus falling far short of a Christian position.[25]

These neo-pagan and Hebraic movements are further characterized by their legalism in the areas of morality, ritualism, and exclusivism. Antagonism toward the white race is not uncommon, and there is a tendency to venerate the so-called Black Messiah as their messianic hope, at the expense of traditional Christian belief in the position of Christ.

While it is true that the Hebraic movements as a whole use some parts of the Christian Bible, none of these groups could be considered fully Christian. This distinction is helpful in that it allows one to distinguish between those within the African Initiated Churches that are classified as

23. Examples of revivalist groups would be those who have made a concerted effort to revive traditional religion via "a combination of tradition, training of priests and the creation of sanctuaries" (Daneel, *Quest for Belonging,* 35). Nativistic groups are represented by those who have become conscientized to their racial identity and nationalistic pride in the face of foreign influences and therefore endeavor to purge all that is foreign. Vitalistic groups have a tendency to use some elements of the Christian faith in their traditional religious practices. As for the *syncretistic* groups, both pagan and new religious elements coalesce so much so that the Christian elements are unrecognizable, thus rendering them un-Christian. See Daneel, *Quest for Belonging,* 35–36; Turner, *Religious Innovation in Africa,* 84.

24. For a fuller discussion on the Hebraic movements, see Turner, "A Typology for African Religious Movements." Turner further delineates the Hebraic movements into two subgroups: Judaistic and Israelitish types (8–10). The Judaistic strand represents those who place "emphasis upon laws, rituals, and taboos, upon baptisms, and purifications and festivals; a sense of exclusiveness may appear in hostility to the white race and in messianic expectations focused upon a 'Black Messiah' who will see justice done at last to the suffering African people of God; finally direct revelation through prophets may have ceased" (9). Turner describes the Israelitish group as "those who reject idolatry and magic, and now feel that the one God of the Scriptures is loving, helpful and speaks to the community through its founder or successor prophets, commanding faith in him (prophet) alone, together with various moral reforms" (8).

25. Turner, "A Typology for African Religious Movements," 8.

Christian and those who are not Christians, or perhaps show tendencies moving away from Christianity to neo-paganism.

The Christian movements within the African Initiated Churches may be divided into three broad categories: *Ethiopian*, *Spirit*, and *messianic* types of churches.[26] The first type, the Ethiopian churches, derive their name from two Biblical passages. The first text is Psalm 68:31: "Ethiopia shall soon stretch out her hands unto God" (KJV). This passage is interpreted as a promise that the oppressed African people have a resonating hope that they will rise and find their place in God's plan of salvation.[27] This idea was borne out, for example, in a sermon preached by James Johnston,[28] when he said, "Africa is to rise once more, Ethiopia is to stretch out her hand to God; her tears are to be wiped off her eyes; her candlestick is to be replaced."[29] The other text concerns the Ethiopian chamberlain in Acts 8:26–40, which shows, it is believed, that the gospel message reached Ethiopia in advance of any European mission. Rising out of this understanding, these movements formulated their own sociopolitical and religious ideology. They are non-prophetic; they do not place much emphasis on the work of the Holy Spirit; and Jordan baptism does not feature as part of their ordinances or liturgy.[30] Turner further nuances this group in terms of their polity that "they imitate the forms of church organization as reflected in the West, and in doctrine and worship they are orthodox."[31]

The second group, the Spirit-type churches, place special emphasis on the work of the Holy Spirit, where the outworkings are discerned in glossolalia, prophetic activity, and faith healing. In Zimbabwe these groups call themselves *maKereke dzoMweya*, meaning "churches of the Spirit."[32] Daneel is more at home with this designation as it accurately portrays these churches. Sundkler, however, prefers the name "Zion," since almost all of these churches, at least in South Africa, have the word *Zion* in their name.[33]

---

26. Daneel, *Quest for Belonging*, 38–42.
27. Ibid., 38.
28. James Johnson, who was a Nigerian bishop, was one of the dissenting voices arguing for what he called "African Christianity" as there is European and Asian Christianity (in Hastings, *The Church in Africa*, 480).
29. Hastings, *The Church in Africa*, 479.
30. Daneel, *Quest for Belonging*, 38.
31. Turner, *Religious Innovation in Africa*, 98.
32. Daneel, *Quest for Belonging*, 39.
33. Sundkler, *Zulu Zion*, 15.

The African Initiated Churches

Turner suggested two further subdivisions within the Spirit-type churches. He nuanced the activity of the Spirit into pneumatological and soteriological subtypes. In the former, it is the work of the Holy Spirit to reveal the will of God to the individual, leading, guiding, and equipping people with powers for prophecy, prayer, and healing.[34] It is the Spirit who empowers the prophet with divine utterances that are meant to regulate both individual and corporate life in the Church. However, the prophetic ministry is not confined to one individual. Others may share in this activity as they are directed and led by the Spirit.[35]

In the soteriological subtype, these churches, having rejected former pagan practices, have turned to the Christian God for healing, protection from evil forces, and salvation. Since salvation is construed as deliverance from all of the above, there seems to be no clear definition of salvation from sin or guilt, and consequently the atonement of Christ seems to be mitigated.[36] Christ, however, is seen as mediator beyond the therapeutic sense.[37]

The whole ethos of these soteriological churches has much in common with the Pentecostal and Holiness churches. There is some affinity with regard to their moral codes, such as the abstaining from alcohol and tobacco, the necessity of tithing according to the injunction in Malachi in the Old Testament, fasting, and scheduled times for prayer.[38] They have incorporated Western liturgical forms in their worship, and there is evidence of "cultural syncretism," where dancing, the use of drums, and clapping seem to be elicited from the remnants of their past.

In addition to these two group types, there is a third distinct group, the messianic churches. They share similar patterns and emphases with the Spirit-type churches, both the pneumatological and the soteriological. There is one major difference, however: their veneration of a leader who is accorded some kind of messianic status.[39] The Mindolo consultation in 1962 described as messianic those groups "which, centered around

---

34. Turner, *Religious Innovation in Africa*, 98.

35. Ibid.

36. Turner, "A Typology for African Religious Movements," 25.

37. Both Daneel and Turner develop this theme more exhaustively. I develop this theme more fully in ch. 7 below. See Daneel, *Old and New in Southern Shona*, 12–124.

38. For other features consistent with Pentecostalism, see Oosthuizen (*Post-Christianity in Africa*, 119–48). Oosthuizen, however, in the chapter "The Misunderstanding of the Biblical Meaning of the Holy Spirit in the Initiated Movements," does not see the person and work of the Holy Spirit as represented in these churches to be consistent with that of Pentecostalism.

39. Turner, "A Typology for African Religious Movements," 31.

a dominant personality, claim for him special powers involving a form of identification with Christ. It should be noted that when this happens the group has . . . moved outside the sphere of the Christian Church."[40] In these movements such a leader, by his mystical powers, miracles, and the mediatorial role he plays between God and his followers, assumes the place of Christ.[41] To what degree this phenomenon takes place varies from church to church. Daneel points out that "in extreme cases where the Christology is manifestly usurped by the Black Messiah, who is to some extent deified, we are in effect confronted with Black Messianism which can be typified only as non-Christian or post-Christian."[42]

All that remains to be said at this point is that although typologies are good efforts to describe the context of the African Initiated Churches, they remain Western constructs attempting to understand these churches. Understandably, the goal of a typology is to differentiate the essential features of these church groups. Within that framework, we recognize that all conclusions are somewhat tentative. Nevertheless, the typology applied to the African Initiated Churches affords the opportunity to embark on a more informed inquiry of where we may place the churches in this study. It also allows one to chart the rise and growth of the African Initiated movement and its proliferation into many streams and variations.

History

In recent times, the African Initiated Churches in South Africa have come to be viewed by some as the most dynamic church movement in the country. They have attracted black South Africans, traditional religionists, and members of mainline churches (or churches that trace their origins to Western churches and missions). Oosthuizen states the following:

> In 1959, fully 75 to 80 percent of all Black South African Christians were members of the mainline churches; only 12 to 14 percent were members of the AICs. By 1980, the mainline share of Black Christian population had dropped to 52 percent, while the AICs had increased to 27 percent; by 1991, the figures were 41 percent and 36 percent.[43]

---

40. Ibid.
41. Ibid.
42. Daneel, *Quest for Belonging*, 41.
43. Oosthuizen, "Indigenous Christianity," 8.

He goes on to predict that by the next century most black South Africans will be members of the African Initiated Churches if present trends continue.[44]

Historically, the roots of the dynamic movement that has come to be known as the AICs go back into the eighteenth century, specifically to a virtually unknown woman, Kimpa Vita, renamed Donna Beatrice after her baptism in 1700.[45] Living in the Portuguese Congo (now Angola), Beatrice claimed that the spirit of Saint Anthony had taken possession of her.[46] Consequently, she dispossessed herself of all material and temporal things and began preaching. According to Jenkins, "An individual is enthusiastically converted through one of the mission churches, from which he or, commonly, she, is gradually estranged. The division might arise over issues of church practice, usually the integration of native practices."[47] Beatrice raised her voice against the Catholic Church and vocalized her displeasure at its formalism and externalism. She canvassed for the removal and destruction of crosses, crucifixes, and images of Christ,[48] not unlike what happened in the iconoclastic controversies that began in the eighth century and continued sporadically up until the time of Luther.[49] To her mind the images could easily become new fetishes replacing the old.[50]

She is, however, more remembered for her messages of liberation [51] and hope in a Black Christ who came to earth as an African in Sao Salvador, and who had black apostles.[52] The Christ of the white Portuguese exploiters, she argued, could not be the Christ of the Bible. At this point the early rise of Black Theology begins. She was later venerated as a saint. Yet, when she later proclaimed a restoration of the ancient Kongo Empire and a new king, she was arrested and imprisoned and condemned to be burnt at the stake.[53] It is said that she died with the name of Jesus on her lips.

44. Ibid.
45. Daneel, *Quest for Belonging*, 46.
46. Hastings, *The Church in Africa*, 104–8.
47. Jenkins, *The Next Christendom*, 48.
48. Isichei, *A History of Christianity in Africa*, 66.
49. Walker, *The History of the Christian Church*, 48–148.
50. Daneel, *Quest for Belonging*, 46.
51. Uzukwu, *A Listening Church*, 28. Uzukwu illustrates the close relationship between religious practices in Africa and liberation movements. See also Okolo, "Christ Is Black," 68–71.
52. Hastings, *The Church in Africa*, 105.
53. Ibid., 107.

The latter part of the nineteenth century was to witness a gathering momentum of the Initiated movement in South Africa and the rest of sub-Saharan Africa.[54]

The Ethiopian-Type Churches

A precursor to the first Ethiopian churches in South Africa was the organization of the first tribal church in 1884 by Nehemiah Xoxo Tile.[55] Up to that time he was an ordained minister of the Wesleyan Mission Church.[56] Tile's breach with the Wesleyan Methodist Church came about because of his involvement in Tembu politics, which earned the ire and disapproval of his Wesleyan superiors.[57] Yet European control and supremacy were not the only reasons that precipitated Tile's secession from the Wesleyan Church. It was "a positive desire to adapt the message of the church to the heritage of the Tembu tribe. As the Queen of England was the head of the English Church, so the Paramount Chief of the Tembu should be the *summus episcopus* of the new religious organization."[58] Tile continued to strive for political freedom and social justice for his people, and in the process he was arrested and jailed.

Tile's contribution to the church and African society cannot be overestimated. His efforts gave rise to the Tembu political protest movement and its concerted efforts to restore initiated rule. Balia says:

> The Tembu church should be seen in the context of the long history of African reaction to White penetration. In the past, increasing White pressure had led Africans on the Eastern frontier to

---

54. Daneel, *Quest for Belonging*, 46–47.

55. Tshabala, "Shembe's Hymn Book Reconsidered," 50. No definitive history of the rise of the African Initiated Churches in South Africa exists. However, the most comprehensive of all written histories is that of Bengt Sundkler. Most scholars rely on his works more than others. See *Bantu Prophets* and *Zulu Zion*.

56. Tshabala, "Shembe's Hymn Book Reconsidered," 50.

57. Balia, *Black Methodists and White Supremecy*, 54. Balia details the issues raised by Tile, especially in the light of the political situation in the country at that time. It seems, according to Balia, that the Methodist Church frowned on Tile's activities as his activities went against missionary and colonial ideology.

58. Sundkler, *Bantu Prophets*, 38. Kiernan, *The African Independent Churches*, 119, speaking in defense of Tile's decision to secede and found the Tembu Church, says, "Within a space of ten years tribal churches of this kind had also emerged among the Tswana and the Pedi. This was an assertion of tribal autonomy against missionary rule and, because the chief of the tribal group was made head of the splinter church, it could not be seen as a bid to increase the personal influence of the instigators" ("The African Independent Churches," 119).

offer resistance by appealing to the shades or ancestral spirits. The founding of the Tembu church marked the trial of a new method, the use of a Christian framework within which to express African equality in an age of White control.[59]

Christianity was seen as the means of articulating people's fears and hopes in a conspicuously racial and hostile environment. However, the paradox was that the very church that raised their hopes for a humane society was very much a part of the root cause of their problems—loss of human dignity, quality of life, and even their land. These brought into question the very presence of the Methodist Church on their land.

Although Nehemiah Tile was responsible for founding the first African Initiated Church in South Africa, which led to a wave of secessions and in a sense liberation from colonial and missionary subjugation, it was Mangena Mokone who founded the first Ethiopian Church.[60] He was ordained as a Methodist preacher in 1888, together with his colleague Daniel Msimang. In spite of being acclaimed a great asset to the Methodist Church and having proved successful in ministry, Mokone soon became aware of the gross discrimination practiced in the Methodist Church system, where he saw a clear distinction between white and black in the church. Mokone was rudely awakened to the fact that "the African missionary was obliged to submit to the European missionary on all points at issue. He found that the privileges White ministers received were denied to his Black brother ministers."[61] The African preacher could no longer sit with his white brethren in the same gathering; the natives had to convene their own black conference and report the proceedings for approval or rejection; and the native preacher was not allowed to enter by the front door of the white preacher—the back door was good enough for him.[62]

Thus, in 1892 Mokone founded the Ethiopian Church in the Witwatersrand (Pretoria, South Africa). Mokone was indeed motivated by the text in Psalm 68:31 and other references such as Acts 8:27, envisioning a grand plan to send missionaries through Africa.[63]

A contemporary of Mokone was James M. Dwane, an ordained Wesleyan minister and a gifted speaker. He was sent to England from 1894 to 1895 to solicit financial support for young students desiring to study

---

59. Balia, 55.

60. Hastings, *The Church in Africa*, 479.

61. Balia, *Black Methodists*, 70; see also p. 81 n. 8, where Balia delineates some of the inconsistencies and harsh treatment that the African missionaries encountered at that time.

62. Ibid., 70.

63. Hastings, *The Church in Africa*, 479.

for the ministry. Upon his return to South Africa, a disagreement ensued over the disbursement of the money received in England; this dispute led to Dwane's resignation from the Mission Church. He found an open door for ministry with Mokone in 1896.[64]

Mokone, via his sister, came to learn about the African Methodist Episcopal Church (AMEC) in the United States and corresponded with them with a view to seeking advice on ecclesiastical matters and a source of support for educating local blacks in the United States. The Ethiopian Church received a favorable response to their request, and the AMEC saw this response as an opportunity to make their presence felt in South Africa.[65]

Dwane was sent to consolidate a union between the two churches. He was appointed as superintendent of the work in South Africa, but this appointment was met with much resistance as many thought that Mokone was the rightful leader of the organization. Further, they had not authorized him to receive an "office" from the AMEC.[66]

On returning to South Africa, Dwane was successful in persuading other Initiated churches to follow him into the AMEC. To this end, he sought government recognition for the church and asked Cecil John Rhodes for the right to expand the church into the neighboring countries of Rhodesia, now Zimbabwe, and the Zambezi, now Zambia. This expansion caused some upheaval among other mission societies such as the Congregationalists and Presbyterians.[67]

In 1898 the AMEC sent Bishop Henry Turner to South Africa, where he held two conferences and ordained a number of ministers. At this time, Dwane was also formally ordained and appointed assistant bishop. It should be noted that this new arrangement with the AMEC was indeed ironic as the very reason, even if not the principal one, for seceding from the Methodist Church was to be autonomous and independent. This newfound marriage, if anything, defeated their original intent.[68]

---

64. Sundkler, *Bantu Prophets*, 39–40.

65. Ibid., 40. The African Methodist Episcopal Church (AMEC) was founded in Philadelphia, USA, in 1816 by the African American preacher Richard Allen. He had earlier withdrawn from the white Methodist Church in 1787 because of race discrimination. The AMEC had started mission work in Liberia in 1820 and boasted of a membership of some 800,000 people. See also Johnson, *African Christianity*, 89–107.

66. Sundkler, *Bantu Prophets*, 40.

67. Ibid., 40–41.

68. Ibid., 41.

Dwane soon became dissatisfied with the AMEC when he realized that "the Ethiopian program, 'Africa for Africans,' conflicted with the linking up of his church with an American Negro Mission Church."[69] In 1900 he and a large number of followers joined the Anglican Church as the Order of Ethiopia.[70] However, the majority of Ethiopians did not go with Dwane but remained in the AMEC.[71]

THE ZION CHRISTIAN CHURCH (ZCC)

The Zion Christian Church, with its current membership of over seven million members, is now the largest of the African Initiated Churches in South Africa.[72] The ZCC in its origins, development, structures, and theology is not only an icon of the independent movement, but it is representative of many other African Initiated Churches in Africa.

There seems to be a lack of consensus regarding the actual dating for the genesis of the movement, but research shows that P. L. Le Roux, a Dutch Reformed minister, figured prominently in the rise of the Zionist movement in South Africa.[73] Dissatisfied with the Dutch Reformed Church and its mission policy, Le Roux resigned from the Dutch Reformed Church in 1901.[74] It was at this time that Le Roux encountered a Zion Church minister, Johannes Buchler, who himself had seceded from the Congregational Church in 1895.[75]

---

69. Ibid. See also Kiernan, *The African Independent Churches*, 119. Kiernan states that "the Ethiopian Church . . . arose not only out of resentment of missionary autocracy, but also out of indignation on the part of defecting ministers at the belittlement of their capacity for leadership."

70. Several other secessions occurring at this time are well documented by Daneel (*Quest for Belonging*, 50).

71. Sundkler, *Bantu Prophets*, 41–42. The Ethiopian contact with the AMEC in the USA had in some way afforded blacks the opportunity to study in America. Many of the Ethiopian leaders had a shorter or longer period of study in the USA. A survey in Natal in 1906–7 revealed that some one hundred fifty Africans from South Africa with definite connections with the Ethiopian Church had gone to the USA for study. The Ethiopian movement seems to have been a catalyst for the opening of a Bantu university in South Africa, and thus was the University of Fort Hare born in 1916, with government approval. See also Sundkler, *Bantu Prophets*, 43.

72. Barrett et al., *World Christian Encyclopedia*, 681.

73. Pretorius and Jafta, "A Branch Springs Out," 217.

74. Sundlker, *Zulu Zion*, 23.

75. Ibid., 29.

Buchler came to know of John Alexander Dowie, from Zion City, IL (near Chicago), and subscribed to his journal.[76] Later, he visited Dowie in America, and under his influence he started a faith-healing practice. Both Le Roux and Buchler were taken up by the teachings that came out of Dowie's church and which conflicted with the Dutch Reformed Church. Some of the issues were the use of doctors or medicines, the teaching that the eating of flesh was against the Holy Scriptures and therefore sinful, the use of tobacco being sinful, and infant baptism being against the teaching of Holy Scripture.[77] However, the main teachings of Dowie, not unlike those of the early Pentecostals, were divine healing, triune immersion, and the conviction that the second coming of Christ was near. Edgar Mahon, a former captain in the Salvation Army, was also influenced by the movement in the same way as Le Roux and Buchler.[78] He initiated his own Zion Church (Christian Catholic Church in Zion) as early as 1902, when he was excommunicated from the Salvation Army.[79]

Dowie, who never visited South Africa, sent one of his overseers, Daniel Bryant, in 1904 as his emissary to establish the Christian Catholic Church in Zion. In Wakkerstroom, Bryant baptized one hundred fifty of Le Roux's Zionist followers in the Slangrivier (Snake River); and in Harrismith, sixty of Mohan's followers were baptized in the Caledonia River. Those events heralded the beginning of the Zionist movement in South Africa. Bryant returned to America in 1908.[80]

Le Roux and other African leaders continued to further the cause of the Zionist movement, and through his influence the organization acquired a marked Pentecostal slant. Le Roux himself claimed to be baptized in the Holy Spirit in 1908.[81] It was not until 1915, however, that Le Roux left the Zion movement to concentrate his work with the Pentecostals. By this time, the sparks of Pentecostalism from the Azusa Street Revival had caught fire in South Africa. Archibold H. Cooper, who was to play a

---

76. Sundkler cites as his primary source *Leaves of Healing*, a weekly paper edited by John Alexander Dowie that began to be published in 1889. This paper along with Daniel Bryant's diary forms the basis for much of Sundkler's historical data for the genesis of the Zion movement.

77. Sundkler, *Zulu Zion*, 29–30.

78. Ibid., 30.

79. Ibid., 33.

80. Ibid., 36–41.

81. Ibid., 52.

leading role in the Full Gospel movement in South Africa, received the first *Apostolic Papers* published by the Azusa movement in Los Angeles.[82]

Although Africans of the Zion movement also claimed the experience and testified to receiving "their Pentecost,"[83] they refused to be absorbed into the Pentecostal movement, as Le Roux had been. As a result and with this new phase of spiritual fervor, they held fast to the name "Zion." Thus the Zion Apostolic Church was formed, and Elias Mahlange became its new leader.[84] After the departure of Le Roux, many new Zion churches were founded.

The main secessions within the movement took place sometime between 1917 and 1920. Paulo Mabilitsa, the most educated among the African leaders at that time, called his church the Christian Apostolic Church in Zion.[85] Daniel Nkonyane, a Zulu, started the Christian Catholic Apostolic Holy Spirit Church of Zion, and upon his death his son Stephen Nkonyane became its leader.[86] J. G. Philips, a Nyasa, founded the Holy Catholic Apostolic Church in Zion, and his leadership was succeeded by M. G. Koza. Fred Luthuli became prominent in the Seventh-Day Adventist secession movement, which also reflected Zion characteristics.[87]

Further splits were to occur within the Zionist churches. One session that was to eventually give rise to the Zion Christian Church was the founding of the Zion Apostolic Faith Mission (ZAFM)—a secession from Mhlangu's Zion Apostolic Church.[88] Subsequently, in 1925 Mutendi in Rhodesia and Lekganyane in Transvaal, South Africa, broke away from the ZAFM, establishing the Zion Christian Church in their respective countries.[89]

The founder of the Zion Christian Church in South Africa was Engenase (Ignatius) Barnabas Lekganyane (1885–1948). He was originally a member of the Free Scottish Presbyterian Church until 1911, but in 1912 he was baptized into the Zionist movement. For a while he was a member of the Zion Apostolic Faith Mission in Lesotho under Edward

---

82. Ibid.
83. Daneel, *Quest for Belonging*, 54.
84. Sundkler, *Bantu Prophets*, 48.
85. Sundkler, *Zulu Zion*, 59.
86. Ibid., 56–59.
87. Ibid., 56–66. Sundkler gives this part of Zion history a fuller treatment than in his previous work (*Bantu Prophets*, 1st ed., 1961).
88. Daneel, *Quest for Belonging*, 55.
89. Ibid.

Motaung and later became a minister in that church.[90] About this time, it is told, Lekganyane went to a mountain near his home to pray. There he had a revelation that "a multitude of people would follow him" and that he would lead a large congregation. In 1917 he prophesied that Britain would defeat Germany, and when this event came to pass, his prestige as "a man of God" increased.[91] In 1925 he returned to Thabakgone (Transvaal, South Africa) and founded the Zion Christian Church.[92] In 1930 he purchased a farm at Boyne, about fifty kilometers from Pretoria, and established his headquarters there.[93]

The Zion Christian Church proliferated rapidly and soon had members in the major urban areas such as Pretoria, Johannesburg, Vereeniging, Germiston, and Kimberley. With fewer than a thousand members in 1925, by 1942 there were more than 27,000. What began as a small Northern Sotho tribal church soon overflowed tribal boundaries and became established among Tsonga, Venda, Tswana, Sotho, and even Zulu people in the cities and homelands.[94]

Many miraculous deeds marked Lekganyane's ministry. Reports of healings of cripples, healings of barren wombs, people finding employment after he had prayed for them, blessing of harvests, and rainmaking brought people to believe that "God had given all power to His chosen prophet, Engenas."[95]

On June 1, 1948, Engenas Lekganyane died, and a leadership struggle arose among his sons. His eldest son, Jesus, had died, and the second, Barnabas, died after serving only seven months as leader. The struggle for leadership then was between his two remaining sons, Edward and Joseph. Joseph and his followers settled on the family farm, but Edward and his supporters established their own headquarters at Zion City, Moria. Edward soon united most of his father's followers, gaining support especially from the urban populations.[96] In 1954 there were more than 80,000 members, and by the time of his death in 1967, the membership rose above the 200,000 mark.[97]

---

90. Anderson, *Zion and Pentecost*, 69.
91. Ibid.
92. Anderson, *African Reformation*, 97.
93. Ibid., 101–2.
94. Anderson, *Zion and Pentecost*, 70.
95. Ibid., 71.
96. Ibid.
97. Ibid.

The African Initiated Churches

Upon Edward Lekganyane's death, his son Barnabas, only thirteen, was appointed leader and bishop of the movement at their Easter Assembly in 1968. In 1975, after he had come of age, he was formally inducted as bishop of the Zion Christian Church.[98]

Beliefs and Practices of the ZCC

Zion City Moria is the headquarters of the ZCC. What Jerusalem and the Wailing Wall is to the Jew, the holy site in Mecca is to the Muslim, and the river Ganges is to the Hindu, Moria is to the ZCC. The name "Moria" reflects 2 Chr 3:1, and other texts that locate the Temple in Jerusalem. The reference in Heb 12:22–23 is also pertinent as it speaks of Mount Zion and the City of God, the heavenly Jerusalem and the assembly of the firstborn.

For the worshippers, Zion City Moria is indeed experienced as a "new Jerusalem." It symbolizes refuge, protection, healing, and cleansing. All people who enter Moria are sprinkled with water to purify them.[99] The presence and power of the prophet is experienced by the sensitive pilgrim; the prophet represents his followers before God, and one feels closer to God at Moria.[100]

Healing ceremonies are an integral part of the religious gathering for AICs. According to Jim Kiernan, "the mainstay of Zionist healing power is their control of spirit (*umoya*) which is identified with the Holy Spirit of Christian belief."[101] A vast array of media serves as ways by which the Zionists attain power or *umoya*. Water is one of the main agents for acquiring power. Members are invited to use it as a medicament, either by drinking it or washing in it. Baptism by immersion in the currents of a swiftly flowing river or in the ocean is conducted for the purpose of cleansing; this baptism is also seen as a means of securing power (*umoya*) for the individual. The stronger the current, the more power one receives.[102]

The regalia worn by Zion adherents also has spiritual significance. The white garments with colored sashes and braided cords are believed to be blessed with spiritual power. They are worn to ward off illness, disease, and evil attacks.[103] It is the function of the prophet at public healing cer-

---

98. Ibid., 72.
99. Anderson, *African Reformation*, 100–101.
100. Oosthuizen, *Post-Christianity in Africa*, 37.
101. Kiernan, *The Production and Management*, 105.
102. Ibid., 106.
103. Ibid., 112.

emonies to recommend to the afflicted member the use of the regalia for a period of time until the illness is cured.[104]

While water and the regalia are important agents for the well-being of ZCC members, the traditional staff also forms part of the basic protective equipment for individuals. Whereas Zulus once used spears when fighting, they now use sticks for protection. For the Zionist, however, the staff is never employed for combat but is used solely to aid in healing and driving out evil spirits: "It is through the acquisition of the staff that each Zionist gains access to this rich diversity of spiritual powers."[105]

At worship services, ministers in the ZCC effect healing through the laying on of hands in accordance with the biblical mandate in Matt 10:7–8 and Mark 16:17–18. In his unpublished work "The Zion Christian Church: A Christian Church with African Characteristics, or an African Church with Christian Characteristics?" Theodor G. Jackel discovered that there was a time when ministers and evangelists in the ZCC laid hands on the sick, and when members recovered from reported illness, the ministers claimed power equal to that possessed by the Bishop Ignatius. The church subsequently issued a communiqué stating that God had vested all power in his chosen prophet Ignatius. Thus, ministers and evangelists were not permitted to use their hands when praying for the sick. Rather, they were provided with a piece of khaki cloth blessed by the prophet. The cloth was said to mediate powers of healing from the prophet to the patient.[106] The founder of the church, Engenas, was also accorded similar status in the eyes of the members of the ZCC. "Members believed that he was a representative of God in the form of a prophet. God had given all the powers to him, and to despise him was to despise God in person. He was mediator not in the theological sense but in a traditional sense."[107] Lukhaimane does not elaborate in what sense Engenas functioned as a traditional mediator but not as mediator in a theological sense. This concept raises the question, in the context of the amaNazaretha Church, whether the current leader, Vimbeni Shembe, functions in a similar role for his people.

The above examples clearly demonstrate that Zionists, while endeavoring to be faithful to the Christian message, do not dismiss traditional healing means and paraphernalia to achieve that end. Thus Kiernan adds, "In effect, Zionism harnesses the distilled spiritual energy of Christianity to respond to modern African needs and channels it through African

---

104. Ibid.
105. Ibid., 118.
106. Jackel, "The Zion Christian Church," 34.
107. Lukhaimane, "The St. Engenas Zion Christian Church," 233.

The African Initiated Churches

thought and action, though without denuding it entirely of Christian categories."[108] Eugene Nida believes that the ZCC exemplifies an indigenized Christianity at least in terms of healing. He writes:

> The Zionist Movements are those typified by emphasis on healing by native medicines, the use of old styled diviners, the local prophet, and the detection of witches by elaborate ordeals. These Zionist groups emphasize the past and appeal to the rural people.[109]

Later, the question of whether the amaNazaretha Church is truly an indigenized expression of the Christian gospel or whether their beliefs and practices have moved them beyond an orthodox Christian position will be addressed. A brief study of the ZCC's theology will later compare and contrast their theology with that of the amaNazaretha Church.

Zion Christian Church: Theology

Any discussion of African theology should presuppose one's affinity, to some extent, to the African worldview. This reality was again brought to the fore at the Mindolo consultation on the African Initiated Church movement in 1962.[110] The consultation admonished that the first requisite should be a sympathetic and careful understanding of the issues that divide Western thinking from that of the African. Concerning the African worldview, the consultation said the following:

> Although in humility we confess that African world-views present intellectual difficulties for some of us, we would emphasize that they need to be taken seriously in Christian practice. The successful cure by traditional diviners of some patients who have been inaccessible to the techniques of Western medicine, suggests that in African culture it is necessary for therapists to enter sympathetically into their patients' beliefs in the objective character of such ultra-human forces as ghosts and witchcraft. This conflicts with the scientific mood, which has excluded all psychic character from the external world. Yet belief in spirit-possession is an ineradicable part of the New Testament thought-forms; it is indeed doubtful whether it is possible to understand some of the experiences therein recorded unless we can enter into the interpretation which the New Testament itself offers. To deny this interpretation is

---

108. Kiernan, "The African Independent Churches," 122.
109. Nida, *Message and Mission*, 139–40.
110. The consultation on the AIC movement was organized by the Department of Missionary Studies of the WCC and was sponsored by the All Africa Church Conference at the Mindolo Ecumenical Centre, Kitwe, Northern Rhodesia (Zambia) in 1962.

> rationalist, rather than Christian; and it is no part of the Christian Gospel to impart a particular metaphysic, but to speak to each man where he is.[111]

As the above quote suggests, any attempt at a theological evaluation of the different trends within the AICs is by no means an easy task. The proliferation of these churches in their large numbers, the various cultural differences and languages, and the extent to which they transform their African traditional religious beliefs into Christianity create considerable problems for the researcher. The biggest hurdle is that so many come to this task relying on the empirical research of others. Hence, the task of missiology today remains to secure more empirical, on-site research over a period of time that would afford a better understanding of where Africans stand in their knowledge of the Christian faith as compared with their traditional religions.

Christology: Biblical Christ or Black Messiah?

The emphasis, or lack thereof, on the person and work of Christ by the AICs seems to have been an important criterion in arriving at a decision about whether the AIC churches are actually Christian churches. Investigators such as Sundkler and Turner, who carried out extensive field work in South Africa and Nigeria respectively, evaluated them very positively without regard to some questionable tendencies. One investigator, Oosthuizen, places some of them as post-Christian.[112] According to Daneel, Oosthuizen characterizes all prophetic churches—that is, the Zionist and Apostolic groups—and messianic movements as nativistic, as opposed to what he calls Christian sects.[113] Peter Beyerhaus provides one set of criteria to accurately evaluate Oosthuizen's claims and the Christology resident in these churches. His criteria for an orthodox Christology are as follows:

1. Christ must be proclaimed as *Christus Victor*, the one who triumphs over evil forces (Col 2:15);
2. Christ must be proclaimed as the *Crucified One* who took the curse of our sins upon himself;

---

111. Hayward, "African Independent Church Movements," 167.

112. Oosthuizen, *Post-Christianity in Africa*, xiv. He argues that while many of AICs are Christian in an orthodox sense, others fall short of the standard of Christian orthodoxy, thus rendering them "post-Christian."

113. Daneel, *Quest for Belonging*, 246.

3. Christ must be proclaimed as the one who is *present*, still working powerfully among his people and assisting them in their need, danger and temptation; and

4. He must be proclaimed as the one *to come* who will appear at the full revelation of God's kingdom.[114]

Beyerhaus's third criterion perhaps is most helpful as it relates to the existential everyday lives of Africans. More than just articulating their beliefs, Africans demonstrate them in and through their practices in daily life. For example, in the face of calamity, illness, and loss of property, to whom do AIC adherents turn?

Ernst Damman, in his study of the African Initiated Churches, concluded that Christ played no role in either the beliefs or practices of these churches. He offers a scale of closeness to orthodox belief as follows:

1. A view of Christ which basically agrees with that of the historical church from which the movement was born (e.g., the African Methodist Episcopal Church);

2. Although Christ is given a place in creedal pronouncements, in the realities of religious experience he is a background figure (e.g., the Musama Disco Christo Church in Ghana);

3. Christ is wholly superceded even in creedal pronouncements (e.g., the Nazareth Baptist Church of Shembe); and

4. Messianic attributes of Christ are transferred to the group leader—the Black Messiah is totally identified with the biblical Messiah (e.g., Simon Kimbangu).[115]

It would appear that the theology of the AICs has received a more sympathetic evaluation from Sundkler[116] than it has from Damman. At this point, I simply note Damman's conclusions. I will discuss my findings from my own field research in chs. 5 and 6 and offer my conclusions on the theology and Christology of the amaNazaretha Church in ch. 7. Comparison between these two approaches in evaluating the Christological

---

114. Ibid., 256. Peter Beyerhaus, Professor of Mission Science and Ecumenics at Tubigen University, Germany, is quoted from his work "Begegnungen mit messianischen Bewegungen in Afrika."

115. Daneel, *Quest For Belonging*, 246. Ernst Damman, who is fluent in Swahili and worked mainly in East Africa, is quoted from his German work "Christusverständnis in den nachchristlichen Kirchen und Sekten Afrikas."

116. Sundkler, *Bantu Prophets*, and *Zulu Zion*.

understanding in the AICs indicates the problem of subjectivity and the bias of the researchers. Here, the Mindolo conference set the tone for any value judgment by issuing the following statement regarding the role of the prophet usurping the place of Christ: "It should be noted that when this identification becomes substitution, in our opinion the group has moved outside the sphere of the Christian Church."[117]

The earlier discussion on typology showed the messianic type of churches, where there appeared to be a kind of veneration to the point at which the Black Messiah may usurp the position of Christ. In attempting to differentiate between Zionism and Messianism, Sundkler reduced the distinction to one fundamental question: "Who stands at the gates of heaven—the Jesus of Scripture or some Bantu Messiah in the person of Shembe, Lekganyane, Khambule or Masowe?"[118] While the Zionist would settle for Christ as Savior, the messianic movements would opt for a black Christ. Sundkler goes on to describe Shembe as a mediator, one who holds the key to heaven,[119] thus excluding the movement from Christianity. Other observers refer to the role of the Black Messiah as the controller of the keys to the gates of heaven, who will admit only his followers to Paradise. Others see Shembe and Lekganyane as kings in their colonies, mediators in their own new Jerusalem. At this point, Jesus Christ as head of the church fades into the background.[120] In Oosthuizen's discussion of Christology in the AICs,[121] he asserts that there is a further devaluing of the person and work of Christ, which are denied by an overt emphasis on the leader's personal powers.[122] The emphasis is also on magic, and magic is a means of enhancing one's power and status. This belief makes it possible to control and monopolize Christ's authority.[123]

Early writers and observers of the AIC movements who previously spoke of Black Messianism, after more extensive empirical research, arrived at different conclusions. Sundkler, for example, in his later work *Zulu Zion and Some Swazi Zionists*, comes to the following conclusion about Shembe and Khambulu, both of whom he had previously classified as Messiah figures:

117. Hayward, "African Independent Church Movements," 167.
118. Sundkler, *Bantu Prophets*, 323.
119. Ibid., 290.
120. Oosthuizen, *Post-Christianity in Africa*, 91.
121. Ibid., 79–106.
122. Ibid., 103.
123. Ibid., 89.

> There is no conscious attempt to minimize the revelation of Jesus. Sermons and testimonies underline that Jesus is the Ultimate Authority and Final Judge. But . . . the Zulu Servant of God has revealed himself in the life of his people, as Healer and Helper and thus of an extraordinary quality.[124]

Daneel, who conducted interviews with Shona Zionists in Zimbabwe, admits that Christ's mediatorship is sometimes misconstrued in Shona churches, or at least that it may function to a lesser degree "in the religious experience of some individuals."[125] It cannot be doubted that both Lekganyane or Mutendi were in some sense "mediators" to some people because of their mystical powers through which they were able to advance the good of their people—for example, faith-healing in their churches. Members saw the prophet as an "emissary, the 'man of God' who listened to their problems and was expected to convey them to God in heaven."[126] It is this role of the prophet that can cause misunderstanding and confusion, as is the case with one deacon who said thus:

> Mutendi is the one who speaks directly to Mwari. We do not address Mwari Wokudenga [the God of Heaven] directly, but we speak to the God of Lekganyane and Mutendi. Minor problems are resolved by us, the office-bearers, without referring to God. The big problems we bring here to Moriah and our leader then presents them to God. We cannot ourselves raise matters to heaven.[127]

This deacon has no illusions concerning the mediatorial role of either Mutendi or Lekganyane. The remote God can only be accessible via these two prophets. This view, however, is not representative of all Zionists. The following view, a sample of several interviews of both clergy and members, reveals the complexities:

> Mutendi is *like* Jesus but cannot take his place. Mutendi is our "foreman," but Jesus is above him. To us Mutendi is like the Pope is to the Catholics and the Revd. Louw [pioneer missionary to Mashonaland] to the DR [Dutch Reformed] Church. He is subordinate to Jesus but in him we see the likeness of Jesus. We venerate Mutendi because he is *like* Jesus, but he himself warns us *not* to compare him to Christ.[128]

124. Sundkler, *Zulu Zion*, 310.
125. Daneel, *Quest for Belonging*, 189.
126. Ibid.
127. Ibid.
128. Ibid., 191.

Daneel admits, "There are no biblical grounds for the leader's function at the gates of heaven,"[129] and the kind of mediatorship espoused by some members is unbiblical. Daneel is clearly more sympathetic to the African view and thus does not see the function of the leader "at the heavenly gates" as an attempt to usurp or supercede the position of Christ. The distinction is that the role of the leader is that of an intermediary and does not imply in any way automatic access to heaven for his followers. The problem arises when the intermediary is elevated to the status above Christ. Then, one begins to question the members' beliefs regarding Christology. Whether this phenomenon in fact occurs in the hearts and minds of the church members may only be verified through field research and interviews.

Anderson, in his study of the Soshanguve Zionists in South Africa, showed that Christ is central in their beliefs and practices. Anderson says, "In every part of the interviews and in every area of life all Pentecostals and Zionist members spoke about the overarching importance of faith in God and in Jesus Christ."[130] He did, however, admit the following:

> The emphasis is often on the presence of the Holy Spirit, through Spirit baptism, healing, prophecy, speaking in tongues, exorcism and other Spirit manifestations. It may not be far off the mark to suggest that theology and Christology are dominated by pneumatology in some of these churches. This does not suggest, however, that there is no clear theology or Christology in these churches or that pneumatology is exclusively overemphasized.[131]

Anderson, in defense of the ZCC's belief in the centrality of Christ, shares some interview data to support his claims. He writes, "Several Zionist church members interviewed shared their faith in Jesus Christ as the basis for their Christian lives. 'Jesus is the one who saves us,' declared one ZCC member. 'He was sent by God to save people from their sins.'"[132] Anderson cites the official magazine of the ZCC, the *ZCC Messenger*, which stated in an article, "The Zion Christian Church is a society of Christians who believe that Jesus Christ is the Savoir and Son of God and that he died on the cross for our sins."[133] Anderson argues on the basis of his interviews that there is evidence of a high Christology in the ZCC.

129. Ibid.
130. Anderson, *Zion and Pentecost*, 222.
131. Ibid.
132. Ibid., 224.
133. Ibid., 225.

Regarding the question of messianic tendencies attributed to the leader, Anderson quotes a ZCC official who said, "The bishop fulfilled the same functions between God and man that the ancestors had done in traditional religion. He was a messiah, a prophet for his followers."[134] Anderson, in mitigation, says that today ZCC members do not emphasize the role of the leader; rather, in their church practices and official news magazines, Jesus Christ is preeminent.

Regarding the role of ancestors, it would appear that ZCC members still have recourse to approaching the ancestors. To quote Anderson on this issue, "People interviewed . . . said that ancestors were mediators between people and God. They were God's helpers and they revealed God's will to people. 'When people wish to speak to God they should go through the ancestors,' said one man."[135] Anderson concludes thus:

> Fundamentally, the Supreme Being is unpredictable and unknowable, and sometimes even dangerous. For this reason, people turn to those nearer home, those more easily related to, more easily understandable, those they can argue with, plead their case with, and even scold—the ancestors.[136]

The above comments from ZCC members relating to ancestors reveal that ancestors still play an important role, both in their religious and cultural practices and beliefs. Further, it seems that Jesus Christ's role and function as one who mediates on our behalf is not an essential or functioning part of the ZCC members' everyday worldview and daily living. Despite what they "said" in their interviews, their daily practices reveal little accommodation for the person and work of Christ. However, Anderson's fieldwork offers us some helpful insight about what ZCC members currently believe and practice.[137] Further, Anderson's work is valuable in that it offers us some insight into ZCC beliefs and practices with regard to the position of Christ, the ancestors, and the leader.

Evaluation

To conclude this evaluation of the ZCC, Mazibuko, a South African theologian, stated that although leaders like Edward Lekganyane and others

---

134. Ibid., 227.
135. Ibid., 175.
136. Ibid., 176.

137. It should be noted that Anderson's fieldwork was confined to one localized group of ZCC adherents. Given the proliferation of ZCC churches all around South Africa, rural and urban, perhaps a wider sample would reveal different results.

rejected receiving a messianic type of homage, they were not always successful in convincing their followers otherwise. To this day many believe that the leaders are omniscient, possessed of extraordinary powers, and able to perform miraculous healings. In other words, they are construed as mediators between themselves and God.[138]

A tentative assessment is that the uniqueness of Christ in the ZCC is compromised in terms of his mediatorial work. Although the ZCC constitution refers to Jesus as the cornerstone of the church, it does not follow that he has retained this position in the hearts of the people.[139] Further, their overt emphasis upon pneumatology has led to a weakening of their Christology. Apart from introducing Jesus as the one who had come to tell the people of the last judgment, there seems to be little in-depth teaching about the implications of Christ's life and work both for the individual and the church. As a result the concept of conversion is seen only as an escape from God's judgment. The attainment of church membership in a sense supercedes the implications of conversion in the individual's relationship with Christ. In the light of such ambivalence in their theological understanding, one solution would be more theological training for the ministers, which perhaps would eventually lead to a more orthodox interpretation of scripture.[140]

Summary

This brief study into the phenomenal rise and growth, beliefs, and practices of the African Initiated Churches in South Africa thus far reveals that, first, the history of this movement has its antecedents in the political, sociocultural milieu of its time. The history of the AICs can only be comprehended in that light. South Africa has had a chequered history. It has endured the scourge of racism, apartheid, and repressive labor policies. All of these forms of prejudice began in 1652 with the arrival of the first Dutch settlers.[141] Today the result is that poverty and degradation coexist in a country where income distribution was racially distorted and where lavish wealth and abject poverty characterized this society. Following his first visit to South Africa in 1985, James Cone, the progenitor of the Black

---

138. Muzibuko, *Missiology*, 39–40.

139. Muzibuko, 42.

140. See Nyamiti, "Contemporary African Christologies." Nyamiti discusses the role of Christology within the field of theology in the African context and suggests guidelines for engaging in more serious study in this area. See also Martey, *African Theology*, 76–81.

141. Pillay and Hofmeyer, *Perspectives on Church History*, 232.

Theology movement compared the apartheid era in South Africa to the civil rights era in the United States. He said thus:

> One factor which partly accounts for the great differences between southern whites and Afrikaners is the absence of the North and the liberal democratic tradition of freedom and equality that is deeply embedded in American history. Afrikaners have no such tradition of freedom which they apply to blacks. Its absence in politics and religion has meant that whites have been able not only to deny the humanity of blacks in the laws that define human relations but to do so without significant objections from any segment of their society. The presence of the North in the United States made this impossible for white southerners.[142]

AICs, among other churches, had their beginning and grew in the context of repression and inhumane laws.

Second, missionaries, true to their convictions and the biblical mandate, came with the gospel and their western baggage. Africa is indebted to the early missionaries who against all odds came with a message of hope.[143] However, many missionaries totally ignored the role that ritual, symbol, and ceremony could fulfill in the lives of Africans. Thus, the "good news of the gospel" became "bad news" for the African. Eugene Nida rightly points out the following:

> Unfortunately some of the unique elements of the gospel are not the things we really talk about. We rather teach people that Christianity involves a new set of taboos: You musn't drink; you musn't smoke; you musn't have more than one wife, etc. And so people often have a very strange idea of what this thing Christianity really is all about.[144]

Third, behind all of the negative causal factors contributing to the rise of the AICs, the genuine missionary fervor and endeavor of certain individuals stand out like beacons on a darkened shore. Le Roux, an Afrikaner coming out of the Dutch Reformed Church, is indeed one such example. As seen here, Le Roux holds an important place in South African mission history, a "white Zion" whose initial efforts gave rise to the Zionist movement. Today the ZCC is the largest AIC in South Africa.

---

142. Cone, *Speaking the Truth*, 164.

143. See de Kock, *Civilizing Barbarians*, especially the chapter "Missionary Heroes and the Miraculous Conversion of Africa" (141–87).

144. Nida, "New Religions for Old," 97.

Finally, Western-oriented churches that Europeanized, intellectualized, and institutionalized Christianity in South Africa perhaps have a different role to play here, since it is the African indigenous churches that are setting the tone for what Christianity should look like in this new millennium.[145] The Zion Christian Church is certainly a vanguard of an indigenous expression of African Christianity. In spite of the movement's theological problems and other weaknesses, these churches can no longer be regarded as a bridge back to traditional religion. All the signs for expansion and advancement are there.[146] Nevertheless, we have shown that the form of Christianity displayed by the AICs, though culturally appropriate and indigenized, may perhaps be wanting in terms of Christological understanding. In this regard the work of missiologists has only begun.

As Walls has suggested, one of the most important events in the whole of church history has occurred in our lifetime; it surely must be that we are witnessing a complete change in the center of gravity of Christianity where Africa is the focus.[147] "Intangible in many of its aspects, the Christian presence has been and remains in the African scene a massive and unavoidable fact and factor."[148]

In the light of the above study, and as further studies of the amaNazaretha Church continue, a fitting admonition comes from Max Warren: "Our first task in approaching another people, another culture, another religion, is to take off our shoes, for the place we are approaching is holy. Else we may find ourselves treading on men's dreams. More serious still, we may forget that God was here before our arrival."[149]

This study of African and Zulu culture and worldview, their religious beliefs and practices, and the brief excursion into the rise of the AICs, their history, and theology sets the foundation for the study of the amaNazaretha Church and its beliefs and practices in ch. 4.

---

145. See Moripe, "Indigenous Clergy in the Zion Christian Church," 103–7.
146. Jenkins, *Next Christendom*, 52–53.
147. Walls, "Towards Understanding," 18.
148. Baeta, *Christianity in Tropical Africa*, xii.
149. Race, *Christians and Religious Pluralism*, 3.

4

The Religious and Cultural Worldview of the amaNazaretha Church

CHAPTER 1 RECOUNTED BRIEFLY the history of the amaNazaretha Church and its succession of leaders. Before embarking on a study of the structure, ecclesiology, beliefs, practices, and theology of the amaNazaretha Church, it is useful to recall some events in the life and times of the founder, Isaiah Shembe, and his successors. These events have an important bearing on how the church views its leaders today—specifically Isaiah Shembe, the founder, and the current incumbent, Vimbeni Shembe.

Antecedents to the Rise of the amaNazaretha Church

While the events surrounding the birth of Isaiah Shembe are well documented in scholarly literature,[1] amaNazaretha members often refer to certain events in the early life of the prophet Isaiah when they speak of the prophet's deification. To substantiate their claims, members recall stories of a supernatural nature surrounding his birth and early life. In so doing they are engaging in what Walter Kaiser[2] has termed *antecedent theology*.

Isaiah Shembe told his congregation how God had prepared him for his ministry in a sermon at Ekuphakameni in 1926:

> In olden times, when Zululand was still ruled by king Senzagakhona (+/- 1816 A.D.), God visited my forefathers who lived in their homes in the mountains of Babanango, serving King Senzagakhona. Mzazela . . . when he was sleeping in the night, the Word of Jehova[h] came to him: "Mzazela, behold I shall raise a king of violent temper (Shaka) . . . who will rule the country with violent temper and will spill the blood of many people. I shall build on him my nation, that all Brown people be united in the Zulu kingdom. I advise you to flee together with your children to the upper

---

1. See Roberts, *Shembe*; Sundkler, *Zulu Zion*; Hexham, *The Scriptures of the amaNazaretha*; Hexham and Oosthuizen, *The Story of Isaiah Shembe*, inter alia.

2. Kaiser, *Mission in the Old Testament*. See also *Toward an Exegetical Theology*.

country in the West, so that the rage of that king may not come down upon you. For from your progeny I shall raise prophets who will save my Brown nation and work with this nation, which I have established and chosen!"[3]

It would appear that the dreams and visions Isaiah's grandfather had prompted the family to move away from Zululand to settle in the hills of Harrismith (Northwestern Natal). Fear of King Shaka caused ordinary people like the Shembe family to relocate outside of the king's reach.[4] Yet, in "re-membering" the event Isaiah restates his story and sets it in the context of the biblical narrative where the baby Jesus is taken away to Egypt for fear of being killed when Herod heard of the birth of a new "king." Isaiah Shembe, speaking in pseudo-biblical language, locates his family's experience in the biblical text, with the result that his followers see him as Jesus' equal or successor.

To show that Isaiah Shembe was more than human to his followers, Mthembeni Mpanza relates several encounters that Sitheya, Isaiah's mother, experienced before his birth, showing Isaiah as one whom God foreordained to be a prophet to the Zulu nation:

> When she was alone in the veld, she would always hear a voice saying to her, "Sitheya, my child, never spoil yourself, for you will give birth to the Messenger of God, Shembe." This voice called out of thin air, but she could not see the person uttering [the words]. She did not know what the voice meant, or where it came from. On another day when she was collecting fire-wood . . . [she] saw a beautiful flower. Sitheya rushed to it, picked it and put it in her mouth. Later on that day she heard a voice saying: What you swallowed was not the flower, but the Holy Spirit."[5]

In a similar vein, Elizabeth Gunner[6] recounts the story surrounding the pregnancy of Sitheya, Isaiah's mother. The Lukan narrative of Mary's encounter with the Holy Spirit before the birth of Jesus (Luke 2) is retold here, only in this instance with reference to Isaiah:

> When Sitheya was already pregnant, a small voice said to her, "You will bear a son who will be a special messenger." She did not

---

3. Hexham and Oosthuizen, *The Story of Isaiah Shembe*, 2–3.

4. The full text of this episode is recorded in Papini and Hexham, eds., *The Catechism of the Nazarites and Related Writings*, 189.

5. Mpanza, "The Biography of Isaiah Shembe," 2–3.

6. Gunner, *The Man of Heaven*.

The Religious and Cultural Worldview of the amaNazaretha Church

though grasp the full significance of the words because she was not a believer.[7]

These stories gain authenticity not only through telling and retelling by amaNazaretha members, but they have become interwoven in the biblical narrative. Consequently, for the amaNazaretha members, Shembe functions today as authoritative "Word" alongside the "Written Word"—the Bible. The events recorded in the biblical text are history; they are in the past. However, Shembe is present *now*, a visible being who meets the everyday needs of his people. Events in his early life that authenticate his calling to prophethood enhance his status to the point that he is deified in the eyes of his faithful followers. Elevating Shembe to the status of Jesus Christ is what Mike Kitshoff calls "jesufication;"[8] to what extent this elevation is evident today in the amaNazaretha Church will be discussed in ch. 7.

History and Ecclesiastical Structure

The Nazareth Baptist Church was founded in 1911 by the itinerant preacher, healer, and prophet, Isaiah Shembe. Isaiah Shembe believed that the Jewish religiocultural ethic,[9] as he understood it from his reading of the Old Testament, was relevant even for his own day and his Zulu Christian community. Particularly, he believed that the Old Testament laws regarding Sabbath rituals should be strictly and meticulously observed. When his views ran contrary to the beliefs and norms of the African Baptist Church and its leadership, Shembe seceded from the church and consequently initiated his own ministry. However, his first initiation to the Christian faith had come through his association with a Wesleyan congregation. He left the Wesleyan Church, according to one account, when the local minister refused to baptize him by immersion.[10] His charismatic gifting soon attracted a large following.

Although the numbers are difficult to quantify, officials of the church now claim a following of some four million members, with adherents in South Africa and the surrounding southern African states. Barrett (his re-

---

7. Ibid., 57.

8. Kitshoff, "From Veneration to Deification," 289.

9. The Nazarite practice is delineated in Num 7:1–20.

10. Hexham and Oosthuizen, *The Story of Isaiah Shembe*, 33. There are several differing accounts as to why Shembe seceded from the Wesleyan Church, and three such accounts are given in this work. One account suggests that the Wesleyan minister asked Isaiah to remove his traditional attire (animal skins) and put on Western clothes when coming to church (32).

search was conducted in 1995), however, offers the figure of 700,000; this number is probably a little low. However, according to Barrett's statistics, the Shembe Church is second only to the Zion Christian Church, which has a membership of seven million.[11]

The ecclesiastical structure of the church is different from other churches in that the leader of the church, Vimbeni Shembe, personally appoints leaders under him. The leadership is divided into three main groups: ministers (*amafundisi*), the highest rank, followed by evangelists (*abavangeli*), and preachers (*mshumayeli*). Others in the leadership structure are the youth, women's, and men's group leaders. The traditional chiefs, who are not part of the ecclesiastical hierarchy, are deemed to rank above the ministers in cultural matters. Two councils are appointed within the church structure. One is a committee of eleven persons—including Vimbeni Shembe—consisting of one chief (*Nkosi*) who is chairperson of the committee, two ministers, two evangelists, two preachers, one layperson (an aide to Shembe), a women's leader, and a men's leader. This committee is appointed by Shembe himself. Evangelist Mpanza reports that the committee convenes at the behest of the leader, Vimbeni Shembe, especially during the month of July, the cultural festival at Ebuhleni. This committee delegates tasks to the ministers' council on an *ad hoc* basis.

The second council comprises all the ministers in the church. Within this council an executive committee is appointed, with representatives from the various geographical regions of the church. The executive committee is elected by the ministers themselves and has thirteen elected members: a chairperson, a deputy chairperson, a secretary, a deputy secretary, a treasurer, and eight members. The ministers' council attends to issues such as disputes in the local temples, disciplinary matters, and development projects in the church. From the above structures it appears that the general membership of the church does not participate in voting on matters of polity and other church business. Thus they are excluded from the decision-making process.

In this predominantly preliterate or nonliterate community,[12] the fascinating oral history as related by the rank and file in the Shembe Church shows that researchers are not simply documenting past and present happenings, but engaging people in conversation about that which they passionately believe. This conversation is more than an exchange of

---

11. Barrett et al., *World Christian Encyclopedia*, 681.

12. From my observation almost all congregants carry a Bible and liturgical songbook to the Sabbath services. Many of them today are able to read from the Zulu Bible and the songbook.

information about personal, ecclesiastical, theological, and mundane beliefs and practices. Narrative, the telling of stories, is the fundamental genus of life. In the words of Walter Ong, people in oral communities "learn by discipleship which is a kind of apprenticeship, by listening, by repeating what they hear, and by mastering proverbs and ways of combining and recombining them, by assimilating other formulary materials, by participation in a kind of corporate retrospection."[13] The more one listens to stories, the more one realizes that stories give meaning to lives, meaning to a people rich in traditional culture yet torn by the paradox of living in two worlds: the nonliterate, rural, traditional third world alongside the literate, urban, modern first world. The resultant disjuncture creates for Shembe members a positive, dynamic forum for telling and retelling their own stories. In such an atmosphere of nostalgia, like-minded people who love and care for each other develop into a close-knit community. This communitarian setting creates for the individual a true sense of belonging in a fragmented world.

Ministers are not chosen because of any specific ability or gifting that they possess, or even through theological training. Rather, long-standing members who are loyal to the church are rewarded by way of promotion, some moving up the hierarchical ladder from preacher to minister over a period of time, others achieving direct ministerial status at the discretion of the leader. For example, Reverend Ngidi, a high school math and science teacher, said he was appointed to the status of minister directly from the rank of member in the church. Ministers who are relatively new to the church gain status on the basis of positions held in their previous churches, thus being rewarded for changing their denominational or church allegiance. Recently, however, some individuals attained ministerial status when they were recommended by older ministers with the approval of the leader, Vimbeni Shembe. The average age of the ministers interviewed was fifty-three years. Many stated that they were "born in the church," meaning that their parents were members of the church before or at the time of their birth. No one had any theological or Bible training. With the exception of the minister who is a schoolteacher, most ministers had minimal schooling or no formal education whatsoever. However, several ministers are successful businesspersons in the city of Durban, and some hold important government, tribal, and state positions.

Perhaps the only difference between this group and the lay people interviewed was that in some instances the ministers articulated more clearly their beliefs, practices, and myths regarding Isaiah Shembe and his succes-

---

13. Ong, *Orality and Literacy*, 9.

sors. Although many of these leaders are nonliterate, they are able to quote Bible passages from memory and tell stories about the founder and his immediate successors. This ability appeared to be part of the time-honored tradition of memorizing the words and works of Shembe, the epistemology of ancient oral tradition. Thus, ministers who had personal contact with the living Isaiah or Galilee Shembe seem to have a more authoritative role in the church. The other factor that would elevate the status of the leaders as compared with the ordinary members is the fact that leaders in their designated geographical locations, in the absence of Shembe, are responsible for assisting members with their everyday problems and needs. The research shows, however, that the content of the responses varied little between one group and the others.

The evangelists and preachers serve in ways similar to the functions of the ministers. In keeping with the hierarchical structure in the church, the evangelist assumes the role of leader in the absence of the minister. Preachers serve under the evangelists with one difference: in a local temple the preacher is in complete control of the service, and he invites ministers or evangelists to participate in the Sabbath service. More often than not, when a minister is present he is given the privilege of delivering the sermon. Youth, women's and men's leaders serve in their respective temples as advisors and leaders at their meetings.

The most important services of the year are when Shembe presides at Ebuhleni during the July celebrations. During the course of the calendar year, two services are held every Saturday, the holy day for the amaNazaretha Church, at nine o'clock in the morning and at one o'clock in the afternoon. These weekly services are convened at various locations throughout South Africa. At the main center, Ebuhleni, the tolling of a bell signifies the beginning of the worship service. At the local temples around the country, the preacher announces the commencement of the service just prior to the starting time, thereby alerting worshippers that the service is about to begin. At the sound of the bell or the call to worship by the announcer, people kneel in silent meditation for approximately one minute. The services are led by the local leader— who holds the title of preacher. Sermons are usually delivered by the most senior minister of the church present.

The Religious and Cultural Worldview of the amaNazaretha Church

Beliefs and Practices in the amaNazaretha Church

To examine the beliefs and practices in the amaNazaretha Church, I have selected the areas that are most critical for solving the research questions: the role of ancestors, the role of Shembe, and the role of Christ.

Ancestors

To determine the role of Jesus Christ in the religiocultural ethos of the Shembe Church, one must discern the status and function that ancestors and Shembe have in the lives of the amaNazaretha. The ancestors are still a vital part of the existential lives of the church members.[14] Oosthuizen already pointed out that "ancestor worship stands at the center of the Zulu tradition."[15] To what extent this cultural practice affects the work of Christ will be studied in chapter 7. While the Shembe church now denounces practices like witchcraft and consultations with *sangomas*,[16] they have not renounced their allegiance to the ancestors.

Shembe members have abrogated some Zulu traditional religious practices, but they still hold to many of the cultural practices. Ancestor "approbation"[17] is still central to them and not any different from the ancestor cult in Zulu traditional belief and practice. To the question "What are you actually doing when you call on ancestors?" interviewees respond first that they do not *worship* ancestors, and then, positively, that they *remember* the ancestors or *talk* with them.

People in this community still live in a symbiotic relationship with their ancestors. The separation between the living and the living-dead is only physical. The living and the living-dead comprise one community, so ancestors are consulted in all matters that concern the living. For example, ancestors are consulted concerning celebrations such as weddings, funerals, births of children, marriages, purchasing and selling houses, moving to new geographical locations, when misfortune is experienced in daily

---

14. In chapter 5, I deal with my research findings.

15. Oosthuizen, *Post-Christianity in Africa*, 3.

16. Oosthuizen describes the functions of the *isangoma* and claims that Shembe now fulfills that role for the amaNazaretha member (*Post-Christianity in Africa*).

17. I suggest the use of the term *approbation* for want of a better term that would more accurately describe the interaction between the living and the living-dead. I have avoided, where possible, the terms *worship* and *veneration*. I believe they do not bode well with the Shembe congregation. The term *approbation* nuances the many practices that inhere in their communication with ancestors and the ancestors' communication with the living. The term may include acts such as approval, consent, praise, esteem, eulogize, and paying tribute to the ancestors by way of animal sacrifices and *nikela*.

life, and when advice is needed. When individuals take a long journey, they invoke the protection of the ancestors. Regarding the importance of ancestors, people state that ancestors mediated between them and God or pointed them to God. Mediation takes the form of requests for everyday needs, healing, and generally whenever people pray.

The symbiotic relationship between the living and the living-dead is a reciprocal one. The living survive in everyday life situations through the intervention of the ancestors. In turn, the living-dead may also call on their living relatives for assistance. The request for such assistance comes mainly through dreams. Sometimes, however, when the living experience illness, loss of economic possessions, or even fracture in personal relationships, the cause for such misfortune is attributed to the ancestors' powerlessness and their lack of ability to help as they themselves are in need of assistance.

When pressed to suggest what kind of assistance ancestors need, people suggest that perhaps ancestors had enemies in their living days and the fracture in that relationship was not mended; thus, the ancestors are rendered powerless to assist others until the broken relationship is restored. Others suggest that because the ancestor had committed certain "sins" or wrongdoing in life and had not repented before death, the ancestor is still in "jail" and needs extradition. The only way the dead ancestor could be assisted by the living is for the living relatives to ask Shembe for forgiveness on behalf of the ancestor. Subsequently, the ancestor would be restored to join his family of ancestors, then becoming effective in his or her role as mediator, guardian, and helper of the living. The process of eradicating the "sins" of the ancestors is made through the paying of *nikela*, a certain sum of money, to Shembe.

This system of payment is akin to the medieval Roman Catholic system of paying indulgences on behalf of the dead. Martin Luther protested against this system in which a ticket of release was bought on behalf of the dead, who were then removed from purgatory. Luther, after reading Rom 1:17, came to the understanding that humankind is saved by faith and not by works. While the Shembe congregants do not use the same terms as the medieval Roman Catholics did, the system is similar to that practiced by members of the Catholic Church in the middle ages. The system of *nikela* is a ritual that is practiced every time the Shembe congregants come together. People come to Shembe at specific times every day of the week to *nikela*. In the absence of Shembe, this duty is delegated to ministers and evangelists. In the local temples the most senior person present, even the preacher, is delegated the responsibility to listen to the petitions from members and respond to their needs. In most instances, Shembe responds by saying, "God bless you." This pronouncement is believed to bring about the required result or need of the petitioner.[18]

When a church member presents a petition or problem to Shembe, he often directs the person to his or her ancestors and suggests that consultation with the ancestor is the appropriate means of solving the individual's dilemma. On other occasions, Shembe undertakes to consult the ancestors in question and request a reprieve for the individual's situation. In most instances, the individuals return to thank Shembe for mediating on their behalf by way of an offering or *nikela*.

Communication between the living and the living-dead is made through animal sacrifices. Cows or goats are slaughtered, and the blood is buried outside the kraal. Zulus have a special hut, *emsamo*, which is dedicated solely for communicating with the ancestors. Shembe members now living in urban and suburban localities dedicate a room in the family home for rituals connected with ancestors. The ceremony is very sacred, and only the head of the family approaches the ancestors. Meat is sacrificed to the ancestors by burning a green herbal plant, *impepho*, producing a pleasant aroma. It is said that the aroma from the plant and the burned meat rises to the ancestors. The meat is left overnight in the ancestor's hut, and during a celebration the next day, the family and friends join to partake of the food.

Vimbeni Shembe, the current leader, perpetuates and encourages the invoking of ancestors, as did Isaiah Shembe, his grandfather and ancestor. This aspect of African Traditional Religion, specifically Zulu Traditional Religion, is still a central part of the cultural and religious ethos of the Shembe Church. The well-being of the Shembe congregants depends on a proper relationship with the ancestors and on reciprocal acts by the living on behalf of the living-dead.

This aspect of Zulu religion and culture becomes most acute when one realizes that Zulus do not have a functionary, such as a priest, who mediates on their behalf, as in other living religions. Zulus do not even have the concept of such a priestly intermediary. Kings and chiefs play that role. In the Shembe Church, Shembe and ancestors assume that responsibility. Perhaps this belief is one of the reasons why the African Initiated Churches, and particularly the Shembe Church, boast such a large following among the Zulus in South Africa and why they are gaining new

---

18. When Shembe grants absolution, it involves three steps: (1) contrition; (2) confession; and (3) satisfaction by means of payment. This practice was evident in early Roman Catholic Church history. However, no individual in the Shembe Church articulated the practice in Roman Catholic terms.

members and adherents even up to the present time: they have revived the ancestor cult while other missionary churches frown upon the invocation of ancestors.

Shembe

Although responses to questions regarding the perception of Isaiah Shembe for the people voiced were cognitively and experientially varied, the general consensus is that he is more than human. Shembe members see Isaiah Shembe as one who is above the ancestors in rank and therefore is able to mediate between the living and the living-dead. For the Shembe Church, Isaiah Shembe is likened to God in the sense that he is able to respond positively and effectively to their needs. According to Zulu culture, God is inaccessible as he is the Supreme Being and too powerful for a mere human to approach;[19] Shembe thus becomes his replacement.[20] In a sense Shembe has become the manifestation of God. The miracle stories as told and retold by members reinforce this idea that Shembe is God in human form. In this regard Mpanza quotes Galilee Shembe as saying thus:

> A God that only stays in heaven, that does not come down to the people and talk, walk with the people, teach the people and is seen . . . with the people, is no God. Shembe came and introduced to you God who stays with the people, God who walks with the people, who listens to people's request; that is the God of Shembe; that is the God of the amaNazaretha.[21]

Stories of Shembe's being omnipresent are told with passion and joy when members come together. Members affirm Shembe's omnipresence as an accepted fact when they compare Shembe with Christ, arguing that nowhere in the Bible did Jesus claim to be in two places, separated geographically by some two hundred miles, at the same time.[22]

The understanding that Shembe is divine is not separated from his role as Holy Spirit. One tangible evidence of this belief for amaNazaretha members is seen every time Shembe congregants come together to worship. In the larger temples, where the physical infrastructure of the temple

19. Oosthuizen, *Post-Christianity in Africa*, 9.

20. Ibid. Oosthuizen adds that in the absence of God, Shembe "can be directly approached, [and] is now in their midst. It is he who has more intimate contact with the ancestral world than anybody else."

21. Mpanza, "The Biography of Isaiah Shembe," 102.

22. I relate the story as told by members of the amaNazaretha Church, where it is purported that Isaiah Shembe was seen by eyewitnesses at two different locations at the same time separated by some two hundred miles.

grounds is more developed, a tabernacle-like structure is an imposing feature. It is here that the current incumbent, Vimbeni Shembe, sits when presiding over the Sabbath worship service. Before the service begins, and before Shembe enters the tabernacle, a huge pillow covered in beautiful embroided material and wrapped in a grass mat is brought into the tabernacle. Congregants kneel while the pillow is carried into the temple. The attendant very reverently, purposefully, and carefully unwraps the pillow. At the end of the service the pillow is wrapped again and returned to Shembe's house. The pillow represents Isaiah Shembe and the Holy Spirit. Shembe members say that *Isaiah Shembe* is not the Holy Spirit, but *Shembe* is the Holy Spirit. As explained by one evangelist, "Shembe existed before Isaiah Shembe was born." This belief is connected with the story told of Isaiah Shembe's mother eating a flower not long before he was conceived. The flower was said to represent the Holy Spirit.

Shembe ministers and members use the Bible to reinforce their belief that Shembe is the Holy Spirit. They refer to the words of Jesus in John chapters 14–16, where Jesus promises the coming of the Holy Spirit after his departure and ascension. Shembe members interpret these passages literally and believe that the reference is to Shembe.[23]

Regarding the role of Vimbeni Shembe today in relationship to Isaiah Shembe and the leaders after him, Johannes Galilee Shembe and Amos Shembe, amaNazaretha members believe that the Holy Spirit that was present in Jesus Christ, Isaiah Shembe, Galilee Shembe, and Amos Shembe is now resident in Vimbeni Shembe. AmaNazaretha members hold to the adoptionist theory that Christ was adopted into sonship at his baptism. Here the outworking of the Trinity comes into focus: the Father speaks to the Son, and the Holy Spirit appears in the form of a dove. For Shembe members, Vimbeni Shembe received the Holy Spirit when he was nominated to succeed his father, Amos, as leader of the Shembe Church. The narrative related by Shembe members is that at the funeral service of Amos Shembe, when Vimbeni Shembe was declared the new leader of the church, a rainbow appeared over his head. This event is interpreted as a sign of the Holy Spirit descending upon Vimbeni Shembe.

Vimbeni Shembe is held with the same aura, dignity, and respect as the previous leaders. His followers believe that he is capable of healing people, removing their sins, and responding to their problems and needs. He is seen as able to mediate effectively between the ancestors and the

---

23. Mpanza, in his unpublished work, "The Biography of Isaiah Shembe," devotes a whole chapter to this discussion (ch. 4). Reference to his work and discussion will follow in ch. 7.

living. Just as Isaiah was considered to be God to the people because of their inability to communicate directly with the Supreme Being, Vimbeni Shembe is cast in a similar role. When asked which Shembe is called upon in prayers and in times of crises, the overwhelming majority believed that all Shembes are one and the same. Older members relate stories about previous leaders while younger members tell stories about the works accomplished by Vimbeni Shembe.

There is the underlying implicit belief, however, that ancestors are more powerful than the living, and thus the previous leaders, especially Isaiah Shembe, appear to be venerated, if not deified. This belief becomes evident in the sermons preached as well as the presence of Isaiah Shembe represented by the pillow in the service. It is also shown when members congregate informally to tell miracle stories that affirm their faith in Shembe and the amaNazaretha Church.

The Holy Spirit

The Holy Spirit plays an important role in the Shembe theology. Central to people's belief is the understanding that the Holy Spirit is a person. Here Shembe clergy and members refer to the words of Jesus to authenticate their belief, using the Johannine passages, especially John 14:26 and 16:7.[24] These biblical passages use the masculine *he* with reference to the Holy Spirit. Shembe members interpret this pronoun to refer to Shembe. The words of Jesus, claiming that he has to go before the Holy Spirit comes, further enforce the members' belief that the Sprit that was in Christ is now in Shembe. However, Shembe members do not believe that they possess the Holy Spirit. The Holy Spirit is given only to certain individuals whom God chooses. God chose Jesus Christ, and now he has chosen Shembe. The miraculous works done by Jesus, and now by Shembe, substantiate this belief. There is a sense of ambivalence when Shembe members say that Shembe "is" the Holy Spirit and also that Shembe "possesses" the Holy Spirit. The underlying belief is that Shembe has his origin in human parents, like Jesus, and when he received the Holy Spirit, he took on a nature that is supernatural, or metaphysical. The concept of the Holy Trinity (Father, Son, and Holy Spirit) is present in Shembe theology, but it is interpreted differently than in orthodox Christianity. God is Father, the Supreme Being; Jesus is the Son of God; and Shembe is the Holy Spirit.[25]

24. Ibid., 90.
25. Ibid., 96–98.

The Role of Jesus Christ

Most of the amaNazaretha believe that Jesus is the Son of God. When pressed to explain, however, people express that he was born of human parents and that at his baptism he received the Holy Spirit. God had sent him to the Jewish nation, who killed him although he performed many miracles and did good works. Shembe members do not have a uniform understanding as to where Jesus Christ is now. Their understanding of his present status, role, or existence is unclear. Some suggest that Jesus has returned to the Father. Others say that Jesus is now dead and does not possess any influence over the living. Generally, though, the amaNazaretha believe that Christians are mistaken in believing that Jesus will return, since Jesus is now present in the person of Shembe, whom God sent to the African nation.[26]

Shembe congregants believe that Shembe has more power than Jesus solely on the basis of the length of time in which Jesus lived and worked on Earth. They believe that all that Jesus did and said is contained in the Bible. Therefore, comparatively speaking, Shembe has done much more than Jesus ever did in terms of miracles and healings, as Shembe is still alive and outlives Christ in terms of chronological age.

To further substantiate the belief that Shembe is more powerful than Christ, Shembe members relate stories of Shembe appearing in two different locations at the same time. They argue that nowhere in the Bible is there record of Jesus showing himself to be omnipresent. This belief elevates the status of Shembe above Christ. Many say that their only knowledge of Jesus is what they read in the Bible, but Shembe is present among them, meets their needs, and performs many miracles in their very presence. The implicit idea for the Shembe members is "We believe that which we see"—that which is visible and tangible is evidential.

The superiority of Shembe to Jesus is also suggested by the Shembe congregants' prayers. The majority say that they pray in the name of their ancestors and Shembe. Jesus does not feature in their prayers. When asked "Who comes to mind in times of need or when problems arise?" people are unanimous that Shembe comes to mind and that they call on the name of Shembe.

Regarding life after death, Shembe members believe that Shembe shows them the way to heaven or to God. He is waiting at the gates to usher them into heaven. Jesus does not feature in this process, although he may be there for his "own people," the Jews. The concept of heaven is

26. Ibid., 90–106.

different from the Christian understanding in that Zulu traditional belief plays a dominant role. Here it is not so much a resurrection of the body but continuity of life and thus immortality. This belief becomes evident in the ceremony of releasing the dead, performed one year after of the death of an individual. The soul of the departed hovers over the grave until such ritual is performed.

Also the belief in the idea of a "jail" holding dead relatives who need deliverance and redemption is rife in the Shembe Church. Reunion with one's ancestors seems to be more dominant than belief in heaven as understood by Christians. Christ does not feature in any of these beliefs.

Summary

The amaNazaretha Church, a predominantly Zulu movement, still maintains many of its Zulu cultural practices in its expression of the Christian faith. To what extent they have contextualized and indigenized the Christian gospel will be studied in ch. 7. What is evident even at this juncture is that the amaNazaretha Church today places a high premium on the status of ancestors and its current leader, Vimbeni Shembe. Shembe's position today appears to be deeply influenced by Zulu traditions and culture.

5

Recounting Stories (Research Findings)

IN JANUARY 2000, EARLY in my field research, I traveled to Durban, South Africa, to begin investigation of the amaNazaretha Church. At that time I thought that the quantitative approach to field research would be an appropriate strategy for gathering data to solve the research problem. Consequently, I prepared a Likert scale instrument containing thirty statements on a five-point scale, ranging from one (not sure) to five (strongly agree). At the amaNazaretha headquarters, Ebuhleni, I invited one of Vimbeni Shembe's close aides, Mr. Sibisi, to fill out the questionnaire. One of the statements in the testing instrument read, "Shembe is God." To this question Mr. Sibisi responded by saying, "It would be wrong to say Shembe is *not* God. It would also be wrong to say Shembe *is* God if we do not explain." He then recounted this story:

> In Zululand (Gingindlovu),[1] 1928, a family planned to attend the July Festival. The money they had saved for the journey was locked in their trunk at home. The daughters of the house went out to collect firewood for their parents, who had already left for the celebrations. The parents were expected back home so that the girls could also attend part of the celebrations. While they were out collecting wood, a burglar entered the house through the window and searched for valuables, eventually finding the trunk with the money. It was a large sum of money. (I am just narrating a story that Shembe is someone else, someone that we don't know.) There was a postcard-size picture of J. G. Shembe lying on a pillow on the bed. When the burglar looked at the picture on the pillow, the man in the picture, J. G. Shembe, walked out of the picture over to the window and closed the window. (You can't believe that!) How can a man rise from a picture and become a person like you? By that time the girls returned from collecting wood. They unlocked the door and found the burglar inside the house. The girls were afraid, but the man said, "Keep quiet, I will not kill you. I will tell you what happened. I came into the room to steal the money.

---

1. This is a small rural town in KwaZulu-Natal dominated by Zulu speakers.

Here's the money. But that man there in the picture walked out of the frame to the window and closed it, and I couldn't open the window until you came." By this time the girls' brothers arrived and listened to the story told by the burglar. They released the burglar after taking back their money. Shembe protects.[2]

Mr. Sibisi went on to relate other stories to make his point that Shembe is an enigma. Responding to the kind of questionnaire I prepared would be totally inadequate; such responses without narrative, commentary, and explanation would misrepresent what the amaNazaretha actually believe and practice.

I realized that the amaNazaretha were not reticent to share their passion, enthusiasm, and exuberance regarding their faith—but that they expressed their faith best through telling stories. I returned to the United States at the end of January 2000 more enlightened about this group of people and revised my questionnaire into a full interview schedule. With renewed hope that a qualitative research methodology would enhance my prospects of gathering data related to the research problem, I returned to South Africa again in June 2000. I was confident that I would be entertained with a rich harvest of stories from an oral culture caught in the throes of a fast-changing political and cultural environment.

My research findings fall under the main areas of inquiry: Ancestors, Shembe, and Christ. Under each of these three categories, my findings fall into two parts: first, responses from ministers, evangelists, and preachers;[3] and second, responses from youth leaders, women's leaders, and laypersons.

The methodology for organizing the data was as follows: First, I typed out the original interviews from the audio recordings on separate pages for each interviewee; I then collected all the data under each of the questions according to the interview schedule; last, I collated the responses under each question, bringing together similar responses and at the same time showing responses that were unusual.

Originally, I had anticipated that responses from people in the church positions would vary from one another, with the most informed

---

2. Mr. Sibisi is fluent in English although English is his second language. Thus, his response is a direct quote. I have edited the stories presented in this work to read better grammatically and more fluently, but also endeavored to maintain the sense and intended meaning each time. We learn from narrative studies that oral societies bring the future into the present, and thus chronology and historical sequence are not primary. The story, or the event, is the central and primary focus (Ong, *Orality and Literacy*, 136–40).

3. I refer to all three in this category of interviewees as "minister."

coming from the highest-ranking officials of the church (the ministers) and the least informed from members. However, the data showed that the responses among the various groups (ministers, evangelists, and members) did not greatly differ in terms of content; one group was not more informed than the other. Exceptions were with four individuals with whom I had extended conversations: the evangelist, Mr. Mpanza, who is credited by many members as being the "theologian" of the church; his brother, minister Mpanza; and two other ministers, Gcwenza and Ngidi.

I found that the data from respondents and their analysis fit generally under the two groupings: (1) ministers, evangelists, and preachers; and (2) youth leaders, women's leaders, and members.[4] The former group represents the official voice of the amaNazaretha Church while the latter represents the folk or popular views regarding beliefs and practices.

The interview schedule of thirty questions covered four topics—the three primary categories, of Ancestors, Shembe, and Christ, and one secondary category, comprising some general questions. The questions were asked of all of the interviewees, including Vimbeni Shembe, whom I had the opportunity to interview in January 2003.[5]

The Role of Ancestors in the amaNazaretha Church

That the ancestors play an important role in the everyday lives of the amaNazaretha became evident when I heard a powerful story told by Vimbeni Shembe's daughter, Lindewe Shembe. I first met her at a Sabbath worship service held in a busy city park cordoned off by a string of ropes, a clear sign of separation of the "sacred" and the "profane." The ropes were substitutes for the whitewashed stones that normally characterize the amaNazaretha places of worship—a familiar sight today in both rural and urban KwaZulu-Natal. This site is behind a row of hotels that line the ocean, Durban's Bay of Plenty, a popular tourist attraction.

Lindewe arrived after the service had commenced, just before the sermon. She joined the women in the front row.[6] At the conclusion of the preaching, she came forward and sat in the open space between the men and women. A small grass basket was placed in front of her as the congregation sang. Both men and women came forward, knelt before her,

---

4. When citing interviewees in the text, I have used the following abbreviations to identify the various groups of individuals interviewed: Minister—MR; Evangelist—EV; Preacher—PR; Youth Leader—YL; Women's Leader (*Umkokheli* in Zulu)—UK; and Members (Lay People)—LP.

5. See chapter 6 for a full account of my interview with Vimbeni Shembe.

6. I describe the seating arrangements for the amaNazaretha worship services in ch. 6.

and placed their offerings (*nikela*) in the basket. My research assistant, Joseph Mhlongo, informed me that it was customary to honor and show respect for the daughter of Shembe as she represented him in his absence. All the money given in the offering that morning was for her benefit. At the conclusion of the service, I asked Joseph if I could request an interview with her. She agreed to an appointment with me for a week later but did not keep the appointment. I called her again at her office in the city and set up a second appointment. It turned out that she had been suspicious of me and the reason for the interview, assuming that if she offered me an interview and entertained my questions, I would misrepresent her views regarding the church and perhaps divulge the text of the interview to the mass media in South Africa. Consequently, her father would not be pleased with her for entertaining me and my questions. Eventually, however, I was able to interview her. My research assistant told me that she had first consulted with some ministers who were close to her father about granting the interview. Also weighing in my favor was the news she learned that I had interviewed several leading members and ministers of the church.

In the interview, Lindewe affirmed her belief in the role of ancestors and Shembe by relating this story:

> I started work in Ulundi [capital of KwaZulu-Natal] for a couple of years and lived in one of the houses shared by four people. I was not serious about church. Even at boarding school I never wore the white gown for church. I did not do the things that we as Nazarites were supposed to do. It so happened that while at work I became ill and was taken home for a week. At this time I was taking driving lessons from an elderly couple. After lessons the lady would drive us back to our place where we lived, and we would talk for some time. One of my roommates also took lessons from her. The driving instructor did not know that I had fallen ill and that I had left for home. But she had a dream. When I returned after my illness, I received a message from my roommate that the driving instructor wanted to see me. I went to visit her, and in our conversation she told me she had had dreams about me and that I was sick. In her dream she came to our apartment and parked at the back flight of stairs to the apartment. She saw a short man with a white gown [presumably Lindewe's grandfather, the late A. K. Shembe and father of the present leader, M. V. Shembe] calling for me, and this lady said I was walking with three ladies from the house. She said the man was calling me by another name that she did not know previously (my nickname normally used at home). I had not told

my friends my nickname, for they would laugh at me; nobody knew it. This lady said she heard the man call me by that name. I said, "I do not believe you because no one knows that name." She said the man called me, and I left the three ladies and walked up the flight of stairs. The man pulled something from under his arm, which I later discovered was a white gown. The man put the white gown on me and said, "I told you long ago to wear this gown. It is the only source of protection you will have from anything, and nothing will ever touch you." She then saw a whole crowd of people dressed like me in a huge field singing and dancing. She could not describe the singing as it was so heavenly. She had never been to our church, nor did she know anything about our way of worship. She said she was worried because white is normally worn by the dead. So that is the only story that I share with you. To me that meant that I must go back to the church and live by the rules of the church. (LP:30)

This story reflects the apparent omnipresence and value the amaNazaretha place on the ancestors in their day-to-day living.[7] Dreams about ancestors also give them a sense of stability and assurance that the ancestors are accessible, involved, and near in times of need. Stories such as Lindewe's are repeated with passion and exuberance by the staunch members of this charismatic church, whether in small group settings or in one-on-one conversations.

To understand amaNazaretha beliefs and practices regarding ancestors, I further subdivided the research focus of the Ancestor category into three questions: (1) whether the amaNazaretha worshipped or venerated ancestors and the type of terminology they used to express such worship and/or veneration;[8] (2) whether ministers and members had diametrically opposing views regarding the status and role of ancestors; and (3) regard-

---

7. The amaNazaretha say that the ancestors are close to God, yet they are with them all the time. Mbiti reinforces this idea of "omnipresence" (he does not use that term though) when he says that the "living-dead" are still people and that they have their "foot in both worlds," guarding the family "activities, traditions, ethics, and affairs" (*African Religions and Philosophy*, 82). One member articulated the presence of ancestors thus: "Generally we believe the ancestors are always with us. Whether you are sleeping, driving, eating, we believe the ancestors are always looking after us on behalf of God. They are like angels. As far as communicating with them is concerned, it depends on why you want to communicate with them. It is either as a way of thanking them for anything that you think they have done for you, or as a way of condemning them for letting evil things happen to you. We believe that they are still bound to look after you. If there is a wedding, you communicate with them, if you are getting a new [wife] *makoti* because you believe that the *makoti* must be an additional member in this family for which the ancestors must care" (EV:3).

8. See explanation of terms for meaning of *worship* and *veneration* in ch. 1.

ing ancestral practices, what role ancestors played in the existential life of the amaNazaretha people. In all, I used thirteen separate questions for the section on the Role of Ancestors. However, in engaging interviewees in dialogue and conversation, I soon found that the questions could not be dealt with separately. The responses for one question were sometimes repeated and articulated differently for other questions. I have not accounted for questions that elicited similar responses in this section, selecting only questions that elicited pertinent responses.

Ministers' Response to Question 1

I interviewed fifteen ministers, eight evangelists, and six preachers for a total of twenty-nine persons in this category. Twenty-three of the twenty-nine interviewees (79%) said they had been raised in the church—their parents were already members of the Shembe church when they were born. None of the respondents had any theological training, and only four (14%) had received tertiary education. The most academically qualified in this group was evangelist Mpanza, who is considered by many members as one of the most knowledgeable regarding the history, ecclesiology, and theology of the amaNazaretha Church. A former magistrate, he is now employed by the KwaZulu-Natal government, where he serves as director of traditional and local government affairs. Apart from my planned interview with him, he granted several more follow-up conversations, during which I learned more about the structure and belief system of the amaNazaretha Church. At public gatherings Mpanza is often called to speak on behalf of the church and is also quoted by scholars of religion who have researched the amaNazaretha Church.

In response to the first part of the question "*When (a) and how (b) do you communicate with ancestors?*" all twenty-nine interviewees reported that they communicated with their ancestors to solicit the ancestors' assistance or that out of obligation they invited their ancestors to be present at family and community celebrations.[9] Communication with ancestors was still an integral part of the amaNazarethas' everyday life. Minister Khanyile responded, "Our belief as Shembe congregants, and also through the teaching of Shembe, is that we speak to them [ancestors] in the morning, day, and afternoon" (MR:5).[10]

---

9. Family and community functions include a variety of cultural and social events such as births and deaths, weddings and engagements, celebrating the purchase of a new home, acquiring a new job, etc.

10. The minister expressed the idea that his ancestors are his constant companions and that he is conscious of their presence throughout the day.

Recounting Stories (Research Findings)

Speaking to ancestors means conducting a conversation, believing that the ancestor hears. It may take place anywhere, given the circumstances that necessitates calling on the ancestor. Interviewees emphatically denied that they prayed to ancestors. They made the distinction that when they talk with the ancestor, they do not close their eyes; when praying, they do. One may also talk with ancestors at home in the room (in an urban dwelling) where no one sleeps, or in a special hut reserved just for the ancestor in rural areas. Occasions that merit invoking an ancestor are many and varied. For example, if an individual has a disagreement with her or his employer, the individual may call on the ancestor to intervene.

In other words, the amaNazaretha call on ancestors when celebrating social occasions, such as the birth of a child, marriage, success in a business venture, or when good fortune comes their way. In addition, "We also talk with our ancestors during ceremonies."[11] On different occasions, for example, when my son is engaged or there is a wedding, we call on our ancestors to come and be with us during these times,"[12] said Reverend Khanyile (MR:5).

Ancestors are also invoked when calamity strikes or when people are in need—material or physical.[13] One minister responded, "In our culture, and Shembe teaches us as well, we must call on them [ancestors] when-

---

11. Remembrance ceremonies are enacted by the living on behalf of the dead. For example, Joseph Mhlongo, my field research assistant, told me of the forthcoming ceremony he will be conducting, the remembrance ritual for his deceased mother, whom he lost when he was barely four months old. The process, as he explained it, is thus: On June 29 he will invite his relatives, friends, and local church community to his home. On this occasion he will sacrifice a goat. On the appointed day, his eldest brother will talk with the ancestors at *emsamo*, asking them to assist Joseph with his problems (difficulty at work with employer; not enough money to support his family). He will sacrifice the animal in the designated room, cut it into several parts, and prepare it in a cooking pot outside the house. The food will be distributed to men and women (each receiving specific parts of the animal), and one part will be brought back into the room and placed before the *emsamo* for three to four days, for the ancestors. The green herbal plant is burned, and the smoke and aroma rise to meet the ancestors. The ancestors may come to Joseph in dreams to acknowledge the sacrifice, but also when Joseph experiences a change in his work and financial situations, he believes that the ancestors responded favorably and that the sacrifice was accepted.

12. It is necessary to invite one's ancestors to a wedding so that the ancestors may shower their blessings on the married couple. If one does not invite the ancestors to the wedding ceremony, it is believed that the marriage may not last, or that the couple will encounter problems. Similarly, when a child is born, she or he must be introduced to the ancestors to ensure protection from ill health and other calamities.

13. Calamities may include loss of a job, sudden illness, fracture in relationships among family or even clans, accidents that cause serious injuries, etc.

ever we have a problem. They can tell us what is going wrong" (MR:8). Another minister said the following:

> There is a Zulu custom that you must perform for a new baby, but I had not done that because I had a problem.[14] In dreams, the ancestors came to the mother of the baby telling her that this custom must be done for the baby. I went to *emsamo* and burned *impepho*[15] in the *big house*. I took an oath with the ancestors and told them that I would do the custom if they heal the baby. (MR:9)

To emphasize the integral place ancestors have in the amaNazaretha community, one evangelist said thus:

> When I am in trouble, I wonder why the ancestors are allowing me to experience hardship. I also think that there is something wrong that the ancestors are trying to highlight to me so I can rectify it. If I need something, like a baby, and I am not getting a baby even though I am married, I will talk with my ancestors. Although you don't get an answer at the same time, we believe that the ancestors are listening to you, and everyone who is around you keeps quiet while you are slaughtering the animal. (EV:3)

This response suggests that family members are obligated to the living-dead and that only when they are appeased are calamity and hardship halted by the ancestors' intervention. In this case an animal had to be sacrificed to appease the ancestor before the situation returned to normal.

Additionally, in response to the above question, some respondents suggested that ancestors communicated with them whenever an ancestor needed assistance from the living relative. Some respondents claimed that ancestors visited the living in dreams and requested food as they (the ancestors) were hungry. More than hunger, the ancestors felt neglected, and one way to regain attention was to ask the living to prepare food for them. This need sometimes requires a special ceremony where sacrificing an animal is not uncommon. It is believed that ancestors communicate such requests through dreams of living relatives.

In response to the second part of the question, "*How do you communicate with ancestors?*" the most frequent response (27 out of 29, 93%)

---

14. The "problem" referred to by the minister is a colloquial term meaning that one is both economically and financially challenged and thus unable to honor his or her ritual obligations.

15. *Impepho* is a green herbal plant that emits a sweet-smelling aroma when burned. The amaNazaretha believe that the smoke from the burnt plant rises to the ancestors as an offering to them.

was that communication takes place via animal sacrifice (cows and goats), which includes burning *impepho*. The understanding is that the aroma and smoke from the burning plant rise to meet the ancestors, a form of offering to them. One interviewee explained:

> When I encounter problems, I go to the grave of my mom and dad. I tell them I am encountering a problem. After that I will see a difference, because they will answer me and help me. The herb *impepho* is used to communicate with the ancestors when it is burned. Then I will slaughter a goat. Later they come in dreams to show their appreciation. (MR:7)

Members' Response to Question 1

The responses to the first part of question one, "*When do you communicate with ancestors?*" were similar to those of the ministers. Here the most frequent response (36 out of 39, 92%) was that the amaNazaretha call on ancestors in times of need and also when celebrating social and community functions.

One example of the amaNazaretha calling upon ancestors in times of need is articulated through this story:

> Recently, in December, I went to the Amanzimtoti area. I had a gun, but I wouldn't let people see it. On the way back home we were stopped at a roadblock, and the police searched our luggage. I prayed to God and to our ancestors. I said, "Oh God of my father and all my ancestors, please be with me now. Don't let me be embarrassed and disappointed in front of these people. I come to you and trust you, my father, that you will send this message to God." You know what happened? Instead of opening my bag, they told me that they were not going to search my bag. They searched everyone else's, but they didn't search mine. Then I said, "Well, isn't that amazing if things can be done this way and a reply comes so quickly from my ancestors!" (LP:15)

This narrative shows that the amaNazaretha firmly believe that they have access to their ancestors at all times, even in mundane everyday situations. In Lindewe Shembe's case, it was her ancestor who caused her to return to the church and respond appropriately by wearing the traditional white gown. For the amaNazaretha the white gown is symbolic of purity, so wearing the white gown obligates the initiate to conform to the rules, regulations, and restrictions imposed by the church upon its members.

Members say that they communicate with ancestors most frequently through animal sacrifices. While this response was the most frequent (26 of 39, 67%), two members stated that they offered the ancestors food as a way of communicating with them.[16] Another five respondents said they offer *nikela*[17] for their ancestors. Another four respondents said they go to the *emsamo* and offer prayers[18] to the ancestors. One respondent who had left the Zion Church claimed that that church disavowed communication with ancestors, and since she holds to that belief, she is now a member of the amaNazaretha Church.[19]

Members present sacrificial offerings to the ancestors on different occasions. For example, one respondent told this story:

> When your first child is born, you must bring a goat and slaughter it and put a bangle on your child's hand. By this you are telling the ancestors that they must take care of this child, guide the child, and make him listen [obey]. Even if I try on my own to put this child on the right path, it will not help him if the ancestors are not involved, because the ancestors will say they don't know him. The ancestors will say, "Who is this? We do not know this child." I have to first introduce the child. It will go on like this. I may have ten children, but I have to introduce them first to the ancestors. The ancestors are so important in everything we do. (LP:22)

While there are ceremonies performed when a child is born, there are also ceremonies for the dead. The ancestors play a pivotal role even in death ceremonies of a family member. This belief was explained by the same respondent:

> If my father has passed away, I will fast for one year. At the end of that year, I must clear [introduce] my father with the other ancestors. I must bring a goat and place it in the *emsamo* and talk. I will say, "Listen! I have my father here. He came to you (the

---

16. One respondent explained that one burns *impepho* and places a piece of meat on the *impepho*. The smoke rises to meet the ancestors, and thus they are happy that they were remembered. The smoke is a gift to the ancestor (LP:8).

17. *Nikela* is the payment of a sum of money (for offences committed and for requests made) to Shembe by the amaNazaretha. *Nikela* is also made on behalf of the dead by their living relatives. It is believed that the sins committed by a departed ancestor can be eradicated and that the said ancestor subsequently joins the company of ancestors where one is in a position to assist the living.

18. This respondent did not differentiate between "praying" to and "talking" with the ancestors.

19. In the section on "The African Independent Churches and Their Views on Ancestors," I discuss the Zion Christian Church, the largest AIC in South Africa.

ancestors)." We are asking our father to take care of us again. For generations this carries on. Shembe said that this was the right thing. Our African history was not written down. It is all left by word of mouth to us. My father left it for me to tell, so I must also tell my sons that if they do bad things it is wrong and you will have bad luck. (LP:22)

One preacher gave an explanation for the sacrificial process:

> In the Zulu custom . . . you prepare some Zulu beer. Call all your family together and tell them that you are going to be greeting your ancestors and feeding them. You slaughter a cow. On this day, you don't take any part of the cow to eat at all. It has to be placed in a position for the ancestors to come and view what has been laid before them. It is at night that the ancestors come and look at the food you left them. This is how we communicate with our ancestors. (PR:1)

There are occasions when members solicit the assistance of ancestors without offering animal sacrifices.[20] One member explained how he sought the assistance of his ancestors in finding employment for his son:

> When my son is seeking employment, even if he is educated, I must first take him to the "Big House" [*emsamo*] where we do all the prayers. I will tell the ancestors, "I have a child looking for a job. You are the ones who are taking care of us as we always hope. Please give him a job." So then my child finds employment. (LP:22)

According to Mbiti, the *living-dead* are those members of the family who, present in spirit, are still considered important in the family structure of

---

20. For example, a layperson said, "When I have nothing to slaughter, I talk to them. I burn *impepho* at the *emsamo*. I pray to them and tell them my problems" (LP:13). Another layperson explained, "Before I left for Ebuhleni [for the July celebrations] I knelt down and called upon them [ancestors] to guide me and go with me. They offer me protection (LP:2). See the story from LP:15 above, a classic example of an individual far away from their home, community, and amaNazaretha temple who called upon God, Shembe, and the ancestors when faced with a difficult situation. No offering was made or promised and no vow taken to offer sacrifices at a later time when his problem was resolved. It was a spontaneous act on his part to call for assistance in a time of crisis. He said, "Oh God of my father and all my ancestors, please be with me now. Don't let me be embarrassed and disappointed in front of these people. I come to you and trust you, my father, that you will send this message to God." Another layperson spoke of a miracle in his own life when he went to Shembe asking for a male child, since at that time he had five girls. After visiting Shembe he went home and invoked the ancestors by burning *impepho* in the *emsamo*. The ancestors then gave him twin sons (LP:24).

Zulu people.²¹ While not explicit in the above account, it is implied that ancestors are mediators²² between the living and God for the Zulu, and that worship is reserved for God only, although the living-dead are respected and honored.²³

Ministers' Response to Question 2

Pursuing the inquiry whether the amaNazaretha worship or venerate ancestors, I posed the question *"What are you actually doing when you call on ancestors?"* Sixty-two percent (18 of 29) of the respondents intimated that they "talk" with their ancestors while thirty-four percent (10) suggested that they "remember" their ancestors. My sense was that all respondents were strongly reacting to the common and often uninformed view by outsiders and non-Africans that the amaNazaretha worship ancestors. In both formal and informal discussions, I was told, "We do not worship ancestors," even before I asked the question. In all of my interviews and discussions with Shembe congregants, I was careful and rarely used the terms *worship* and *veneration*. One evangelist explained, "When I want something from God, I know that my forefathers are close to God because they are dead. I cry to them. Then the ancestors go to God and tell him, 'Our child is crying. Can you give him this and this?'"(EV:7). Evangelist Mkize referred to both the hierarchical order and mediatorial role of ancestors, but made no reference to worship:

> When we pray we don't say, "My ancestors," but we say, "God of my ancestors." We believe that God will always know my ancestors first before he knows me. So between me and Shembe are my

---

21. Mbiti, *African Religions and Philosophy*, 25.

22. One of the functions of ancestors is the mediatorial role they play in the prayers offered by their living relatives. One member described the ancestors' role thus: "Whenever I pray, I first ask them to 'clear the line' [open the way], because when I am praying there is a barrier between me and God or Shembe. So it is these ancestors that clear the line. They are my code number to God" (LP:1). One minister explained further the hierarchical structure of the spirit beings and the place of ancestors thus: "We have physical people down here on earth. Above them we have ancestors. Above the ancestors we have spiritual beings, angels. Above the angels we have God. We believe the ancestors are the conduits between us and God. We can never do without them." (MR:8). A medical doctor, member of the amaNazaretha Church, reaffirmed the view that ancestors mediate between the living and God. He said, "My father is a means of communication. He is a conduit. Whatever we report to the ancestors, they pass it on to a higher being before it gets to God Almighty" (LP:16).

23. See Mbiti's, *African Religions and Philosophy*, chs. 7–9, pp. 58–97, for fuller discussion on the concept of worship, respect, and honor. I also explain the terms in ch. 1 above.

ancestors. So that is why I always mention them first. I believe that by first calling my ancestors, God recognizes that I am calling for attention. And God will say, "There is the son of 'so-and-so' who I know I am working with." Therefore, if God wants to do anything for me, he will send my ancestors. God will tell the ancestors that he heard my cry and ask the ancestors to go and do this for me. And my ancestors may say, "No, we cannot do such a good thing for him because he is not taking care of us [the ancestors]." (EV:3)

The evangelist earlier in the interview had placed Shembe under God and above the ancestors in the hierarchial order. There was always a measure of ambivalence as to whether Shembe or the ancestors approach God independently or jointly on behalf of the living. The question this situation raises is whether the traditional Zulu customs and the Christian religious beliefs coalesce to the point that even after almost one hundred years the amaNazaretha do not differentiate between religious and secular cultural dynamics. Does the Zulu worldview take precedence over Christian teaching regarding mediation? Yet, since we know that for the African all of life's activities are viewed through religious eyes, so much so that "religion penetrates and propels all of life,"[24] this distinction is difficult to pursue.

Members' Response to Question 2

In this category, respondents (22 of 39, 54%) emphasized that they "talked with" their ancestors while many emphatically denied that they worshiped ancestors. A typical response coming from a medical doctor was thus:

I believe that ancestors are around us at all times. It is not a matter of ancestor worship. I think we have parallels also in other religions. Jesus Christ himself is an ancestor. In African religion, we believe that my father is not a demon after he dies. My father is a means of communication. He is a conduit. Whatever we report to the ancestors is passed on to a higher being [Shembe] before it gets to God Almighty. (LP:16)

From his response, I gather that the amaNazaretha talk with their ancestors out of respect, devotion, and duty, believing that ancestors have the capacity to mediate between the living relatives and God.[25] The responses

---

24. Stine and Wendland, *Bridging the Gap*, 19.

25. The hierarchical system (patriarchal) as it functions in a Zulu family was explained to me by a member by way of an analogy. He said that just as a child would first go to its mother with a request, and such request would be taken by the mother to the father, likewise with our ancestors. People cannot approach God directly, and their only communication

here were similar to those of the clergy in that some individuals answered the question by talking about sacrifices to and for ancestors.[26]

Ministers' and Members' Response to Question 3

One response recurred in almost all of the interviews (67 of 68), the belief that the relationship between the ancestors and the living is reciprocal. Inasmuch as the ancestors meet the existential, everyday needs of the living, the living likewise should offer their ancestors assistance. One respondent claimed that ancestors also encounter problems and consequently solicit the assistance of the living. He said, "Through *nikela* we communicate with the ancestors. When they are in trouble they come to us in dreams" (MR:2). Another minister added, "We also sacrifice for the ancestors if they have problems, like when they have done something wrong [while alive on earth]. We sacrifice something for the ancestors in the form of *umnikelo*—we slaughter a goat or cow" (MR:4). Sins committed by the dead ancestors are remitted when the living offer the necessary payment (*nikela*) to the church.

Although I had not initiated the question, members said that while ancestors guided and protected them, mediated, and satisfied their everyday needs, the relationship with ancestors was reciprocal. In light of the new information, I added subquestion (3a) to the interview schedule: "*Can you assist ancestors in any way?*" To this question the response was that the living could assist the ancestors through sacrifices and *nikela*. *Nikela* in this instance took the form of the payment of a sum of money to Shembe, and thus the ancestor in question was relieved of the problem.

Members articulated various kinds of problems ancestors encountered. One respondent explained, "We believe that if the ancestors have gone from here, it is not over. The ancestor's soul is still living. So whatever sins the ancestor has done in the physical life can be forgiven" (MR:4). Another informant said, "The ancestors tell of all the wrong things they have done. Then the families must go to Shembe and ask for their forgiveness. After that, the sins of the ancestors will be removed" (MR:5).

From my interviews I learned that ancestors, if not remembered, inflict hardship on their living relatives. Only when the living offered animal sacrifices on behalf of the offended ancestor would living conditions be

---

with God is through the ancestors and Shembe. Further, just as children respect, honor, and approach their parents with their needs and wants, the ancestors are still part of their family and are approached in a similar manner.

26. Their responses and discussion are included in my first question above.

restored to normality. Others suggested that if the ancestors had been involved in factional fighting, wars, and tribal conflicts, they were separated from other ancestors of the clan. When people died unnatural deaths by motor accidents, suicide, and even diseases such as AIDS,[27] these ancestors were considered unclean, and as such they needed to be purified so as to join the realm of the ancestors.[28] In the interim, however, they were confined to a locality referred to as "jail." Still others may have left this world not having repaired fractured relationships; consequently, they also have been confined to "jail." It is here that the reciprocal relationship between ancestor and the living relative comes to the forefront. One interviewee demonstrated the reciprocal relationship that exists between ancestors and their living relatives in this way:

> When I started selling [as a curio street vender] at the Beach Front, there were problems. People would not buy from me. I do not know my mother, because she died when I was a small child. One day my mother came in a dream and said, "Where are you living?" I told my mother that we are living with our father at home. My mother asked, "Why don't you give me water? You have given me nothing." I told her I did not know that my father was not doing that for her. My mother said, "Tell your father to do something for me, and then your problem will be solved. You will see the people buying from you." My father did those sacrifices, and now things are going right. My father has no work; it is only me. (LP:27)

The same respondent further lamented her present predicament regarding marriage. She stated the following:

> They [ancestors] can make problems for you. I have been engaged for five years with my husband but not wedded. *Labola*[29] is paid in full, but when it comes to doing the wedding, I am prevented from getting married because of problems. People tell me that my

27. Statistics (1990s) show that two out of every five people in South Africa are HIV positive. The pandemic is most rife in KwaZulu-Natal, the province where the amaNazaretha Church has the most members.

28. It is believed that the soul of the dead will need to be released from the place where the person died in order to be sent back to the community of ancestors. The ritual performed here is that a goat or cow is sacrificed at home, and the blood is sprinkled at the place where the individual died. Alternatively, if the place of death is unknown, the living would ask Shembe to release the soul of the dead ancestor. This act is performed by means of *nikela*—the payment of a certain sum of money for the release of the ancestor's soul.

29. *Labola* is a Zulu cultural custom having economic implications where in a marriage ceremony, the father of bride receives cows from the bridegroom, which traditionally is a payment for the bride. This is called *labola*, or bride-payment.

> mother was not wedded. So my mother is the one obstructing everything. (LP:27)

I then raised a follow-up question: "What can you do about your mother obstructing your wedding?" She responded:

> My father took another woman after my mother died. This lady has married my father, but my mother did not wed my father. We can do something, but the problem is we don't have enough [money]. We can do the wedding for my mother who is dead. I can stand in my mother's place on the dancing ground and do the wedding. The father or brother will be the husband. If the father is dead, the brother will represent the father for this wedding. We can then do the wedding for my dead mother. (LP:27)[30]

Marriage is related to the ancestor cult in this instance since the mother's rights were infringed while she was alive. She was deprived of a proper cultural wedding that involved *labola*. The amaNazaretha Church facilitates such as weddings of departed ancestors through the dance ceremonies on Sundays. This practice again is a classic example of the church living out its existential life through Zulu cultural norms. This cultural act raises the question as to how such practices in the church are biblically mandated and acceptable.

One of the respondents, a medical doctor, described further how living relatives may assist the ancestors. He explained the belief in "cleansing" ancestors:

> People might have died by car accidents or been eaten by crocodiles, so those people are unaccounted for. So we have a *cleansing ceremony* so that they stand right with God. Even to the point that if you are a diabetic or have an amputation, then when you come to God you must come whole. If you have a rotten eye, we have a special offering so that it will be put back. We have this belief that most of the hardship you find in families is because of those ancestors whose problems are not made right by their descendants. (LP:15)

---

30. Although Zulus may be legally married (civil law) and have children, culturally they are not considered married until the male has met the required payment of an agreed-upon number of cows. The problem with this interviewee is that her parents were not married according to cultural laws; hence her mother appeared to be preventing her daughter from being married until the living daughter performed the wedding ceremony on her behalf.

Regarding the belief that because of misdemeanors or unnatural death ancestors are not with the community of ancestors, respondents explained that the method of removing an ancestor from "jail" required the living to make a payment of a sum of money to the present Shembe. Shembe then released the ancestor from his or her place of suffering to join their clan ancestors, a place that is believed to be close to God. Respondents claimed that the ancestor came back to the living relatives in dreams to offer their thanks and appreciation. The ancestors, now free, were again in a position to assist their living relatives. Other respondents said that improvement in their own situations, plus the fact that their requests have now materialized, showed that the living had successfully met the demands of the ancestors, most often by the payment of money (*nikela*) to Shembe. One minister explained:

> If a person died in a tribal clash, or fight we must do *nikela* for him and ask Shembe to cleanse him. Only then will he be fit to join the other ancestors and go to a good place. If they are not in a good place, they cannot help us. Therefore it is important to take them out of jail, and Shembe can help us do this. (MR:8)

Respondents generally alluded to some form of request that ancestors initiated. When living relatives give these requests their due response, usually in the form of *nikela* or animal sacrifices, the situation is resolved. For example, one evangelist said, "Some are languishing in hell, and we have to plead to Shembe to release them through *nikela*. They come back in dreams and thank us" (EV:4). Another said the following:

> When they [ancestors] were living they quarreled. They died and didn't sit down and discuss their quarrels. It is for the living to bring the two sides together [the living in this instance act as peace brokers on behalf of their dead relatives by approaching the offended party] by bringing a goat or anything they can afford to rectify the situation. When we have peace amongst the living, there will be peace with the ancestor as well. (EV:8)

The amaNazaretha believe that ancestors call for the assistance of their living relatives in the same way that the living call on them for help.

These beliefs and practices raise several issues for further discussion. First is the idea of "jail" and its effects on the afterlife. This concept parallels the idea of purgatory as understood by Roman Catholics. Second is the belief that one may atone for the wrongs committed by the dead through the payment of a sum of money. This belief parallels the doctrine of indulgences as taught by the Catholic Church in the medieval period of the Western Church. Third, is the power of Shembe to forgive sins. The following chapter will explore some of these ideas believed and practiced in the amaNazaretha Church.

Ministers' Views of Shembe as Ancestor

Evangelical Christians in South Africa, especially those who come into contact with amaNazaretha members daily, claim that the amaNazaretha believe that Shembe is God, and thus they deify and worship their leader. To test this perception, I raised the question in a way that would not appear to be confrontational. I asked, *"How would you differentiate between Shembe as an ancestor and God?"* [31] Of the twenty-nine respondents only four (14%) claimed outright that Shembe is God, while others said that he is more than an ancestor—he controls the ancestors to the point that Shembe mediates between the people and the ancestors. Minister Mjadu told this story to attest his belief that Shembe is God. To my follow-up question, *"Is Isaiah Shembe then God?"* Mjadu responded thus:

> If he were not God he could not be at Inanda while my forefathers were accompanying him to the station here in Zululand. That is why he is God. He was here *and* at Inanda at the same time. Shembe wrote a letter to my grandfather and gave it to *mkokeli* [women's leader]. He said to Ida, "Go give this letter to Mjadu." But before she arrived here Isaiah himself was here already. He was at Ekuphakameni talking to the people. Isaiah told them he had just come back from Zululand to see if Mjadu was doing his [Isaiah's] work. The people asked, "How could you have gone to Zululand when you were here all the time with us?"[32] (MR:4)

Mjadu did explain, however, why he perceived Shembe as God. He said, "We don't say Shembe is God because God came all the way from heaven down to this earth. It is the work that is given to Shembe by God that makes us believe Shembe is God." Minister Mpanza believed that since Shembe is omnipresent, he is far superior to the ancestors. He explained the following:

---

31. Isaiah Shembe may be considered an ancestor because of the belief held in Zulu Traditional Religion that important figures in the community, such as chiefs and kings, still guide the lives of the community and societal traditions long after their (ancestors') death.

32. The distance from Inanda to Zululand is approximately two hundred kilometers. In those days a trip by train would take a whole day's journey.

In 1998, we were in Manzini, Swaziland, where there are hot springs. We met some people there who asked us why we were there. We told them, "We are here for religious purposes. We are coming from the Church of Shembe." The people knew about the Shembe Church already. They joked about this, saying, "You Nazarites call a person [Shembe] God. We had an argument with one, and it turned out to be intense. We left the man there but told him that because he didn't believe us concerning Shembe, there were severe consequences for his words and actions. In 2000, the same man came here [Ebuhleni]. The man said he came to apologize to Shembe. He said that from the time he had the argument with us about Shembe, he has not been able to sleep. All his possessions were gone. He had cars and cows, but now they were all gone. We asked the man which Shembe would come to him in dreams. We showed him a photo of the three former leaders. We asked him which of these three he saw in his dream. (They have already left so we think they are ancestors.)[33] The man looked at the photo and said that Shembe was not here. Then we took him to M. V. Shembe, and the man said that this Shembe is the one who came to him at night. The man said to M. V. Shembe, "Oh my king, I come to apologize. You are the Lord." We also were confused because we did not tell M. V. that we had an argument in Swaziland. Now we began to believe that M. V. is also doing the same thing as the other Shembes. Shembe is omnipresent. There is the belief that when we were arguing, Shembe was there with us. Then M. V. went to this man—not in the physical, but in the spiritual—and talked to this man, telling him that he was Shembe. (MR:4)

Reverend Mpanza's belief is consistent with those of the amaNazaretha in that the attribute of omnipresence residing in the person of Shembe sets him apart from other human beings and all the other ancestors. There are several similar stories told of attributes specific to Isaiah Shembe and the succeeding leaders. I was often told that Shembe is an ancestor to his own family, but more than an ancestor to the followers of amaNazaretha.

Members' Views of Shembe as Ancestor

Among the lay people only seven of thirty-eight persons (18%) claimed that Shembe is God. The remainder of responses were similar to those in the ministers' category. One respondent told his story of the time he went to Shembe on behalf of his ancestors, and that his ancestors came back to

---

33. This comment is that of the narrator of the story.

him in a dream and said, "*Siyabonga*, thank you." Relating the story, he said the following:

> When I joined this church I knew that one of my sisters, Katazile, who died of poisoning, could be helped by the church. I went to A. K. Shembe and paid R20 *nikela*. It was on the Sabbath. On Monday, my sister came to me in a dream. She said, "Thank you." She told me that after she was poisoned she could not drink water. But by paying the *nikela* to Shembe, he removed the poison that she had eaten. Then she said to me, "Can you make a cup of tea? I have not had any since the poison prevented me from drinking anything." I went home a week later to visit my mother. She is a member of the Methodist Church. When I came by the gate, she was there waiting for me. With a smile she asked, "What were you doing in Durban? I have not dreamed of your dead sister before. I saw her in my dream on Saturday. She was inside the house here. Your sister was dancing like the girls of Ekuphakameni. She wore a white gown and covered her head." Later I went to visit my sister who told me she also dreamed of our sister who had been poisoned. This place is fifty kilometers apart from my mother's house, so no one had seen each other. She asked me, "What did you do right in Durban, because my dead sister said we should thank you [the brother] because you are the one who helped her by paying *nikela* to Shembe?" (LP:21)

This story, like many others, not only reveals the amaNazaretha's staunch belief in ancestors, but also their reliance on Shembe to communicate with and "assist" the ancestors. This story further reinforces the idea among the amaNazaretha that Shembe is far superior to the ancestors. Yet, one respondent believed that Shembe and the ancestors are equal in stature since the ancestors have the power to refuse any request made by Shembe. He did, however, qualify this statement:

> We can say that they are equal, yet by paying *nikela* Shembe can change the decisions of ancestors. Shembe is the God of the ancestors and us on earth. For us on earth there is no communication with the ancestors without Shembe. Whatever they do, they do through Shembe. In the Bible when Moses was looking after his father-in-law's cattle [sheep] he heard God say, "I am the God of your forefathers; go and release the people of Israel." Likewise, Shembe is the God of our forefathers, and he is the link between our forefathers and us. (LP:2)

This statement raises the question of mediation[34] both on the part of the ancestors and Shembe. It suggests the critical roles held by both ancestors and Shembe in the life-world of the amaNazaretha. Yet, there is the underlying belief that God ultimately meets their specific needs. This belief was eloquently stated via analogy by one minister:

> If you write a letter, and there is no [return] address where it comes from, it can reach the place [it was sent], but it will never come back because the one who is to write back to you has no address for you. The ancestors are our address to God. (MR:6)

Another respondent said, "Ancestors are very important to us because they are next to God. [35] We cannot talk to God, but the ancestors and Shembe can" (MR:12). Regarding the mediatorial interaction between ancestors and Shembe on behalf of the amaNazaretha, one evangelist said the following:

> The ancestors are ones who communicate [more] effectively to Shembe than the living ones. Shembe can listen to them more than he can listen to you. Shembe knows the ancestors' language much better than our language. (EV:6)

Based on observation and conversation with the amaNazaretha, I have hypothesized that the distinction between ministers and members, as understood and enacted in the church both traditionally and historically, does not exist in their church. Yet their rigid hierarchical system clearly draws boundaries between the ministers and members. I wanted to discover whether the members and ministers espoused different views on the status and role of ancestors. Thus, to both groups I raised the question *"How would you characterize the status and role of ancestors in your cultural and religious practices?"* Among the clergy, 21 of the 29 respondents (72%) stated that ancestors were near to God and thus were in a better position to communicate with God and the current Shembe. One minister said, "The ancestors are close to God, and they are my parents physically. They have

---

34. Mediation occurs on several occasions in the religiocultural ethos of the amaNazaretha. Ancestors mediate in the healing process, family disputes, and economic and financial stringency, among other situations.

35. The amaNazaretha believe that ancestors and Shembe are nearer to God than the living. Their status and presence give them greater access to God. John Mbiti, in *Concepts of God in Africa*, argues further that the ancestors have acquired a bilingual language, of human beings they left behind, spirits whom they have joined, and God to whom they are closer than when they were physical people (236).

more power than we [on earth] have. In my opinion, the ancestors can ask God to hurt you or bless you" (MR:9).

Apart from the mediatorial function of ancestors, six respondents also claimed that ancestors guide and protect them.

Among the members, twenty-one of thirty-eight persons (54%) described the status and role of ancestors as being their protectors, while twelve (31%) respondents described ancestors in the role of mediator. One respondent spoke of the time her ancestor warned her of impending danger:

> I dreamed of my grandmother telling me that I must immediately leave the place where I was staying. My husband wanted to kill me so he could get the insurance money. I left the house at 3:30 in the morning carrying my child on my back. No one knew where I went. I went to my friend's place and stayed there. Then I heard the rumors that my husband was looking for me. I hid myself to where he could not find me. Then the man who was paid to kill me came back and told me. He told me that my husband said if I got killed he would receive more money from the insurance policy and he would buy a car. Then I believed that because my grandmother came to me in the dream and told me to wake up and leave that place, I was saved. She came three times to me in a dream. It was as if someone was shaking me and I just woke up and went away. I knelt down and prayed to say thank you. I think it was God's power to send someone that looked like my grandmother in my dream. (LP:31)

To ascertain whether the amaNazaretha invoked Isaiah Shembe as their ancestor, I raised the question "*Who do you invoke in your prayers—Isaiah, Galilee, Amos, or Vimbeni?*" In the ministers' category, twenty-seven of the twenty-nine respondents (93%) said that no particular Shembe comes to mind as all the Shembes are the same; they possess the same Spirit. However, only two respondents said that they visualize Isaiah Shembe when they pray. Among the members, thirty-five respondents (90%) answered in a similar way to those in the clergy category. Three respondents said that Vimbeni comes to mind when they pray, and 1 respondent said again that she "prayed in the name of Jesus." The belief among the amaNazaretha is that the physical person is not as important as the spirit resident within him (Shembe). Therefore, when the amaNazaretha pray, no particular Shembe comes to mind, but it is Shembe the Holy Spirit. Evangelist Mpanza reminded me that Shembe is a surname (family name), and Shembe is also the Holy Spirit (EV:1). Thus, the amaNazaretha do differentiate between Shembe the person and Shembe the Holy Spirit when speaking. The belief that Shembe is the Holy Spirit, with no differentiation in status among the four Shembes,[36] came home to me in the following narrative. My research field assistant told me the following:

> Isaiah, J. G., Amos, and Vimbeni, these are people, humans. When we talk about Shembe we don't talk about Isaiah, J. G., Amos, or Vimbeni. We talk about the Spirit. That is what was amongst each one of them. It did not leave them. From the first to the present leader, each had the same Spirit in them. The same Spirit. When we call them we don't pray in their names. We pray in the Spirit. That is why when I am standing in the mountains, I don't expect Vimbeni to come and help me on this mountain. I expect the Spirit of Shembe to come and help me. (LP:1)[37]

The belief that Shembe is the Holy Spirit and that the same Holy Spirit once imparted to the founding Shembe is transferred to the succeeding Shembes seems consistently present in the religious ethos of the amaNazaretha church. A further question this belief raises is whether there is any room for discussion about the three persons of the Christian Trinity.

In contrast to the above, two respondents claimed that they prayed in the name of Vimbeni Shembe. One of them believed that the previous three leaders delegated their powers to the current leader; therefore, he concluded it was appropriate to call on him. The thinking among some of the amaNazaretha is that Shembe is the Holy Spirit, and consequently the physical Shembe is merely the successor who now possesses the Holy Spirit that was resident in past leaders.

To inquire whether ancestors mediate between the amaNazaretha and God, I raised the following question: *"Do the amaNazaretha talk to God directly or do so via ancestors?"* In the ministers' category, twenty-four of twenty-nine respondents (83%) said they called on both their ancestors and Shembe. Three respondents said that the ancestors talked to God on their behalf, while one respondent believed that he only called on Shembe. In the members' category, thirty-eight of thirty-nine respondents (94%) claimed that they approached God through ancestors *and* Shembe. One respondent, however, said she prayed in the name of Jesus. The latter, who

---

36. Evangelist Mkize made an interesting comment regarding the four Shembes being one and the same when he said, "Shembe is one in four" (EV:3). I wondered if the Christian understanding of the Trinity—the "three in one" and the "one in three"—has influenced the evangelist's belief. I will raise this question in a later study.

37. I capitalize *Spirit* when reference is made to Shembe as the amaNazaretha believe Shembe is the third person of the Trinity.

had been healed of cancer when Shembe prayed for her, said she still believed that God heals and that in her situation God had used Shembe to perform the healing. She had not as yet committed herself to membership in the amaNazaretha Church.

There was no unanimity as to who was called upon first, Shembe or the ancestors, and also as to who approached God on their behalf, Shembe or ancestors. What was confirmed consistently was that both Shembe *and* the ancestors were responsible for mediating between the living and God. One respondent explained the amaNazaretha's morning devotions:

> We put on our gowns, took the hymnbooks, and read the liturgy for the morning prayers. Then we prayed. After reading the morning prayers, we opened hymn 234. I began with thanking God for giving us the night we had, and I asked Shembe to bless us and our family in Bulwer. Then I asked Shembe to heal my mother and give her more days, so that she will attend my wedding. When we pray we say, "God of Shembe, God of *amakosi* [chief], God of our ancestors," then I mention the things I want from God. We use the same procedure that is used in Zulu culture. When a child wants something it will first go to the mother. We sometimes ask the ancestors first because we believe they are close to God, but Shembe is greater than all my forefathers and chiefs. They all listen to him. (LP:26)

Mbiti suggests that Africans generally feel that out of respect they should not approach God directly, so they need an intermediary, either a living person—a chief, king, or priest—or the living-dead.[38] Zulus believe that the living-dead are closer to God and thus are more effective in communicating the needs of their living relatives to God and also in carrying back responses from God to the living via dreams. This belief raises questions for further study: When does a cultural norm mitigate or supercede biblical norms? Would the cultural norm of ancestor mediation in prayers, healing, and everyday problem-solving be consistent with biblical teachings of Jesus Christ as the mediator?

I recorded some of the prayers to verify if what was articulated in the interviewees' responses was the same as what was actually practiced in the Sabbath services.[39] The following prayers were recorded at Ebuhleni during the July Festival in 2002:

---

38. Mbiti, *African Religions and Philosophy*, 67–68.

39. I joined Reverend Gcwenza and his family at their home for the Evening Prayer in August, 2002. The opening prayer was read from the liturgical hymnbook (9–14). Then the family engaged in corporate prayer. I was able to discern one person's prayer that went

Recounting Stories (Research Findings)

> Father Shembe, Lord of Lords, we are coming. Lord of the Sabbath, strengthen your word that it would be accepted in the world. Secure us, Jehovah. Amen. [Prayer by a minister]
>
> God of our forefathers, we thank you for the day you gave us. We ask you to give us more days. We thank you for good things you do for us. We ask you to give us courage to do the good things for you. All this we ask in the name of Shembe. Amen. [Closing prayer at Sabbath service by Vimbeni Shembe]
>
> Thank you, Shembe, for inviting me to this temple. Please, Shembe, look at me and love me. Make me to stick to you. Please, my Lord, erase my sins. Shembe, my thoughts must always be according to your ways. [Prayer at the end of the service by member]
>
> We thank you, Lord, for this day. We ask you to give us more days. We thank you for keeping us [un]til this day of remembrance. We ask you to be present [un]till the next one again. Give us more days and the power to defeat the devil. All this I ask in the name of our Lord, Shembe. Amen. [Benediction by Vimbeni Shembe]

I invited two ministers and several members of the amaNazaretha to my lodgings in South Africa one Sunday for discussion and dialogue. At the end of the day, when my visitors were ready to leave, they requested permission to pray. I gladly consented. Minister Ngidi concluded in prayer after we sang a hymn from the amaNazaretha liturgical book:

> Holy Shembe, we are here at Phoenix at the house of Moodley. We are asking you to love us and protect us and secure this home we are under and give us the day which is protected by you and the blessing, in the name of Shembe.

Consistent in all of the prayers by members was the name of Shembe, and in two prayers the names of the ancestors and clan chiefs. I discovered that prayers are also given spontaneously and extemporaneously. Shembe and the ancestors are always conscious in the minds of the members. I noted especially that when Vimbeni prayed he concluded his prayer with the

---

like this: "God of our ancestors, we are in your face [come before you]; we ask you to be with us this night. We are praying, O Lord, show your greatness; we ask you to show us the work you were sent for by God. In the name of Shembe, Amen." They then sang a closing hymn (no. 195). A closing benediction was offered by Reverend Gcwenza: "God who has all power, we are in your face this evening. We thank you for keeping us on the way we have been. You have protected us. We ask your love, which has no end, to be with us this night. We ask for your love, which has no end, to be with us this night in the name of Shembe. Amen."

words "In the name of Shembe." This practice would confirm the belief that when the amaNazaretha pray, they are praying in the name of and with reference to the living Spirit of Shembe and not the person Shembe. From the data recorded in the research, it would appear that in religious settings (the Sabbath services) the amaNazaretha more often call on Shembe and not the ancestors, but at cultural events and celebrations, the ancestors feature prominently in the prayers. I have already alluded, however, to the ambivalence where sometimes the ancestors are named and then Shembe, and, at other times, Shembe first and then the ancestors.

The above prayers in different settings raise the question as to whether the amaNazaretha community of believers, even after almost one hundred years since the founding of the church, is still grappling with the issue of when and how to invoke the ancestors, given the presence of the physical and spiritual Shembe in their midst. As is evident from the above prayers, the amaNazaretha call on God, ancestors, and Shembe, sometimes all three; and at other times, Shembe and God with the exclusion of ancestors. It would appear that the *written* liturgical songbook brings God and Shembe into focus, and the unwritten cultural traditions and beliefs regarding ancestors, "always present in the cultural psyche of the individual,"[40] coalesce in the corporate worship experience. When do the cultural norm and religious belief coalesce in the amaNazaretha beliefs and practices? Does such coalescence result in mixing of beliefs from Christian faith and Zulu culture? I will give attention to this critical aspect of amaNazaretha life in chs. 6 and 7.

Ancestors still remain central in the religious and cultural beliefs of the amaNazaretha, even given their current transitions from rural to urban life and from European dominance to living under a black democratic government, and also given the fact that they are moving from an oral, nonliterate society to a scripted, literate world. They also use the Old Testament to support their reasons for including ancestors in their beliefs and practices.[41]

My findings on the role and status of ancestors in the amaNazaretha Church raise two important questions:

---

40. Ong, *Orality and Literacy*, 73.

41. Evangelist Mpanza stated that there is no direct reference to calling the ancestors in the Old Testament. However, by deduction, there are several references that allude to the importance of ancestors. For example, he referred me to the scriptures where God speaks to Moses with words: "And God said moreover unto Moses, Thus shalt thou say unto the children of Israel, the Lord God of your fathers, the God of Abraham, the God of Isaac, and the God of Jacob, hath sent me unto you" (Exod 3:15 KJV).

1. Since the ancestor cult is still well-established in the amaNazaretha, and is indeed in the mindset of its members, to the extent that members offer sacrifices and give restitution payments (*nikela*) to Shembe, is there a way of accommodating these beliefs and practices without mitigating the fundamental tenets of the Christian faith?
2. Since the amaNazaretha look to the ancestors as mediators in terms of healing, prayers, and salvation, what role, different from Shembe, could Jesus Christ have as mediator?

Research Findings: The Role of Vimbeni Shembe

An essential component in my research was to raise the question of mediation by discovering the status and role of Vimbeni Shembe in the religious and cultural ethos of the amaNazaretha Church. The enormous corpus of literature on the movement written over a period of seventy years says very little about the present leader, Vimbeni Shembe. He assumed leadership by popular choice when his father, Amos Kula Shembe, died in 1995. Earlier conclusions about the theology of the amaNazaretha Church were based on data from the preaching, teaching, songwriting, and miracles performed by the founder, Isaiah Shembe, as well as the ministries of Johannes Galilee Shembe and Amos Shembe. For example, Oosthuizen's work, *The Theology of a South African Messiah*, studied the hymns composed by Isaiah Shembe. He concluded that Isaiah Shembe was both mediator and messiah to his people. Oosthuizen states, "Shembe I is not only Mediator but is Messiah, the manifestation of God . . . . Shembe I is to the Nazarites the personification of Supreme Power."[42] With this background, therefore, it was necessary that I discover the status and role of the current leader, Vimbeni Shembe, the grandson of Isaiah Shembe, serving in the amaNazaretha Church some seven decades after Isaiah's death and after three changes in the leadership.

This section of my findings, like the previous section, is divided into two parts: the responses from ministers, evangelists, and preachers (ministers), and the responses from laypersons, including youth leaders and women's leaders (members). As in the previous section, I selected questions that offer the most pertinent data to make clear the status and role of Vimbeni Shembe in the amaNazaretha Church. The following derived questions from the interview schedule provide helpful clarifications:

42. Oosthuizen, *The Theology of a South African Messiah*, 4.

1. Would there be a time when you would talk with Shembe and Christ in the same conversation or prayer? Explain.

2. How would your words of address be different when you talk with Christ or Shembe?

3. What are the functions and roles played by Vimbeni Shembe, the living descendant of Isaiah Shembe?

4. Would you say that Vimbeni Shembe is more than a human being? In what way?

5. How is Vimbeni Shembe related to Christ, and does he possess the Spirit of Christ or is he the Christ?

6. Is Vimbeni Shembe capable of removing your sins or does he ask Jesus to forgive you? And is Vimbeni Shembe without sin? Why?

7. There is a story told that Isaiah Shembe was present at Creation. Would you cast Vimbeni in the same role? Why?

To ascertain whether Shembe and Christ are treated alike, or if Shembe is elevated in the amaNazaretha prayers above Jesus Christ, I raised the question *"Would there be a time when you would talk with Shembe and Christ in the same conversation or prayer? Explain."* Among the ministers, the most frequent response (twenty-four out of twenty-nine, 83% of respondents) was that the amaNazaretha leadership address their prayers to Shembe or include Shembe among multiple addressees. Four respondents claimed that they did not pray in the name of Jesus Christ. One minister believed that Jesus and Shembe possess the same Spirit, although Jesus is absent and Shembe present physically.

Among the members, seven respondents stated that they prayed in the name of Shembe, while ten respondents believed that Christ, upon his departure, left his work to Shembe. Another six respondents said that Shembe and Christ are one and the same person, while another nine said that they did not know Jesus Christ. In effect, it would appear that in the most frequent responses (thirty-two of thirty-nine, 82% of respondents), members addressed Shembe and not Christ in their prayers. However, one layperson said that she prayed in the name of Jesus, not Shembe.[43]

---

43. This interviewee, at the time of the interview, was an adherent but not a full member of the amaNazaretha Church. She was healed of cancer when Shembe prayed for her. However, she believes that ultimately it was God who healed her and that Shembe was only the instrument.

One minister used this story to explain the interaction between the ancestors and Shembe, excluding Jesus Christ from requests and prayers. He said the following:

> Whenever you pray, you first call the ancestors. The ancestors have to determine if you are worthy of the request you are asking of Shembe. The ancestors are the ones who talk to Shembe and say, "He is good, and you can give it to him." But if you are not good[44] to the ancestors, they will tell Shembe that you are not good and that he should not grant you your request. There was a line of people going to *nikela* to Baba [Shembe]. Among them was a man who was coming to Shembe for the first time. The man thought that Shembe did not know him. Shembe called him by name. The man just looked at Shembe amazed because he knew Shembe did not know him, and how could he call him by his name. The man came to Shembe, and Shembe said, "Your grandfather (ancestor) has come here and told me that you do all these wrong things. So how can you come and ask for good luck now? I must not give you anything that you are asking for." That is why the ancestors are there to ask for us, because even Shembe respects the ancestors' wishes. The ancestors are next to Shembe. The Nazarite Church has grown in this way, because more people come here on instructions from their ancestors. That is why we believe the ancestors can help us, but Shembe is above the ancestors. (MR:4)

The above shows that the amaNazaretha believe that Shembe and the ancestors feature prominently in their everyday religiocultural life. Seeing that the ancestors are repositories of ethical, juridical, and sacred traditions in the Zulu ethos, the ancestors are in a position to either allow or disallow one's request. It would appear that when the needs of an individual are not met by invoking the ancestors, people approach Shembe. In the above story, Shembe had prior knowledge concerning the man's misdemeanor and fault in the eyes of the ancestors, so Shembe would not allow his request until the fracture in relationship with the ancestors (and consequently living parties as well) was repaired. The story also shows the strategic role Shembe plays in the religio-ancestral cult among the amaNazaretha. Shembe is positioned to hear from the ancestors and relate their messages to the living. He thus functions as an intermediary between the living and the living-dead. While the above story shows the importance of Shembe and ancestors in the everyday affairs of the

---

44. When the interviewee uses the word *good* in the text, he is referring to the living and their respect and obedient response in meeting the ancestors' requests that come to the living in dreams.

amaNazaretha, it also suggests that Shembe's status and role among them lessens the importance of the person and work of Christ. If Jesus Christ does not feature in the existential "salvation" of the individual, as Shembe and the ancestors do, how do we characterize the amaNazaretha (adherents) in terms of their religious affiliation?

One member explained why the amaNazaretha called on the ancestors and Shembe and not Jesus:

> There was King Shaka in Zululand, and now there is our present King Goodwill. That does not mean that Shaka was not the king. Likewise we cannot ignore the presence of Shembe. Shembe's name heals us, so we can't go and call the name Jesus. Shembe knows Jesus. But we only know about the name Shembe, which heals us.

By analogy, the member suggested that just as King Shaka existed historically, so did Jesus. Politically and culturally members do not doubt or dispute the existence of past kings, but they respond to the current incumbent, King Goodwill. Likewise in the church: while they do not doubt that Jesus Christ lived and helped people in his time, his departure opened the way for Shembe, who now is capable of responding effectively to people's requests and wishes.

My follow-up question, *"How would your words of address be different when you talk with Christ or Shembe?"* yielded similar responses to the first question among both categories (ministers and members) since the amaNazaretha do not address Christ in their prayers. The following prayers demonstrate the consistency between the responses from the interviewees and the actual prayers recorded during my participant observation at the July 2002 Sabbath services:

> Father, God of Ekuphakameni, we are asking for your angels to come and stop the anger which is finishing the family of your son.[45] Give long life in the name of Shembe. Amen. [Prayer by Vimbeni Shembe]

> Father Shembe, Lord of Lords, we are coming. Lord of the Sabbath, strengthen your word that it would be accepted in the world. Secure us, Jehovah. Amen. [Prayer by a minister]

> God of our forefathers, we are in front of your face [come before you] as sinners. We do wrong things daily. We ask you to forgive us

---

45. This prayer was prayed by Vimbeni Shembe in the Sabbath service when the congregation was asked to remember the family of the late J. G. Shembe, whose youngest wife had died.

our sins. Make us to forgive each other where we do not see eye to
eye. Give us the power to sit down and settle our problems. All this
I ask in the name of Shembe. Amen. [Prayer by a member]

In the first prayer above, when Vimbeni Shembe begins, he addresses the "God of Ekuphakameni"—referring to the Supreme Being, Unkulunkulu or Jehovah.[46] It is not clear whether Vimbeni uses the term "God of Ekuphakameni" to refer to Shembe or to the Supreme Being. The prayer ends with the words "in the name of Shembe." As the research findings strongly suggest, Shembe is not referring to himself here; neither is he referring to Isaiah Shembe, but the reference is to Shembe the Holy Spirit, transcendent and immanent.

The second prayer by a minister, which begins with "Father Shembe, Lord of Lords," is directed to God Jehovah through the name of Shembe. As was told by most interviewees, not one Shembe comes to mind when they pray. Their prayers are directed to God but go through Shembe the Holy Spirit, the supreme mediator of all prayers. This belief is also evident in the final prayer with the proviso that the member calls on his ancestors as well.[47]

Because of the framing of the next question, "*What are the functions and roles played by Vimbeni Shembe?*" many interviewees misunderstood it. Consequently, I restated it as "*What are the various duties carried out by Vimbeni Shembe?*" In the ministers' category, I received a total of forty responses since some interviewees offered more than one answer. The most frequent response (twenty-eight, 70% of respondents) was that Vimbeni Shembe was no different from the previous three leaders, who addressed peoples' everyday problems, afforded counsel and advice, healed, and gave leadership to the congregation. Four respondents indicated that Vimbeni Shembe was their mediator,[48] representing them in the presence of the ancestors *and* God, advocating on behalf of the people. Additional responses included descriptions of his functional attributes as leader, such as proph-

---

46. Oosthuizen discusses these terms for the Supreme Being as used in prayers and in the Shembe songbook. He states that Isaiah Shembe claimed to be the revealer and personification of Jehovah and that he claimed messiahship for himself—he claimed to be the Christ (*The Theology of a South African Messiah*, 32–33).

47. I make the point earlier (ch 4) that from my interviews the amaNazaretha believe that the ancestors are closer to God, understand the "heavenly language," and are better positioned to petition on behalf of the living relatives.

48. Although interviewees did not use the exact term *mediator* throughout the interviews, this was stated or implied by means of analogy or story. In articulating the function and role Vimbeni Shembe plays in the life of the amaNazaretha, it became apparent that Shembe functions in such a role.

et, savior, and Holy Spirit. One respondent believed that those leaders who succeeded Isaiah Shembe (the prophet) are not prophets themselves; rather they *remind* people of the deeds of Isaiah Shembe. That interviewee saw Vimbeni as a lesser leader than Isaiah.

In the member category, several offered more than one answer to the question just as the ministers did. The most frequent response (twenty-seven of fifty, 54% of respondents) also was that Shembe was no different from the previous three leaders. However, here there were fifty responses to the question. Again, the less frequent responses concerning his duties, as with the ministers, was the mediatorial role of Shembe (twelve, 24% of respondents). Less frequent responses were that Shembe was reconciler, messenger from God, prophet, and priest.

Minister Ngidi succinctly defined the status and role of Vimbeni Shembe when he said, "As our leader, we go to him with our problems, sometimes for advice, and as I said we can go to him to *nikela* for our dead relatives (ancestors). He is the Spirit of God among us. That's why our people call him God, because we can't see God, and he does all these miracles for us by asking God" (MR:8). Minister Gcwensa further explained the following:

> In May 1935 Isaiah's flesh was suffering [Isaiah was ill]. He called his ministers around him and said, "My flesh is tired and will soon be in the grave. But my soul will rise and will cover new flesh." The same Spirit which worked through J. G. Shembe is the Spirit which worked through A. K. Shembe and is now working through M. V. Shembe. He is our leader . . . . He has the Holy Spirit to heal, solve problems, and communicate with our ancestors and God for us. (MR:9)

A layperson (LP:1) described Vimbeni as one who is capable of reconciling the two wings of the church that split after the death of J. G. Shembe:

> He [Vimbeni Shembe] called for peace and forgiveness after the church divided into two parts. But he *can* reconcile the church. Reconciliation was the first thing that he called for [when he assumed the leadership]. We have one father who started this church. If he could come back to us in person, he will [be] ashamed of us. I see him [Vimbeni Shembe] as a reconciler. I see him as a leader like the others. (LP:1)

From the interviews it became apparent that the current leader, Vimbeni Shembe, is treated with awe and respect, no different from the previous leaders, and that the amaNazaretha accord to him a status that is equal to those of the past leaders. Vimbeni Shembe's role among the amaNazaretha is no different from that of the past leaders as he functions in a similar role as one who mediates healing, prayers, and communication with the ancestors.

So as to elicit responses to the question of Vimbeni Shembe's status as divine,[49] I asked the question *"Would you say that Vimbeni Shembe is more than a human being? In what way?"* Among the ministers, nine respondents out of a total of twenty-nine (31%) believed that Vimbeni is God, while eight (28%) respondents claimed that Vimbeni either *possessed* the Holy Spirit or *is* the Holy Spirit. A further five respondents (17%) said that Vimbeni is the living embodiment of Isaiah Shembe. However, these responses cumulatively suggest that interviewees saw Vimbeni as one who is more than human and thus deified in some way.

Responses among lay people differed in that more respondents, twenty-three of the thirty-nine (59%), believed that Vimbeni is God, while four respondents claimed him to be the Holy Spirit, and yet another four respondents said that he is a prophet. A comparison between the two categories reveals that lay people tend to divinize Vimbeni more than the ministers, but more ministers express that Vimbeni is the Holy Spirit. One layperson described Vimbeni Shembe in the following way:

> When they say *God* in Zulu it is *Unkulunkulu. Unkulunkulu* is something bigger than you can describe. So we just call M. V. *Unkulunkulu* because of the work he does among us. That is why people call him God. He has led the Nazarites for only a few years. He has done great things. When he went to Gospel [temple], people just threw away their wheelchairs. (LP:22)

When the amaNazaretha refer to Vimbeni Shembe as God, it is not as though people are oblivious to the reality of the transcendent being *Unkulunkulu*. But in the absence of God as a physical being, Shembe assumes that role for them. The following observation from a youth leader in the church sums up their understanding of how and why Shembe is called God:

> There is a distinction that I want to point out. We believe that God who sent Shembe is using him. God is Shembe himself. This is how God shows himself to the black people. To us God came as a Shembe. That God, that Spirit, came and covered Shembe. There

---

49. By divinization I mean Vimbeni Shembe is believed to possess supernatural power that elevates him to the status above a human being, yet he is not God. The amaNazaretha believe that God does exist separately from Shembe.

is confusion about this belief. People who are not members of this church wonder why we call Shembe God. It is because God, the Spirit of God, came to the flesh of Shembe and now rules him. So Shembe does not do anything he likes to do. Shembe only listens to the Spirit that rules him. That is why I call Shembe God though I still mean that he is the Spirit of God. (YL:3)

The "theologian" of the church, evangelist Mpanza, described Vimbeni thusly:

> Vimbeni Shembe, our leader, is the symbol of the presence of all our leaders as a successor. But I cannot say that there is anything peculiar with him other than the peculiarity based on the embodiment of the Spirit. He is a human being and Isaiah Shembe was a human being. They may not have the same character, but all that we know is that they have the same Spirit. (EV:1)

To pursue further the question of Vimbeni's divinity, relating Christian beliefs and the practices of the amaNazaretha, I raised the question "*How is Vimbeni Shembe related to Christ, and does he possess the Spirit of Christ or is he the Christ?*" The most frequent response (eighteen of twenty-nine, 62% of respondents) from the clergy was that Vimbeni possessed the Spirit of Christ, while eight leaders (27% of respondents) believed that Vimbeni Shembe *is* Jesus Christ. Three respondents said that they had no knowledge of Christ.

In the laity category, first, eleven of thirty-nine respondents (28%) believed that Vimbeni Shembe and Christ are one and the same person, while another eleven interviewees (28%) understood Vimbeni Shembe and Christ to possess the *same* Spirit. Second, nine respondents (23%) claimed that they had no knowledge of Christ. Finally, three respondents said that Shembe and Christ are different people. A tentative response to the question came from a minister who mused thus:

> The problem is [that] I do not know what they mean by Christ, whether the name was given by his mother or whether it came to him when he was baptized by John, since he only received the Holy Spirit after his baptism. If Christ is the name of the Holy Spirit, Vimbeni is the Christ. (MR:1)

Another minister explained how Vimbeni Shembe and Christ are the same person:

> My belief is that when Jesus was going [away] he said he will send another person, the Holy Spirit to us. That person is Shembe today. (MR:12)

It would appear that the majority among the amaNazaretha connects the person of Jesus Christ with Vimbeni Shembe through the Holy Spirit, whom they claim Jesus promised before he departed. Since Vimbeni Shembe possesses the Holy Spirit, that elevates him to a status above a human being. From their theology, it is not really clear what that status may be.

With the next two questions I tried to elicit a clearer response to the question of Vimbeni's divine status among the amaNazaretha. I asked, "*Is Vimbeni Shembe capable of removing your sins?*" The ministers were almost unanimous that Shembe had the power to forgive sins. Only one leader said that Shembe was incapable of removing sins and that it was God's prerogative to forgive.

Among the laity, again, the overwhelming response (thirty-three of thirty-nine, 85% of respondents) was that Vimbeni possesses the power to forgive sins. Three did not respond to the question.

I pressed the question further and asked, "*Does Vimbeni Shembe live without sin?*" The ministers responded overwhelmingly (twenty-one of twenty-nine, 72% of respondents) that Vimbeni had no sin, arguing that one who possesses the Holy Spirit cannot sin and that the miracles Vimbeni performs could not happen if he had sin. Two respondents believed that Vimbeni was human, therefore capable of sin, while another two respondents argued that Jesus said that no man is without sin, and thus Vimbeni cannot be without sin. One interviewee said that it was possible for Shembe to have had sin before he received the Holy Spirit in 1995, when he assumed leadership of the church.

The most frequent response from lay people (nineteen of thirty-nine, 48% of respondents) was that Vimbeni was without sin. Five respondents said that they could not judge Vimbeni Shembe, and a further two claimed (as stated previously) that Jesus said that there was no one without sin. I did not elicit responses from twelve interviewees (31%) to this question. However, from the above responses it would be fair to propose that the amaNazaretha firmly believe that Vimbeni Shembe is capable of removing sins and that he is not currently capable of sinning himself.

My conclusion is based on the statements of the amaNazaretha members. One interviewee commented that "God does not send many prophets to earth. People confessed to the one prophet then before Isaiah's day, but now people confess to Shembe" (MR:2). Another minister said the following:

> He [Shembe] can forgive sins. He communicates with the Creator, God. If he said to God, "Please forgive this person," if he says to you, "You are cursed and I will not see you in heaven," it will happen as he says. (MR:12)

In response to the question about Vimbeni himself possessing sin, one member said thus:

> We are talking about the Spirit of God, so I don't think the Spirit of God can have sins. If you are talking about M. V. Shembe, then I can say that he had sin before the Spirit of Shembe came into him. But since the Spirit entered into him, M. V. Shembe does not have any sin. (LP:1)

Concerning the sins of those who died before Shembe came, one respondent explained thus:

> I don't think that the Zulus will be penalized because there were no rules then. But when Shembe came he told us what we can do for our ancestors who died without knowing Shembe. We go to Shembe and *nikela* for the ancestors. The ancestors say, "Go to Shembe and do *nikela* for me so that I [the ancestor] too may join the church." The ancestors also say, "Join the Shembe Church, because when you join you do not go alone, but we go with you." That is why we say that the ancestors are not penalized because they did not know. That is why the ancestors encourage us to join the church. (MR:13)

I framed my final question in an endeavor to test the thinking regarding the divinity of Isaiah Shembe among the amaNazaretha and whether such divinity is believed to have passed on to Vimbeni Shembe. I inquired, "*There is a story told that Isaiah Shembe was present at Creation. Would you cast Vimbeni in the same role?*" In the ministers' category eighteen of twenty-nine (62% of respondents) responded in the affirmative, with the qualifier that it was not the physical Shembe but Shembe the Holy Spirit, and thus all four Shembes are included. However, one respondent did not believe that Shembe was present at Creation. I was unable to ask this question of all ministers.

Among the laity I only raised the question nine times. Eight of the 9 respondents believed that Shembe was present at Creation and that all Shembes are one. Therefore, Vimbeni would have been present too, in the Spirit. One minister explained, "My belief is that Isaiah, the Holy Spirit, was there, not the physical Isaiah. As I have previously said, the Spirit is one, whether Isaiah, J. G., Amos, or Vimbeni. We can say that Vimbeni the Spirit was there too" (MR:8).

There are several stories that the amaNazaretha relate to vouch for their belief that Isaiah Shembe is God. The amaNazaretha, when preaching at the Sabbath services, in informal conversation, in small groups, or when family and friends gather at social events, share stories that relate to the miracles performed by the Shembes. These stories and narratives act as points of reference to deepen faith. They also offer members some semblance of solace, assurance, and stability in the fragile and harsh world that confronts their daily existence. These are stories of healing, deliverance, and mighty acts done in the supernatural that cause the amaNazaretha to regard their leaders, past and present, with an aura of spiritual power to the point of divinization.

One minister recounts, "When Shembe decided to baptize my forefathers, he went to the Umlazi River. Here he stopped the river from flowing into the sea. A pool was formed, and in it he baptized them. After he had finished baptizing them, the river went back into the sea" (MR:2). To point further to Isaiah Shembe's "presence" at Creation, one minister related this story:

> One day Shembe said to us [members of the church], "This is the fifth time that I have come to be here [on earth]." Here at South Coast when Shembe came and preached, the people came, listened and joined him. Then Shembe wanted to baptize them, but there was no river close to them. Shembe then asked, "Who is the oldest here? If you are the eldest in this place, what is underneath the earth?" But the people did not know what was underneath. Shembe said, "When you dig here, you will find six stones which *we* put when we were creating the earth, me and my father. Those six stones are holding the other stones, underneath them. Dig here and you will find the 6 stones. When you come to the seventh stone, water will gush out." When they dug they found water there as he said. Those 6 stones are still present. Tourists come to visit this place in South Coast next to [evangelist] Mkhize's place. This gives us the hope that Shembe is not here for the first time. He came to other places but with a different name, not Shembe. (MR:4)

Healing is also integral to the amaNazaretha community as it is in African culture generally. Africans believe that any illness is attributed to a disturbance of the balance between people and spiritual forces. The goal of healing is to restore the equilibrium. Shembe and the ancestors facilitate and mediate in the process. I specifically asked the interviewees about the role Shembe played in healing among the amaNazaretha. Members related several stories to demonstrate Vimbeni Shembe's healing powers.

When I asked a minister what miracles he had witnessed Vimbeni Shembe perform, he told me of the occasion when Shembe visited the church in Johannesburg, some six hundred kilometers from Durban, where he healed two girls who were crippled. The minister claimed that Shembe commanded the girls to walk, and they were instantly healed (MR:5). Another minister told of the time when a leading academic came to Shembe for healing. He had visited the traditional healers without success. While the minister did not specify the man's illness, he recalled Shembe saying to the man's wife, "Go and buy him some soup, boil it, and have him drink it." The man replied, "I always drink soup. What kind of soup will heal me?" Shembe replied, "The soup you buy, I will be in it." The man's wife prepared the soup, and the man drank it and was healed. The man responded, "Shembe is God" (MR:7).

I asked one minister if Shembe possessed the power to heal. By way of analogy he explained thus:

> When I pray I do not say, "God of Reverend Gcwenza." There is a difference. I say, "God of Shembe." As God said to Moses, "I am the God of your forefathers." People will not be healed if I pray in the name of Reverend Gcwenza. (MR:13)

The minister spoke of a delegated responsibility given to him (the minister) where, in the absence of Shembe (physically), he calls on the name of Shembe and healing takes place.

I then raised the question about why Vaseline and water were used in the healing process. Interviewees said that Shembe used these as aids to increase faith in the people, and when they were physically separated from Shembe, the use of the Vaseline and water represented him. Vaseline and water in and of itself possessed no healing power or value. One minister explained it thus: "What heals the people in the Vaseline is the fire of God. Shembe himself is the fire of God, which burns all diseases" (MR:11).

One minister explained how Shembe heals individuals even without seeing them. My question *"When did you last witness a miracle by Vimbeni Shembe?"* prompted this response:

> At the temple Gibizisila, Esikaweni, where the remembrance prayers for Isaiah are held on the second of May, I took my fellow workers to M. V. [Shembe]. While we were standing in line, some people came with a girl twenty-one years of age. She could not walk and was carried in a blanket. They reported to him [Shembe]

that this girl was not walking since birth and is now twenty-one. I want you to understand that Shembe does not only use Vaseline and water. Sometimes he uses his own spirit. Shembe was inside his house when this young girl came. When Shembe was told about the girl's condition, he said to them "God will make her to walk." He said, "God will bless her." They said, "Thanks." The people who brought her were lifting her up to leave when she shouted, "I want to urinate." She stood up and walked in the presence of all the people.

Healing in the amaNazaretha is also performed through *nikela*. Members come to Shembe with an arbitrary sum of money and mention their needs to Shembe. Shembe responds by saying, "God bless you." Members testify to the effectiveness of this method, and they believe that it is their faith in Shembe that heals them.

To summarize, Shembe's followers in the amaNazaretha Church believe him to be more than human. Consequently, he is able to serve them in a mediatorial capacity where he brings healing and salvation and also answers their everyday prayers. While the members of the amaNazaretha Church believe that there is a God above Shembe, Shembe himself, by virtue of his miraculous deeds and by meeting the existential everyday needs of his people, further has become to his followers the god and savior they see. This fact leads to a further question: If Shembe functions in this critical role for the amaNazaretha, is there still a place for Christ in the beliefs and practices of its members?

Research Findings: The Role of Jesus Christ

The purpose of this study was to discover if the amaNazaretha Church is a Christward movement. A Christward movement is one that recognizes and acknowledges that "Jesus Christ is Lord." To ascertain if Jesus Christ is central in the amaNazaretha's beliefs and practices, I first had to discover the status and role that the ancestors and the leader, Vimbeni Shembe, hold in the church in its beliefs as well as in its practices. The above two sections in this chapter report my research findings on these prior questions.

In this third section I ask specifically about the amaNazaretha's official position regarding the person and work of Jesus Christ. In Christian orthodoxy one espouses first the words and work of Jesus Christ in terms of his past deeds, especially his atoning work. Second, Christians believe in his present mediatorial role and intercession on their behalf. Finally, Christians hold to a resounding future hope in Jesus Christ's return. To discover the Christology operating in the amaNazaretha Church, I raised a series of questions on the status and role of Jesus Christ, vis-á-vis the ancestors and Vimbeni Shembe:

1. Christians generally pray in the name of Jesus Christ. Do the amaNazaretha pray in the name of Christ or in the name of the ancestors?
2. Are the ancestors more important than Christ?
3. How do you characterize your religious affiliation?
4. The bumper sticker says, "Shembe Is the Way." What do you understand by this statement?
5. Who possesses more power—Vimbeni Shembe or Christ?
6. When a member of your family is ill, whom do you go to for healing?
7. When you pray, do you pray in the name of Vimbeni Shembe or Christ?

To ascertain whether Jesus Christ mediated prayers in the amaNazaretha Church or if ancestors fulfilled this role, I asked the question *"Christians generally pray in the name of Jesus Christ. Do the amaNazaretha pray in the name of Christ or ancestors?"* Among the ministers, the most frequent response (fourteen of twenty-nine, 48% of respondents) was that they do not pray in the name of Jesus but in the name of their ancestors *and* Shembe. A further twelve respondents (41%) said they pray only in the name of Shembe. Three respondents said that they had no knowledge of Jesus Christ.

Among the members, the most frequent response (twenty-four of thirty-nine, 62% of respondents) was that they pray in the name of ancestors *and* Shembe, while five respondents claimed that they pray only in the name of Shembe. A further nine respondents claimed no knowledge of Jesus Christ.

From the above responses in both groups, it would appear that prayers are mediated by both Shembe and ancestors. When respondents said that they pray only in the name of Shembe, I think that if I had phrased the question differently to include both Shembe and ancestors, the outcome may have been almost unanimous.

The following question elicited identical responses in both groups, leaders and lay people. I asked the question *"When you pray, do you pray to Vimbeni Shembe or Christ?"* to ascertain whether the amaNazaretha specifically invoke Vimbeni Shembe in their prayers or Christ. Both ministers and members said they pray in the name of Shembe the Holy Spirit and not any one Shembe. However, among the lay people, one respondent said she prayed in the name of Jesus.[50]

I raised the next question to ascertain in what way ancestors affect the person and work of Jesus Christ. I asked, *"Are the ancestors more important that Christ?"* The most frequent response (sixteen of twenty-nine, 55% of respondents) from the ministers was that Jesus was more important than ancestors, while the less frequent response (thirteen, 45% of respondents) was that the ancestors were more important. Members responded in the majority (twenty-nine of thirty-six, 80% of respondents) that ancestors were more important; seven respondents believed that Jesus Christ was more important.

I sensed that lay people responded out of their existential everyday experience, where ancestors are believed to be actively involved in all of their affairs, while Jesus Christ is considered to be one whom Shembe replaced. Therefore, Christ plays no direct part in their lives and well-being. The ministers who claimed that Jesus was more important than ancestors were arguing from the perspective that if Shembe is above the ancestors and more important, then Christ is also more important than ancestors as he is Shembe's equal.

My next question was to ascertain if the amaNazaretha considered themselves Christian. I asked the question *"How do you characterize your religious affiliation? Are the amaNazaretha Christian? What are the differences?"* In both groups, ministers and members, the overwhelming majority (65 of 68, 96% of respondents) argued that there were several differences between the amaNazaretha Church and Christians, and thus they are Nazarites, not Christians. Three interviewees did not respond to the question.

So as to elicit responses about the amaNazaretha's belief about the afterlife, I raised the question *"The bumper sticker, 'Shembe Is the Way,' what does it mean to you?"* The overwhelming response (sixty-four of sixty-eight, 94% of respondents) in both groups, leaders and lay people, was that Shembe is the only way to heaven and to God. Four responses were unclear.

My next question received mixed responses. To the question *"Who possesses more power—Vimbeni Shembe or Christ?"* leaders (seventeen of twenty-nine, 58% of respondents) stated that Shembe had more power

---

50. I have discussed this one respondent earlier. She had not yet committed to membership in the amaNazaretha Church.

than Christ, while ten respondents (35%) in this category believed that both Shembe and Christ were equal. Lay people were equally divided, where seventeen respondents (44%) believed that Shembe was more powerful, and another seventeen (44%) said that both Shembe and Jesus Christ were equal. Four respondents claimed that they had no knowledge of Christ, while 1 respondent believed that Jesus had more power than Shembe.

In a follow-up question I asked, *"Who is a more powerful healer—Shembe or Christ? When you or a member of your family is ill, whom do you go to for healing?"* To this question leaders were unanimous that Shembe is their healer and that they call on him. Among members I raised the question thirty-three times, and thirty-two respondents (97%) answered that Shembe is the one they call on and that he is their healer. On six occasions I did not raise the question or did not receive a response.

A secondary question that I raised was *"How would you characterize the movement? Is the Shembe faith for blacks only?"* The most frequent response (twenty-five of twenty-nine, 86% of respondents) from leaders was that the church was for all nationalities, while four respondents thought it was for Africans only. Members in the majority (eighteen of twenty-two, 82% of respondents) believed that the church was for all people, while 1 respondent believed that the church was meant for Africans only. I did not raise the question on seventeen occasions, and three did not respond to the question.

My final question was *"When you encounter problems or are in want, who comes to mind first—Vimbeni or Isaiah Shembe?"* Among leaders the most frequent response (twenty-eight of twenty-nine, 96% of respondents) was that Shembe is one; therefore, it is neither Vimbeni nor Isaiah, and 1 respondent believed that Isaiah Shembe comes to mind. Lay people gave a similar response (thirty-three of thirty-nine, 85% of respondents) as the leaders. I did not secure responses from six interviewees.

From the previous sections concerning the role of ancestors and the role of Shembe in the amaNazaretha Church, one could well foresee the results of the third section, the role of Christ. People's perceptions of the role of the ancestors and Shembe left little room for Christ in the church's practices, beliefs, and existential life. However, in answering the questions about the role of Christ, they made it clear as to why they place more emphasis on ancestors and Shembe than on Jesus Christ.

The amaNazaretha seek a faith that is practical, and if Jesus is to be a practical reality, a theoretical, abstract Christology will not bring to the fore something that works for them. In this instance it is Shembe and the ancestors who, as mediators, can effect healing, deliverance, and salvation in the here and now as well as in the afterlife. Any illness or misfortune that befalls the amaNazaretha opens the question "How did it happen?" and then "Why?" Such illness or misfortune involves the whole person, and then not only the person alone, but the community as well. It goes further to involve the living-dead. A healthy body or life is symptomatic of a right relationship with people and the environment, under the watchful eye of the ancestor.

Summary

In summary, my research via interviews brings to the fore the following six observations, concerns, and challenges:

First, the amaNazaretha Church is more pneuma-centered than it is Christo-centered. Pneumatology for the amaNazaretha is the embodiment of a person, Shembe, a living person. Biblical references, especially John 14–16, are interpreted in an unorthodox fashion.

Second, the amaNazaretha gravitate more to the Old Testament than the New Testament. Thus very little reference is made to Jesus Christ in their beliefs and practices. Some members of the amaNazaretha Church have no knowledge of Christ.

Third, while the amaNazaretha have a firm belief in a transcendent Being, they believe culturally that they do not have the capacity to approach such a Being. Mediation is achieved through the ancestors and Shembe: ancestors, as they are still an integral part of the community and family; and Shembe, as he is the Holy Spirit sent by God. Therefore, Jesus Christ has no role to play in the lives of the amaNazaretha.

Fourth, the Zulu culture and tradition supersede biblical injunctions. Any semblance to biblical norms is taken literally out of the Old Testament. Examples are animal sacrifices, funeral rituals, and food taboos.

Fifth, the amaNazaretha have a different view of the Trinity. They believe that the third person of the Trinity is a living person that Jesus promised before he departed, namely, Shembe.

Finally, Christian Sunday worship is changed to Saturday "Sabbath" in keeping with the Old Testament. Further, they strongly present themselves as a Nazarite movement, not a Christian church.

The challenge for Christian mission is how to identify Christianity with African culture without obfuscating essential elements of both culture and Christian religious norms. Is there room in Christian theology for the role of ancestors, and what form should such a role take? Finally, the status and role of the leader, Shembe, has to be clearly discerned both culturally and theologically. Chapter 7 on Shembe Theology and Christology will hopefully address these and other pertinent issues.

I discuss the findings from my participant observation in the activities of the amaNazaretha Church in ch. 6.

6

Participant Observation in the amaNazaretha Church and an Interview with Vimbeni Shembe

Religious and Cultural Events in the Church Calendar

THE AMANAZARETHA CHURCH HOLDS two important annual gatherings when members from all over South Africa and neighboring countries congregate for a time of religious and cultural celebration. The first of these is the January celebration that commemorates the founding of the church and Isaiah Shembe's call to the holy mountain Nghlangakasi. This event is convened over a two-week period beginning early in January each year. At the end of the two-week mountain vigil at Nghlangakasi, congregants walk back to Ebuhleni, where the celebrations continue until the last day of January.

The Sabbath service on the mountain does not vary from the weekly Sabbath service held during the rest of the year. Vimbeni Shembe convenes the meeting and sometimes preaches; at other times he invites other ministers, evangelists, and preachers to deliver the sermon. Shembe often selects individuals who can report miraculous happenings in their local congregations; others have had visions or dreams that Shembe deems worthy of proclamation to the assembly. Such miraculous happenings, dreams, and visions become the centerpiece of the sermon that day.

The annual journey to the mountain takes approximately two hours by taxi traveling through very rugged and at times impassable terrain. About midway through our journey, Joseph, my research assistant, instructed the driver to stop the vehicle as he wanted to point out a huge pile of rocks on the side of the road. This spot is called *Isivivane*, meaning a heap of stones. According to Joseph, the stones are placed at this point to demarcate the journey, which the Shembe pilgrims make on foot. On their return these stones become a reminder that they had journeyed to the mountain to meet with God and Shembe. The pilgrimage is also a commemorative act.

People remember that Isaiah Shembe, the founder, was faithful in obeying the voice of God, and, subsequently, he experienced a theophany that in similar circumstances each pilgrim may also experience.

Pilgrims stop at seven prayer stations on their way up to the plateau, a journey that takes approximately an hour from the base of the mountain. A series of white stones marks these prayer points. Joseph said that Isaiah Shembe prayed at these points before his encounter with God. One of these prayer stations is different from the others. It resembles a huge cement flowerpot, approximately six feet in diameter, out of which hang bunches of colorful wildflowers. At the base of the pot, and all around it, are heaps of *impepho* flowers placed by pilgrims. According to Joseph, this place was where Isaiah Shembe descended to meet with his congregation for their Sabbath services. It would only be some years later that the congregation was allowed to ascend to the plateau of the mountain. The burning of *impepho* flowers is representative of a form of cleansing for the pilgrims as they approached the highest point of the mountain, symbolizing the highest point in their spiritual journey as well.

The other annual gathering is the midyear cultural celebration held for the whole month of July at the church headquarters at Ebuhleni, some thirty kilometers outside the Durban city limits. Thousands of members gather on the campgrounds, bringing with them their supplies for the entire month. Members have constructed specially designated living quarters, *idogolo*, of wood, iron, and mud. As many as five or six people live in one hut during the month of July. Women and men remain separated during this time, and the women's quarters are distanced from those of the men. This is a time of fasting when the amaNazaretha refrain from eating foods containing leaven.[1] Thus, their food is cooked at home, and bread is baked without yeast.

During the month of July, several cultural and social events take place. Among them are weekly dances, marriages, men's circumcisions, and girls' virginity tests. Weekend activities attract many people from the community, international visitors, and the media. Sabbath services attract as many as 100,000 participants throughout the month, members coming from all over South Africa and the neighboring states.

The amaNazaretha are Sabbatarians in that they follow the principles, practices, and observances pertaining to the Jewish Sabbath as mandated in the Old Testament. Some time after initiating his own movement,

---

1. Fasting, in the context of the July celebration for the amaNazaretha Church, requires the initiate to abstain from sexual relations and maintain a restricted diet where leaven is excluded. Members are required to keep this fast for the whole month of July.

Isaiah Shembe changed Sunday worship to Sabbath worship. He called his followers together and said the following:

> My children, I have been called by God, and he informed me that . . . he prefers you worship him on the Sabbath Day. But the Sabbath is difficult to keep. If you choose to be his children, he would like you to worship him on the Sabbath Day and keep it holy as he commanded the children of Israel.[2]

Mpanza records that some members had doubts about Sabbath worship but deferred to the wisdom of Isaiah Shembe, as he claimed to have received the message from God. It was in this context that Isaiah was inspired to write the Sabbath liturgy, which is used three times each Sabbath—Friday at six o'clock in the evening (start of the Sabbath) and Saturday at nine o'clock in the morning and at one o'clock in the afternoon.

While ministers and evangelists are assigned specific areas of jurisdiction, they visit temples, sometimes unannounced and at other times by invitation. Vimbeni Shembe rotates visiting the temples in the larger areas, and more than likely he will spend at least one month at each location. Most of his time during the week, however, is spent at Ebuhleni, the church's headquarters in Inanda, some thirty kilometers from the city of Durban.

The service described here was observed at Ebuhleni on July 5, 2001, at nine o'clock in the morning. Approximately twenty thousand worshippers were present. From about eight o'clock in the morning, people began streaming into the worship center to take their places. Worshippers brought their own grass prayer mats on which they sat.

Women were seated in four groups in front of and on the right side of Shembe. Distinctions were made; married women who had already borne children were seated together. Then, married women who had not as yet borne children sat behind them. Behind them were unmarried women who had borne children. The young women were seated on Shembe's right side. Men were seated on Shembe's left side. Closest to Shembe were the ministers, followed by the evangelists and the preachers, then the lay members. The chiefs were seated behind Shembe. Visitors were seated behind the ministers, and sometimes they are seated behind Shembe.

All these groups were seated under open skies, in neat rows, the shade from the trees providing the only protection from the elements. Shembe, by contrast, was seated in a brick structure, likened to the tabernacle in

---

2. Mpanza, "The Biography of Isaiah Shembe," 52.

the Old Testament.³ Symbols in the Nazarite "tabernacle" include an oak table covered with a colorful cloth, a vase of artificial flowers, one oak cane chair, a lectern on which is placed Shembe's hymnbook and Bible, and finally a huge pillow covered with beautifully embroidered material and wrapped in a grass prayer mat.⁴

The service is preceded by a selection of organ music. The organ, which is a contemporary keyboard, and the organist are situated below the tabernacle, facing Shembe. During this time the processional begins. Two helpers unroll a red carpet onto the concrete-paved pathway where Shembe will walk. The carpet begins from the periphery of the temple worship area, demarcated by white-painted stones, and ends at the entrance to the tabernacle. Next, the table and chairs are brought in by Shembe's helpers, some of whom are young girls with their heads and faces covered. Then the vase of flowers, the lectern, and Shembe's hymnbook and Bible are brought into the tabernacle. Finally the pillow also is brought in. The pillow, for the amaNazaretha, represents Isaiah Shembe, the Holy Spirit.⁵ Inside the tabernacle itself the helpers do not stand, sit, or walk, but move about on their knees.

Congregants at the service remove their shoes upon entering through the outer gates to the demarcated area of worship. Shembe's aides assist him in removing his shoes when he enters the temple structure's precincts.

During this ceremonial procession, all worshippers remain on their knees, and the ministers also come in to take their seats. The bell rings at nine o'clock in the morning, at which time people kneel as Shembe enters. They exclaim in unison, "*Ameni, Oyingcwele!*" meaning "Amen, He is Holy."

The service begins when Shembe announces the person who would lead the liturgy and conduct the singing for the morning service as prescribed in the hymnal. The liturgical readings and singing usually take some twenty-five to thirty minutes. After this time, the leader invites the congregation to join in corporate prayer. The designated person, announced earlier by Shembe, then delivers the sermon. The sermons are

---

3. The term *tabernacle* is not used by amaNazaretha worshippers. They do not have a name for the building. However, in my conversation with evangelist Mpanza, he assured me that my term *tabernacle* accurately represents the building, its structure, and its symbols.

4. A set of two microphones was brought into the tabernacle with the symbols previously mentioned. The microphones and their tripod stands were also wrapped in grass prayer mats when brought into the tabernacle.

5. From my interviews, I gather that the pillow was used by Isaiah Shembe. Adherents believe that Isaiah is present in spirit at their worship services. Some interviewees believe that the pillow is representative of the Holy Spirit, interpreted to be Shembe himself.

based on the ethical teachings of the Bible, with particular reference to Sabbath Day observances. Most sermons are crafted around the miraculous deeds of the leaders (Isaiah Shembe, Johannes Galilee Shembe, Amos Shembe, and Vimbeni Shembe). At the end of the preaching, Shembe concludes the service by calling for a closing hymn.

Next, announcements are made by those appointed by Shembe. Most often they deal with monetary issues. There are prescribed fees for different activities in the church. Each member is expected to contribute. After these announcements, Shembe prepares to leave the temple and retire to his house, located some fifty yards from the temple area. Again, all the worshippers kneel and exclaim, *"Ameni, Oyingcwele!"* or "Amen, He is Holy!" Shembe is met outside the tabernacle by a young virgin who assists him with his shoes. When he has finally moved beyond the view of the members, they take their seats again. More announcements follow. Then Shembe's helpers remove the symbols from the tabernacle. During this recessional, the members kneel again.

The final ceremony is *nikela*, a ceremony when members are invited to make offerings for various projects and also when people pay a sum of money for their needs to be heard.[6] This ceremony is conducted by selected ministers who listen to the requests of the members and respond by saying, "God bless you."

At the conclusion of the service, people leave the worship area via the main exits, indicated by the larger breaks between the white stones. Many congregate outside the church office, where vendors sell church calendars, photos of the Shembes, Vaseline, handcrafted book covers, and the church's liturgical songbook. "Tickets," which are taken to Shembe for the release of the ancestors from "jail," are also purchased at the church office.

The officially printed book *Izihlabelelo ZamaNazaretha*, or *Nazarite Hymns*, functions as the formalized liturgy for the amaNazaretha. The hymnal contains 242 hymns, of which the last twenty-two were composed by Galilee Shembe. The *Izihlabelelo ZamaNazaretha* was first published in 1940 under the supervision of Galilee Shembe. It contains the meditations and songs composed by the founder, Isaiah Shembe. The faithful, young and old, literate and illiterate alike, carry both the hymnal and the Bible

---

6. *Nikela* is a ceremony where worshippers have the opportunity to bring an offering to the church when requests are made for healing and for family need. Members also bring offerings when the church is in need of financial resources for specified church projects. *Nikela* is also an offering ceremony one makes on behalf of one's ancestors. The belief is that ancestors appear in dreams, requesting assistance from living relatives. In this instance members purchase a ticket of release for the ancestor from the church office and approach Shembe, who mediates on behalf of the "troubled" ancestor.

to their places of worship with the utmost care and dignity.[7] Members come to the worship center with their Bibles and hymnbooks wrapped in embroidered cloth or with attractive plastic cellophane covers bearing pictures of the founder or one or more of the succeeding Shembes.[8]

The hymnal contains liturgies for both morning and evening prayers and also the Sabbath services. Its format and style resemble the formal liturgies used by Western churches today. According to Bongani Mthethwa,[9] "Isaiah Shembe was strongly influenced by the format of Protestant religious worship, particularly as he experienced it as a member of the Baptist and Methodist churches."[10] This influence becomes evident when one reads the acknowledgment at the end of hymns 184 and 194, *Izihlabelelo Sama Wesile* ("Hymn of the Wesleyans").[11] However, as Carol Muller notes, the hymns bear close resemblance to the Psalms in the Old Testament.[12] The *Izihlabelelo ZamaNazaretha* becomes a sacralized corpus of writing more important that the biblical text. Isaiah's words and works that are now committed to writing take on supra-biblical import. Time and again in my conversation with evangelist Mpanza, he alluded to a "third testament," meaning that Isaiah Shembe's words and works should be treated as *inspired* works no different than the Bible.

The Sabbath liturgical prayer from the hymnal combines the Old Testament laws and rules for observing the Sabbath, forms of worship incorporating citations from the Psalms, along with aspects of Zulu socio-religious traditions expressed through music, drums, and dance.[13] Several Old Testament texts demonstrating the worshipper's religious identity and experience are quoted in the liturgy. While Jehovah is invoked, the name of Jesus Christ is conspicuously absent. Isaiah refers to the ancestors in the

---

7. Muller, *Rituals of Fertility and the Sacrifice of Desire*, 98.

8. A member of the church presented me with a copy of the hymnal and encouraged me to purchase a cover for the book. I have my copy of the book, and on the cellophane jacket is a picture of Vimbeni Shembe and myself outside his residence at the Ebuhleni compound.

9. Bongani Mthethwa was the son-in-law of J. G. Shembe. Prior to his murder by unknown assailants, he was the church's chief organist. He studied music at Natal University, where he obtained his B. A. in music. At the time of his death, he was writing a master's thesis at the University of Natal.

10. Mthethwa, "Music and Dance as Therapy," 2. Hans-Jurgen Becken also completed a translation of the hymnal, "Nazarene's Hymns with Sabbath Liturgy and Morning and Evening Prayers."

11. Ibid.

12. Muller, *Rituals of Fertility and the Sacrifice of Desire*, 88.

13. Shembe, *Izihlabelelo ZamaNazaretha*, 15–23.

liturgy when he calls the congregants "children of *Senzangakhona*" (stanza 19). Common in the liturgy, as the following quote shows, is the mention of "Nazaretha," "Sabbath," and "Jehovah." Stanza 19 reads, "Today is the Sabbath for all people who fear Jehovah. You and your children must heed the law of the Sabbath because it is a great joy to God when the Sabbath is observed. As for me, I beg you, Nazaretha, in the name of the Lord Jehovah, do not harden your hearts, children of Senzangakhona."[14]

The selection of the hymns seems to bear no connection with the sermon or the occasion when the service was convened. Hymns selected made reference to Jehovah, Ekuphakameni, legal and moral issues, and the consequences for disobeying the Sabbath and other moral codes. From my observation, the *Izihlabelelo ZamaNazaretha* is valued above the Bible and is referred to more often than the Bible. This veneration becomes evident when one observes the morning and evening prayers conducted in the homes of the amaNazaretha. Only the *Izihlabelelo ZamaNazaretha* is used on these occasions.

The centerpiece of the Sabbath service is the sermon delivered by the person whom Shembe chooses. The preacher faces in the direction of Shembe, who is seated in the *tabernacle*, and the preacher remains on his knees for the whole duration of the sermon, while the congregation is seated. The preacher, out of honor and respect for Shembe, addresses him as a subject would approach Zulu royalty—on one's knees.

Sermons

I recorded and analyzed twelve sermons to ascertain the amaNazaretha's beliefs regarding Shembe, the ancestors, and Christ. Preachers made reference to Shembe on forty-six occasions; there were four references to ancestors and three references to Christ in the sermons. On ten of the twelve occasions, preachers referred to a biblical text in the sermon. The Old Testament was quoted twenty-seven times, while the New Testament was quoted eighteen times. Sermons usually addressed moral issues in the church and the consequences of disobeying the law. Other sermons centered on miracle stories and the life and times of the Shembes, especially Isaiah Shembe. The chart below depicts the data extrapolated from the twelve sermons.

14. Ibid., 18.

Table 2. Data from Sermon Extrapolation

Sermon	OT Refs.	NT Refs.	Refs. to Christ	Refs. to Shembe	Refs. to Ancestors	Hymns	Theme	Sermon Prompted By...
#1	3	3	0	2	1	13; 110	Loving relationships; the consequences of immoral living	Current malaise in church
#2	7	1	0	3	0	74	Vimbeni Shembe weeps over the sins of his people	A vision from an ancestor (Amos Shembe)
#3	4	3	0	1	0	69	You wear white gowns but are still sinners	Sinful deeds of congregants
#4	0	1	0	3	0	160; 32	Self-aggrandizement	Pride of positions
#5	4	2	0	5	0	213; 127	Listening to the voice of Shembe is listening to God	Dreams and visions
#6	0	0	0	4	1	110; 89 104; 98	Behavior at July celebrations	July celebrations
#7	0	1	0	2	0	208	Love one another; it is safe to follow Shembe	Nazarites' exemplary lives; witness to the world
#8	4	4	0	10	0	39; 148 107	The uniqueness of Shembe	The incomparable Shembe
#9	1	0	0	4	0	94; 54	Words and works of Shembe	Pure motives for worship on the mountain
#10	4	1	1	3	1	107; 64	Abstinence; endorsement of polygamy in the church	Immoral lifestyle of certain individuals in the church
#11	0	0	0	5	1	45	Preparation for the July celebrations; stories of the life and times of Isaiah Shembe	Isaiah Shembe is sent by God to the Zulu people
#12	0	2	0	4	0	164; 153; 39	Miracles performed by Isaiah Shembe, J. G. Shembe, and A. K. Shembe	Shembe: God's promise to the Zulus
Totals	27	18	3	46	4			

For the amaNazaretha, Isaiah Shembe functions as their enscripurated Living Word. For people in this oral culture, Shembe is in a sense divine and is present in their midst through the telling and retelling of stories about his miraculous and humane deeds. Worshippers believe that Isaiah Shembe's presence is pervasive throughout the Sabbath service, as represented by the pillow in the tabernacle. In many instances, the biblical text is used to support and authenticate the view of the preacher regarding Isaiah Shembe, his words, and miracles. For example, an eighty-three-year-old preacher, Nyaba, selected Isaiah 41:25 and 43:5 for his sermon (Sermon 8). The former text reads, "I have stirred up one from the north, and he comes—one from the rising sun who calls on my name. He treads on rulers as if they were mortar, as if he were a potter treading the clay." The latter text reads thus: "Do not be afraid, for I am with you; I will bring your children from the east and gather you from the west." Preacher Nyaba is illiterate, so he called on members to read the text after he cited the biblical reference. With reference to Shembe, he said, "People will say Shembe is not mentioned in the Bible. Read Isaiah 41:25 and 43:5. According to Isaiah 43:5, the verse says that God said to Shembe, 'Wherever you go I will go with you. I will bring your generations from the east and the west. They will come to Ekuphakameni.'" Preacher Nyaba then cited examples of people coming to Shembe from the neighboring countries and provinces, north and south (Sermon 8). Shembe thus functions as a subtext not only in the Sabbath services but throughout the fabric of the amaNazaretha religiocultural life. In the preaching, the name of Jesus Christ was not mentioned except when "Jesus" was part of the biblical text.

Prayers

Prayers in the Sabbath service are spoken in concert and are led by Vimbeni Shembe. The only individual, free prayer is said by Vimbeni Shembe at the end of the service. At the local temples, the service concludes with prayers in concert. These prayers, spoken by individual members in concert, consist of one's personal and everyday family requests and are always prayed in the name of the ancestors and Shembe. Jesus is not usually mentioned in any of the prayers. Vimbeni Shembe himself prayed in the name of Shembe.

Minister Gcwenza and his family are an example of a typical evening family prayer meeting. Before the evening meal, the whole family congregated in the living room, all wearing their white gowns. Minister Gcwenza invited Joseph, my research assistant, to read the lesson for the evening prayer. At the conclusion of the reading and songs, the whole group prayed in concert. The prayer was not different from that of the Sabbath service. The family members prayed to God in the name of their ancestors and Shembe.

On another occasion two ministers, their families, and three members of the church were invited to my missionary cottage in Phoenix, Durban, one Sunday for lunch. After a discussion on issues regarding the church structure, beliefs, and practices, all shared a meal. When the church members were ready to leave, one of the ministers suggested that the group should pray before they left for home. The invited guests put on their white gowns and knelt down to pray. Minister Gcwenza read the evening liturgy, and minister Ngidi prayed, thanking God for the hospitality shown to them and praying for the host's well-being and for their safe journey home, concluding his prayer in the name of Shembe. As a rule, only the names of ancestors and Shembe are mentioned, never the name of Christ. The recorded prayers are listed below:

> Closing prayer at the temple at Ebuhleni: Vimbeni Shembe
>
> God of our forefathers, we thank you for the day you gave us. We ask you to give us more days, we thank you for good things you do for us. We ask you to give us courage to do good things for you. All this we ask in the name of Shembe. Amen.
>
> Prayer at the temple at Ebuhleni
> Prayer offered by Vimbeni Shembe for the family of J. G. Shembe
>
> Father God of Ekuphakameni, we are asking for your angels to come and stop the anger which is finishing [destroying] the family of your son. Give long life in the name of Shembe. Amen.
> [This prayer was offered following of the death of one of J. G. Shembe's wives.]
>
> Benediction by Shembe
>
> We thank you, Lord, for this day; we ask you to give us more days. We thank you for keeping us till this day of remembrance. We ask you to be present till the next one again. Give us more days and the power to defeat the devil. All this I ask in the name of our Lord Shembe. Amen.
>
> Members' prayers at Ebuhleni

Father Shembe, Lord of Lords, we are coming. Lord of the Sabbath, strengthen your will that it would be accepted in the world. Secure us, Jehovah. Amen.

God of our forefathers, we are in front of your face as sinners. We do wrong things daily; we ask you to forgive us our sins. Make us to forgive each other. Where we do not see eye to eye, give us the power to sit down and settle our problems. All this I ask in the name of Shembe. Amen.

Thank you, Shembe, for inviting me. Please, Shembe, look at me and love me; make me to stick to you. Please, my Lord, erase my sins, Shembe. Shembe, my thoughts must always be according to your ways.

Evening prayer in Gcwenza's house
Opening prayer: Reading from liturgical book (9–14)

Corporate prayer: God of our ancestors, we are before your face; we ask you to be with us this night. We are praying, O Lord, show your greatness. We ask you to show us the work you were sent for by God [reference to Shembe]. In the name of Shembe. Amen.

Closing Hymn 195

Closing prayer: Benediction: Father, God who has all power, we are before your face this evening. We thank you for keeping us on the way we have been going; you have protected us. We ask for your love, which has no end, to be with us this night. In the name of Shembe. Amen.

Sunday Prayer at my rented residence with the ministers Gcwenza and Ngidi and their respective families, Hymn 242

Prayer: We are here we ask you to remember the good we try to do.

Ngidi's closing prayer: Holy Shembe, we are here at Phoenix at the house of Moodley. We are asking you to love us and protect us and secure this home we are in. Give us the day protected by you and blessing in the name of Shembe.

Significant in all of the prayers is the fact that Shembe features so prominently. As one devotee in his prayer asked, "Please, Shembe, look at me and love me; make me to stick to you. Please, my Lord, erase my sins, Shembe. Shembe, my thoughts must always be according to your ways." While it is likely that the reference to "Father God of Ekuphakameni" in Vimbeni Shembe's prayer is a reference to God, one is left in doubt whether the person praying such a prayer has Shembe in mind. What does become evident is that initiates pray both *to* Shembe and also *in* the name of Shembe to God. Petitions are also made in the names of ancestors, as is evident in the above prayers. However, absent from all prayers is any reference to the name of Jesus Christ. This absence also becomes evident when one considers the morning, evening, and Sabbath liturgical prayers recorded in the amaNazaretha hymnbook, *Izihlabelelo ZamaNazaretha*. The following chapter will refer to the prayers and hymns to determine the Christology present in the beliefs and practices of the amaNazaretha Church.

At the Shembe Sabbath services, one can witness the amaNazaretha's devotion to and respect for the current leader, Vimbeni Shembe, and also the special place accorded to Isaiah Shembe, the founder. However, the person and work of Christ was absent from the sermons, songs, teaching, and beliefs. In their practices, the amaNazaretha invoked the ancestors and Shembe rather than Christ.

Healing Ceremonies

Every service, irrespective of venue or occasion, concludes with a healing ceremony. At the local temples the most senior person presides. Various sizes of grass containers are placed in front of the person presiding. Congregants come forward kneeling and announce their requests to the person presiding, who is also on his knees. He offers a word of encouragement to the congregant and says, "God bless you." The congregant places a sum of money in the grass basket and resumes his or her place in the congregation. Some congregants carry with them Vaseline and a bottle of water. The presiding official takes a spoonful of Vaseline from his own bottle and mixes it into the congregant's bottle. The same procedure is carried out with water. The belief is that in the name of Shembe, the Vaseline and water now possess curative powers to heal the individual of his or her infirmity. The presiding official (minister, evangelist, or preacher) mediates power and authority from Shembe to the congregant.

At the church headquarters in Ebuhleni, Vimbeni Shembe also conducts healing ceremonies, usually twice each day, apart from the regular service times. He sees members and visitors outside his cottage. As many as two hundred to three hundred people congregate outside his cottage at each session. Those who have come to solicit his assistance remain on their knees awaiting their turn to approach Vimbeni Shembe at his table. Shembe has two young women who collect the *nikela* offerings from the congregants. Similar to the regular healing services, each person mentions his or her need to Shembe, and he responds by saying, "God bless you." As with all other healing services, for those who come with illnesses, Shembe adds Vaseline or water to their bottles with instruction on its use. Healing for the amaNazaretha initiate is not confined to the physical. Financial stringency, economic hardship, fractures in relationships, and breakdown in communication with ancestors are not unrelated, and thus healing has to be holistic. It is Shembe who is believed to be the one empowered to bring about restoration, relief, and satisfaction for the amaNazaretha adherent.

An Interview with Vimbeni Shembe

On the first visit to the Shembe compound, I sought to meet with Vimbeni Shembe, but the senior ministers closest to Shembe would not allow me access to him. However, in June 2000, through invitation granted through an attorney who was doing some legal work for Shembe, I was able to meet with Vimbeni Shembe.

On that cold winter's morning at the Ebuhleni compound, Shembe was seated at a table in the courtyard of his cottage. Some two hundred people, on their knees, waited for the opportunity to share their grief, sorrows, and illnesses with him in the hope that their needs would be met. When the group entered the courtyard, he beckoned us to come to the table, waving his hand. It was assumed that we should also move toward him on our knees. However, Shembe asked us to walk over to his table. I was introduced to him by my attorney friend, and Shembe offered to see us after the lunch hour.

After lunch, a maid announced our arrival. Shembe met us at the front porch of his house. He stood inside the porch with a wrought-iron fence separating us from him. He was told that I had come to see him for two reasons: first, to seek his permission to conduct field research at the amaNazaretha church, and second, to interview him. He granted the first request by stating that I was free to talk with any member of the church and also attend the worship services. To the second request he responded, "I have no time for an interview, but anything you need to know [pointing to one of his aides] he will tell you. He knows everything about the church and me." With that remark Shembe dismissed us, but not before I stretched out my hand to him. Surprisingly, he withdrew, taking a few steps back, and with a smile he said, "God bless you" without shaking hands. I later learned that Shembe does not shake hands with the rank and file of ordinary people, as in their eyes he is believed to be God.

The aide, I later came to learn, was Rev. Sibisi, whose main function in the church is to ensure that before Shembe visits a temple or goes to a worship site, the infrastructure is set in place, and that Shembe's personal needs are met. Sibisi was very responsive to questions and assisted in networking with other ministers and church officials.

In 2002 I spent five months in South Africa doing field research. One of the goals was to interview Vimbeni Shembe himself. The opportunity to achieve this goal came about when minister Mpanza said that he had spoken to Vimbeni Shembe and that Shembe was willing to grant the interview. Upon minister Mpanza's advice, two sets of interview questions were prepared, a long version (the original) and a shortened version, in the event that Shembe offered only a limited amount of time.

On the day the interview was supposed to have taken place, a group of ministers who heard that the interview had been secured called me to a meeting with them. They did not want Vimbeni Shembe to be interviewed. Their argument was that since many of them had been interviewed, Shembe would not have anything different or more to offer. I sensed that the underlying issue was that I had not consulted with the ministers before securing the interview with Shembe. Nonetheless, I left South Africa after urging my contact, minister Mpanza, to pursue my request with Vimbeni Shembe, and that a special trip to South Africa would be made to see him.

This opportunity presented itself in January 2003, the month when the amaNazaretha meet on Nghlangakasi Mountain for the Firstfruits Celebration. The appointment with Vimbeni Shembe was scheduled for ten o'clock on a Tuesday morning. We arrived at Ebuhleni at approximately quarter of ten only to find that in the courtyard Shembe was surrounded by hundreds of people waiting on bended knees for him to attend to their many diverse needs. He stated that he would only be able to see us later that day. We returned, and he invited us into his house. Minister Mpanza and I were on our knees in Shembe's living room while he was seated on an exquisite brown leather couch. He was again reminded that he had invited me to come to interview him. I stressed the fact that I had spent much money and time just to return to South Africa to interview him. He asked me if there was a questionnaire. Then he asked for a copy of the interview schedule. He promised to answer the questions and stated that I should return the following week to see him again.

We returned to Ebuhleni the following Tuesday. Again Vimbeni Shembe appeared, surrounded by a sea of people, all waiting with keen anticipation for him to speak a word of encouragement to them. When he recognized our presence, he came over to where we were kneeling and said, "I have answered all your questions. But as you can see I am so busy. Could you come back later?" I had learned that to be persistent was the best way to achieve my goal, so I asked rather confidently, "What time would you like for us to return?" He responded that three o'clock that same afternoon was a good time.

We returned earlier than the appointed time and waited for Shembe to grant us an audience. At half past three in the afternoon, the maid in attendance invited us to enter Vimbeni Shembe's living room. This time he invited me to sit beside him on the couch while minister Mpanza remained on his knees. Shembe handed me a manila envelope that contained a neatly typed document with all the questions answered. The conversation with Vimbeni Shembe was rather brief. I raised some questions (bold), and his responses follow (normal text):

> Q: How did you receive your calling to be leader of this great movement?
>
> A: Only Isaiah Shembe was appointed by God on the mountain Nghlangakasi. The word of God sent him all over Zulu Natal preaching the word of God and God showed him the holy mountain Nghlangakasi, where God gave him all the ways to run this church. He was just alone, and he appointed his son Bishop J. G. Shembe after him, and said when he passes away the younger son Bishop A. K. Shembe will lead the church. And my father appointed me to lead the church.
>
> Q: I have spoken to many ministers and lay people who have been in the church for a long time, and they have been kind to answer all my questions. One of the things I wanted to know is this: They tell me that Shembe is the Holy Spirit. How do you explain that? What does it mean to you?
>
> A: We believe that, because God appointed him as the leader of the church. And he was given all the powers, and he prayed for the people who are sick and they get help. And that is how we took Shembe as the blessed name.
>
> Q: Now if I may ask you, is it only the leaders who can possess the Holy Spirit, or I as a person? What I was told was that when Jesus left he promised in the Word, John 14:16, that he would send the Comforter, the Holy Spirit, and that the Holy Spirit is Shembe now.
>
> A: We think so, but we do not know. Everything is known by God. We only think that it is like that, but God knows everything.

Q: Can Reverend Mpanza have the Holy Spirit?

A: Yes, God can do that. God can give that person power.

Q: But right now he does not possess that power because it resides in one individual.

A: YES. God can turn it. It is his power.

Q: But two people cannot have the Holy Spirit at the same time?

A: No, no it follows one after the other.

Q: One question about ancestors: How important are they to you as an individual?

A: We send our ancestors to the Almighty God whenever we pray. We believe in that.

Q: Do they assist you in any way?

A: We pray sending them to the Almighty and we get answers, and in that way we feel they help us.

Q: Can you do anything for them?

A: No, no, no, because they are in the world to come; they are not living in this world.

Q: I have been told that people can come to the leader, and if the ancestor has come to an individual in a dream and said that they are in a bad place and they want to be removed from there, they can come and make offerings for the ancestor, and that ancestor can be removed from what they call "jail" and be reunited with the other ancestors.

A: We do that by prayer, asking the Almighty to take them out of that bad place.

Q: How would one know that they have been removed from there and have been reunited with the other ancestors?

A: That dream comes back again, a return dream.

Q: Now I have been told by your theologians and especially evangelist Mpanza, who has written much on the church. He said, "The Shembe movement is not a Christian church because the traditional religions and Zulu traditions are important. You take the teachings from the Old Testament and even the ethical teachings of Jesus, so bringing that together this is a new religious movement that started in 1906/7 and officially in 1913/14.

A: Yes, we are not Christians. We are Nazarenes, but we do follow the advices given by Christ. Some of them are written in the Bible. We respect Christ.

Q: But he does not have any significant role because he has come and gone?

A: Yes, that is correct, but we respect him.

Q: When people come for healing, they say, "I came to Baba, made an offering, and Baba said, 'God bless you,' and a miracle followed." So one of the questions I ask is, "Who heals?" Does Baba heal, or does God work through him to heal, or is it Jesus Christ? Every time I have been told that God heals through you. . . .

A: Yes, that is correct.

Q: So it is not Jesus Christ?

A: No.

Q: I also ask about the Vaseline and water? When you put your finger into the Vaseline, it is only a means to enhance their faith, and it is not the Vaseline that heals but it is their faith.

A: Yes, that is correct—it is their faith and prayer.

Q: Is the church only for Africans?

A: It is a church for anyone.

Q: The bumper sticker "Shembe Is the Way." What does it mean?

A: They like Shembe and they like to follow him; that is the way to go.

Q: Many people said that it means Shembe is the way to heaven.

A: Yes, we believe that is so.

Q: I would like for you to tell us your story of how you came to be the leader of the church . . . . I am told that when you were elected as leader, people saw a rainbow over your head, and this told them that you received the Holy Spirit to lead the church.

A: Yes (pointing to minister Mpanza), they can tell you about this. I did not see the rainbow; they saw it.

Q: Just as when Jesus was baptized, people saw the dove appearing and the voice of God saying, "This is my believed son in whom I am well pleased."

A: That is correct, and I believe that that is true.

Thank you for taking the time to talk with me.

Shembe shook hands and I took some pictures. I gave Shembe a personal monetary gift before leaving his presence. Perhaps Shembe saw the gift as *nikela*, an offering to the church.

Vimbeni Shembe, who trained to be a school teacher but never actually taught a class, herded his father's cattle before coming into the church leadership. He has had no formal theological training, and it is possible that this lack precludes him from addressing theological matters in the church.

Summary

Participant observation at the amaNazaretha Church services afforded me the opportunity to take part in the Sabbath services at various temples during field research. To obtain data to solve the research problem, I listened to and recorded sermons, songs, and prayers and observed healing ceremonies. Finally, I had the privilege of interviewing Vimbeni Shembe after several disappointing attempts.

The data collected from those interviewed and from observation demonstrates that the amaNazaretha Church uses the Bible, with an emphasis on the Old Testament, and their liturgical songbook (mostly composed by Isaiah Shembe) in their Sabbath services. As noted above, Isaiah Shembe also functions as the authoritative Word alongside the biblical text. The Bible becomes secondary in the light of the words and works of Isaiah Shembe and the succeeding leaders. Consequently, very little room is allowed for the person and work of Christ in the sermons.

In the prayers that were recorded, it is evident that all prayers are offered to the Supreme Being, God. However, prayers are mediated in the name of ancestors and Shembe. In some instances the prayers are made directly to Shembe. As was discovered in interviews, *Shembe* is more than a name, more than a physical person; Shembe represents or *is* the Holy Spirit. Thus, praying to God is likened to praying to Shembe. The hymns have an emphasis on Jehovah, God, and in some instances Jesus Christ (as shall be pointed out in ch. 7) and are psalmodic in nature. Shembe is central in the healing process, whether he personally conducts the ceremony or delegates the duty to other officials. Chapter 7 offers an evaluation of the theology and Christology evident in the amaNazaretha Church.

7

Theology and Christology in the amaNazaretha Church

THE BURDEN OF THIS study has been to discover if the amaNazaretha Church is a Christward movement. In chapter 1 a Christward movement was defined as one that recognizes that "Jesus is Lord." The amaNazaretha Church could be considered a Christward movement *if* it affirms, "Jesus is Lord," in the sense that adherents of the Christian faith acknowledge and receive the person and work of Christ on the basis of the past (his work of atonement), present (his mediatorial role and intercession on our behalf), and future (his second coming in glory as our hope).

So as to discover the Christology espoused by the amaNazaretha, this study considered the extent to which the church positions the leader, Vimbeni Shembe, and ancestors as mediators between the living and the Supreme Being. Through interviews and participant observation, it was discovered that Vimbeni Shembe and ancestors still occupy a significant place in the everyday lives of amaNazaretha members. Consequently, there is little or no room for the central role of the person and work of Jesus Christ in the lives of amaNazaretha adherents. It is to these results that this study is directed for further analysis and reflection. First is a look at the status and role of Shembe, then the Ancestors, and finally Christ in the life of the amaNazaretha Church.

Christ and Shembe

The importance of the subject of Christology in the African context cannot be overestimated. It is more than a truism to say that "the concept of ancestors is as popular among traditional Africans south of the Sahara, as the name of Jesus Christ in the Church in Africa."[1] Muzorewa adds, "Christian Church membership is growing like wildfire. . . . It is growing faster than the development of African theology."[2] Perhaps, herein lies one

---

1. Muzorewa, "Christ as Our Ancestor," 255.
2. Ibid.

of the clues as to why members of the amaNazaretha Church hold to non-orthodox views regarding Christology (the person and work of Christ), pneumatology (the role of the Holy Spirit in the lives of people and in the world), and the Holy Trinity. Because of the rapid proliferation of the amaNazaretha Church beyond the province of KwaZulu-Natal and even to neighboring African countries, discipleship and training has not kept pace with the growth of the church. However, of primary importance, as I have discerned, is the lack of a clear articulation of the basic tenets of the Christian faith, specifically the doctrine of God, Christ, and the Holy Trinity.

Responses to Research Questions

To ascertain the place of Jesus Christ in the amaNazaretha beliefs and practices, there were three questions that invited interviewees to compare the position Vimbeni occupies in the amaNazaretha Church to that of Christ. The questions posed were: (1) *Would there be a time when you would talk with Vimbeni Shembe and Christ in the same conversation or prayer?* (2) *How would your words be different when you talk with Christ or Shembe?* and (3) *How is Vimbeni Shembe related to Christ; does he possess the Spirit of Christ or is he the Christ?* As the research has shown (ch. 5), the majority of respondents affirmed Vimbeni Shembe at the expense of Jesus Christ in that Jesus Christ does not feature prominently in their prayers. Others suggested that Vimbeni and Christ are equal in status, arguing that Jesus, before he departed, promised that he would send the Holy Spirit, who, the amaNazaretha believe, is Shembe.[3] The mediatorial role of Shembe is discerned in the prayers offered by amaNazaretha members, both formally and informally.

Prayers in the amaNazaretha Church

With regards to prayer, amaNazaretha ministers' and members' unanimous claim was that they prayed in the name of Shembe. As participant observer, I recorded several prayers offered during the amaNazaretha Sabbath

---

3. The amaNazaretha appeal to the Johannine texts to stake their claim that it is Jesus who told of Shembe's coming. They thus develop their theology on their understanding that when Jesus referred to the Holy Spirit, the Counselor, as "he," Jesus was referring to Shembe. For example, in John 16:7, Jesus says, "But I tell you the truth: It is for your good that I am going away. Unless I go away, the Counselor will not come to you; but if I go, I will send him to you." AmaNazaretha members believe Jesus sent them Shembe.

services that substantiate this claim. For example, one congregant in his prayer said thus:

> Father, God who has all power, we are in your face this evening. We thank you for keeping us on the way we have been; you have protected us. We ask for your love which has no end to be with us this night *in the name of Shembe. Amen* [emphasis mine]. (Congregant: 2002)

Two observations are in order here. First, the worshipper's prayer was directed to God; he affirms that blessings and protection ultimately issue from the hand of God.[4] Second, such blessings and protection, while proceeding from God, are mediated through Shembe. For the Zulu, God is acknowledged as the ultimate Supreme Being—culturally, the Supreme Being is at the apex of the hierarchy. Then there is a series of mediators in the persons of ancestors who arbitrate between the Supreme Being and the living. For the amaNazaretha, the Supreme Being is the God of the Old Testament, Jehovah, whom they worship. Yet, this Supreme Being cannot be approached directly by mere humans, and thus an intermediary is necessary. In this instance the intermediary is Shembe, who approaches God on behalf of the amaNazaretha adherents.

The theory used to evaluate the amaNazaretha prayers is the model suggested by Shorter.[5] In terms of Shorter's typology,[6] research shows that amaNazaretha prayers are directed to God, the Supreme Being, but through Shembe, thus interfacing with what Shorter calls symmetrical mediation. The figure below demonstrates this model of prayer:

---

4. According to Oosthuizen, "Shembe uses the word *Baba* [father] in a much broader connotation than 'my father' in the Western sense. Shembe uses it in two senses: 1. earthly people; 2. the Supreme Being as in the Zulu Bible translations" (*The Theology of a South African Messiah*, 24). Oosthuizen shows how the term *baba* is used to refer to the Supreme Being on one hand and to Isaiah Shembe on the other in the Shembe hymns (for example, see hymn 26, stanza 3, and hymn 32, stanza 3 in Shembe, *Izihlabelelo ZamaNazaretha*). Vimbeni Shembe is also called *Baba* by the congregants today. The relationship between Isaiah Shembe and God the Father is viewed in an unorthodox way among the amaNazaretha for the following reasons: (1) Isaiah Shembe himself claimed equality with God when he once made the statement that he was present at Creation, and in so doing he aligned with the supernatural world; (2) members of the amaNazaretha Church see Shembe as a personification of God. As my interviews showed, people claimed, "He is God to us by the very miracles he does for us." The role of the Holy Trinity in the amaNazaretha requires a separate study as there does not seem to be any crystallization of the doctrine presently.

5. Shorter, *Prayer in the Religious Traditions of Africa*, 9.

6. See ch. 1 above for his typology.

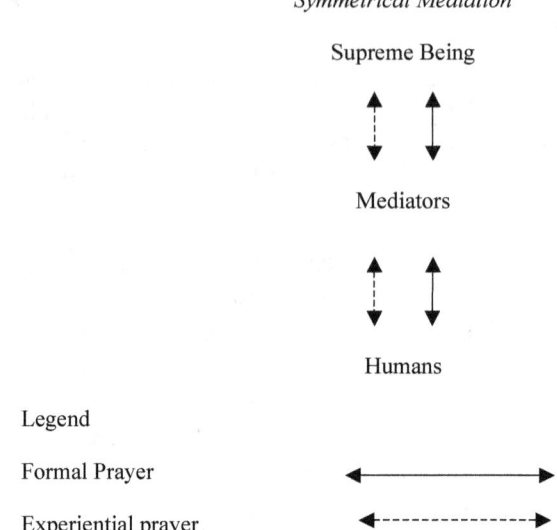

Figure 8. Symmetrical Mediation[7]

The second frame of reference to evaluate amaNazaretha prayers is Hexham's work, *The Scriptures of the AmaNazaretha of Ekuphakameni* (1994), which contains the prayers and writings of Isaiah Shembe, the founder of the amaNazaretha Church. Two excerpts of Isaiah Shembe's prayers show first how Isaiah Shembe prays in the name of ancestors and second that he believes himself to be mediator between his people and God, Jehovah. The first is the prayer he offered at Ekuphakameni for the forgiveness of sins. One excerpt of the prayer reads:

> My prayer Nkosi that I pray when I am alone
> In the corners of my heart,
> Which no one knows about,
> Which I do not pronounce with my mouth
> May it come to you Thixo of our fathers:
> Let nothing hinder it on the paths along which my prayers travel,
> When they come to you [NKulunKulu of Dingane and
>   Senzangakhona][8]
> Hope of all hopes.
> May I be accepted and rejected before your face Father.
> What will become of me.

7. Shorter, *Prayer in the Religious Traditions of Africa*, 10–11.

8. NKulunKulu is the Zulu name for God or the Supreme Being; Dingane and Senzangakhona are ancient Kings of the Zulu nation.

Theology and Christology in the amaNazaretha Church

There is no other NKulunKulu
To whom I can call and who would respond except you.[9]

The above prayer suggests that Isaiah Shembe articulates his heart's desires directly to God (NKulunKulu, Thixo), asking God that nothing should hinder his prayer from reaching God, and more than what his mouth utters, that God would cleanse his heart. The prayer also reveals that Isaiah Shembe was conscious of the mediatory role his ancestors played culturally in communicating with the Supreme Being. This role becomes evident in the prayer when he says, "May it come to you Thixo[10] of our fathers," and also in his reference to "NKulunKulu of Dingane and Senzagakhona." Here he makes reference to the hidden things within the sanctum of his own heart that may be revealed to God through the ancestors. In these instances it would appear that Isaiah Shembe, although calling on the God of the Old Testament, fuses his prayer with the Zulu traditional approach when he calls on God through the ancestors. This phenomenon will be discussed at the end of this chapter.

The prayer by Isaiah Shembe below was offered at Zibone[11] in 1927. In this prayer, Isaiah Shembe articulates his belief that God is transcendent and consequently cannot be understood by mortal humans. Shembe thus appeals to God, asking that he (Shembe) be the people's representative to God and also mediate God's presence to the people. Isaiah Shembe prays:

> Jehovah be you my friend. If I call you do not hide yourself from my calling you. You called me with your voice and with your glory. Because you did not hide yourself from me the nations are murmuring about you.
>
> Because you did not hide yourself from your slave many Nations have feared your name, because of the wonders and the signs that you have performed through me today Nkosi Jehovah.
>
> I have extended the length of my heart to you in my prayers for the sake of your name.
>
> So that which is good to you Jehovah may come to your Servant because you have called him. It is my prayer that you be as you are in the presence of the Nations.
>
> You are a myth and yet you exist, Jehovah. You are terribly beyond what is terrifying. You may be understood by no man. The thou-

---

9. Hexham, *The Scriptures of the AmaNazaretha of Ekuphakameni*, 61.
10. Thixo is another name for the Supreme Being used in the Zulu Bible.
11. Zibone is a small town in Zululand, the province of Natal.

> sands of your being NkulunKulu cannot be understood. There is none among those born of man and woman under the sun who may pray to you, Nkosi Jehovah. You appoint your own times according to your own consent during which you may be praised so that it may be pleasure in your heart.
>
> ... Write Nkosi Jehovah on the tablets of the heart of your slave Shembe, the times when he may praise you: times that you have appointed. That it may become a sweet odour to you Nkosi Jehovah. Like the odour of the incense that was burnt by your servant Moses and Aaron on your altars (Numbers 16:41–46).[12]

Isaiah Shembe prayed this prayer in the latter part of his ministry (he died in 1935). A brief analysis of this prayer reveals that Isaiah Shembe appeals to his calling, that God called him through an audible voice and amidst God's glory.[13] The prayer goes on to affirm that God revealed God's will for the nations through Isaiah Shembe when the nation experienced "signs and wonders." Isaiah Shembe was speaking in the context of a troubled South Africa where political strife, the negative effects of colonialism, the consequent economic hardship, and the fracturing of Zulu society were taking their toll on his people. He prays reminding God that God had specifically chosen him, Shembe, for times like these. He goes on to suggest that since God's transcendence disqualifies mere mortals from approaching the Supreme Being, Shembe offers himself as the intermediary, just as Moses functioned between God and the people of Israel in the wilderness.[14] God's transcendence is one explanation why adherents of the amaNazaretha Church today pray in the name of Shembe. Isaiah Shembe's prayers are models and teaching tools that people have passed on from Isaiah's generation to this day. It is Shembe who acts as mediator for the Zulu person when she or he prays to God. However, the prayers offered by the current leader, Vimbeni Shembe, add to the complexity as to who mediates the amaNazaretha prayers since Vimbeni calls on both his

---

12. Hexham, *The Scriptures of the AmaNazaretha of Ekuphakameni*, 102.

13. I earlier recounted Isaiah Shembe's experience when he believed God called him through thunder and lightning and a series of divine revelations (see chs. 1 and 4).

14. When asked by some white ministers in South Africa, "Of all of the prophets, which one are you?" Shembe replied, "I am not Jesus, I am not Jeremiah, nor any other, but I am Shembe." When provoked further to reveal his "true" identity with the question "Where do you come from?" Shembe responded, "My children, I cannot tell you that. All that I can tell you is that when Moses saw the burning bush, I was there" (Loubser, *A Critical Review of Racial Theology in South Africa*, 274). Shembe not only identifies himself with Moses but perhaps takes upon himself a deified role superior to Moses.

forefathers and Shembe, who is both his ancestor and (in the belief of the amaNazaretha) the Holy Spirit.

Vimbeni Shembe prayed this prayer at the conclusion of one of the Sabbath services:

> God of our forefathers, we thank you for the day you gave us. We ask you to give us more days, we thank you for good things you do for us. We ask you to give us courage to do good things for you. All this we ask in the name of Shembe. Amen. [July 2002]

Two observations about this prayer show a double mediatorial role—ancestors and Shembe. First, Vimbeni Shembe begins his prayer in the name of his ancestors—forefathers. This beginning is consistent with the prayers by members of the amaNazaretha Church generally. Also, Isaiah Shembe's recorded prayers[15] reveal a similar characteristic. (The ancestors' mediatorial role in prayer is discussed in greater detail below in this chapter.) Second, Vimbeni Shembe concludes his prayer with the words "in the name of Shembe." One explanation for this addendum to his prayer comes from his response to questions in the interview schedule. First, "How would you differentiate between Shembe as ancestor and God?" Vimbeni Shembe's written response to the question was as follows:

> There is always the confusion arising out of the ambiguity in the name of Shembe because even before one renders that Shembe is a particular surname, the Holy Spirit that resided in Shembe was also called Shembe. Insofar as the Holy Spirit being called Shembe, there is no difference between it [Holy Spirit] and God; taking into account also that God is said to be a Trinity (Father, Son, Holy Spirit).[16]

Second, to a specific question on prayer, "Would there be a time when you would talk with Shembe and Christ in the same conversation or prayer? Explain," he offered this response:

---

15. Hexham, *The Scriptures of the AmaNazaretha of Ekuphakameni*.

16. Although I did not study specifically the role of the Trinity in the amaNazaretha belief system, from my research I discovered that the amaNazaretha understanding of the Holy Trinity does not emerge clearly, as Shembe is said sometimes to be *the* Holy Spirit while at other times he is said to *possess* the Holy Spirit. Further, from the above response to my question, the respondent draws the conclusion that since there is no difference between the Holy Spirit and God, Shembe occupies all three positions—Father, Son, and Holy Spirit. I comment further on this issue in my conclusions to this study in ch. 8.

> We pray to Shembe the Holy Spirit who was in Christ and appeared in the form of a dove; the dove descended on him during baptism in the Jordan River.

The belief that Shembe is *the* Holy Spirit or that he *possesses* the Holy Spirit will be discussed later in this chapter. However, the above responses show that the amaNazaretha, including Vimbeni Shembe, believe that their prayers are mediated through Shembe the Holy Spirit and not through Jesus Christ. My research has already discerned that the amaNazaretha do not differentiate between the Shembes, as they believe that the Holy Spirit who resided in Jesus Christ was transferred to Shembe upon the ascension of Jesus and then to his successors. As the interview has shown, Jesus has no relevance for the amaNazaretha today because he came to earth at a specific point in history for a specific group of people, the Jews.

There is precedent for the belief that Jesus reincarnated in other religious traditions as well and that it is not only a cultural phenomenon but that it transcends culture. Snyder offers one example from the life and times of the Chinese revolutionary leader Hong Xiuquan (1814–64), where, after his conversion to Christianity, he "later saw himself as God's special emissary, a sort of second Christ, sent by God to establish *Taiping Tienkuo*, the 'Heavenly Kingdom of Eternal Peace and Prosperity.'"[17] Like Isaiah Shembe, who claimed to have received divine revelations from God, Hong Xiuquan also received visions of God:

> He saw a venerable old man and his middle-aged son and received a commission to rid the world of demon worship. . . . He identified the old man . . . with God the Father and the son as Jesus Christ. Hong thereafter saw himself as the Younger Brother of Jesus, sent to earth to establish God's kingdom.[18]

Another example from history that shows how religious movements begin with mere mortals who claim divine revelations and thus gain a following is the rise of the Shaking Quakers. Ann Lee is credited with bringing the Shaker Movement to the United States of America. She claimed to have received visions and heard voices as a child. However, the definitive breakthrough and God's calling came when she was thirty-four, in 1770, when Shakerism began. Her mystical visitations brought her to believe that she was the female Christ.[19] Her visions brought her to believe that in the Second Coming Jesus would appear as a woman. Her conviction was that

---

17. Snyder, *Models of the Kingdom*, 94.
18. Ibid., 95.
19. Campion, *Ann the Word*, 39.

Theology and Christology in the amaNazaretha Church

God was both male and female. When arrested and put in prison for her extreme views and teachings, she had a divine revelation in which "she saw the Lord Jesus Christ in his glory."[20] She went on to make a bold claim:

> Jesus revealed to her that *she* was his anointed successor on earth. He told her she must carry his Truth to the world and promised her divine protection. Henceforth, she was to be the incarnation of the word of God, the second coming of *Christ as a woman*.[21]

The above two illustrations suggest, at least, that Isaiah Shembe and his successors share similar experiences with others in religious history and that to arrive at a state of apotheosis is not uncommon, nor is it limited to certain cultures.

My conclusions regarding mediation in prayers are based on two theories used in this study. The first is Shorter's taxonomy of symmetrical prayer where mediators act reciprocally between the Supreme Being and people,[22] which is evident in worship and prayer in the amaNazaretha Church. Shembe's mediation is imperative in the light of God's transcendence and lack of direct involvement in the worship experience of the amaNazaretha.

The second is Hexham's work on the prayers of Isaiah Shembe,[23] which points to Shembe's mediatorial role. Shembe pleads his people's cause in the presence of God, not unlike the way Moses did in the Old Testament. Isaiah Shembe, thoroughly immersed in the Old Testament tradition and taking on the likeness of Moses as mediator, and also acting culturally in a kingship role (the Zulu king or chief), "links his nation with the supernatural forces" as Moses did for Israel.[24] Here Zulu tradition and Old Testament paradigms coalesce to produce a mediator who usurps the place and the work of Christ. Shembe in one sense parallels the position and work of Moses in the Old Testament. One example is the function of mediation. Exodus 20:18–21 reads:

> When the people saw the thunder and lightning and heard the trumpet and saw the mountain in smoke, they trembled with fear. They stayed at a distance and said to Moses, "Speak to us yourself and we will listen. But do not have God speak to us or we will die." Moses said to the people, "Do not be afraid. God has come

20. Ibid., 41.
21. Ibid., emphasis added.
22. Shorter, *Prayer in the Religious Traditions of Africa*.
23. Hexham, *The Scriptures of the AmaNazaretha of Ekuphakameni*.
24. Oosthuizen, "The Theology of Londa Shembe," 33.

to test you, so that the fear of the God will be with you to keep you from sinning." The people remained at a distance, while Moses approached the thick darkness where God was.

It is clear from the passage that Moses' sacerdotal and prophetic role between the people and God is established. God speaks through Moses to the people, and Moses approaches God on their behalf. Isaiah Shembe also functioned in a similar role, as we have noted in his prayers. He is also the giver of the law for the amaNazaretha when we consider the liturgical reading of morning and evening prayers and also the Sabbath liturgical. Shembe sets out the rules and regulations in accordance with the Ten Commandments and also the Levitical laws of the Old Testament to which the amaNazaretha Church must conform. In this respect Shembe is likened to the Moses in the Old Testament in the role of mediator and one who pronounces God's laws to the people.

Christians, however, pray in the name of Jesus. That Christ mediates the Christian's prayer is replete in scripture, especially in the Gospels. For example, in the Fourth Gospel Jesus invites his disciples to make requests in his name. Two clear references to asking "in my name" in John's Gospel are John 14:13–14, where Jesus says, "Whatever you ask in my name, that I will do, that the Father may be glorified in the Son. If you ask anything in My name, I will do it" (NKJV), and John 16:24, where Jesus says, "Until now you have asked nothing in My name. Ask, and you will receive, that your joy may be full" (NKJV). Leon Morris, commenting on the importance of prayer "in Jesus' name," says that the name of Jesus should not be used as a mere formula.[25] He adds:

> It is prayer proceeding from faith in Christ, prayer that gives expression to a unity with all that Christ stands for, prayer which seeks to set forward Christ Himself. . . . We should not overlook the importance of the fact that Christ says He Himself will answer prayer.[26]

The older manuscripts citing v. 14 as "if you shall ask [*me*] anything in my name . . ." suggest that Jesus was specific that prayer should be made in his name and, further, that he himself will answer.[27]

In the second verse (John 16:24), the question of Christ's mediation comes to the fore as Jesus reminds his disciples that in the pre-Resurrection era they either asked Jesus or the Father directly. Now Jesus, in the post-

---

25. Morris, *The Gospel According to John*, 646–47.
26. Ibid., 646.
27. Ibid., 647.

Resurrection era, affirms that Christians are at liberty to ask anything of the Father. However, this asking is through the Son.[28] Jesus' finished work (his death, resurrection, and ascension to the Father) qualifies him as mediator.

In the Christian understanding of the words and works of Jesus in regards to prayer, it is Christ who mediates between people and God. The Christian belief in one mediator thus precludes all other mediators. Therefore, praying "in the name of Shembe" disqualifies the amaNazaretha prayers as being part of the Christian tradition. This aspect of the amaNazaretha Church's beliefs and practices places them outside of orthodox Christianity.

Healing

When the questions were raised, "Who is a more powerful healer, Shembe or Christ? When you or a member of your family is ill, whom do you go to for healing?" both ministers and members overwhelmingly responded that Shembe heals, and when calamity strikes they call on Shembe.

In a conversation with an elderly woman in a rural amaNazaretha congregation, I raised the question about healing by telling the story of Jesus healing the blind man in the miracle recorded in John 9.[29] John reports in specific detail the means by which Jesus heals the blind man and also comments on the man's faith when Jesus commands him to go and wash in the pool of Siloam. Morris, in his commentary, notes that in curing the man, "He chooses to do this by making clay of His spittle, putting it on the man's eyes and bidding him wash it off. Questions arise, like 'Why clay?' 'Why spittle?' 'Why wash in Siloam?'"[30] In the ancient world it is known that curative powers were attributed to saliva.[31] While the man's faith may have been enhanced by this act, it was Jesus who healed him by this method, although he was not confined to it.

The interviewee responded by saying that, for her, it is Shembe who heals. She went on to describe Shembe's way of procuring healing. Shembe said, "God bless you," and then gave her Vaseline and water. She explained that Shembe places his finger in the bottle of Vaseline, and when she applies the Vaseline to her body, she is healed. The woman said she had

---

28. Ibid., 708.

29. Verses 6–7 read as follows: "Having said this, he [Jesus] spit on the ground, made some mud with the saliva, and put it on the man's eyes. 'Go,' he told him, 'wash in the Pool of Siloam' (this word means Sent). So the man went and washed, and came home seeing."

30. Morris, *The Gospel According to John*, 480.

31. Ibid.

suffered from abdominal problems for some time, and when she had drunk the water that Shembe gave her, she was relieved of her illness. She went on to say that when she prayed in the name of Shembe, she would also experience healing. When the question was raised as to why she did not pray directly to God, she responded, "Only Shembe knows God."

Another story that suggests healing powers are transferred from the founding leader, Isaiah Shembe, to his successors is evident in the testimony told by one minister in the church. He claimed that he had died in a train accident and his body was sent to the local hospital mortuary. However, the mortuary could not accommodate more bodies, and so the corpse was left overnight on a gurney. The minister said the following:

> In September 1, 1973, there was a train accident at Mondani. I died at nine o'clock in the morning. At three o'clock in the afternoon the next day, J. G. Shembe came and woke me up. Shembe said to me, "I want you to go back to your physical life because I want you to be a minister." There was a paper written that I was dead [death certificate]. Even the newspaper reported that I was dead. When J. G. Shembe came he was carrying the book and opened it. He read from the book my name. I then woke up in my physical body. (MR:2)

This miracle testimony given by the minister took place in the tenure of J. G. Shembe, the immediate successor to Isaiah Shembe. When asked how Vimbeni Shembe heals, the minister responded that Vimbeni Shembe uses the words "God bless you," and said that he sometimes uses Vaseline and water. The minister explained that Vaseline was also used in Bible times. He referred me to the book of James where we are encouraged to anoint the sick with oil.[32] The minister believed that healing in Shembe's name was possible because it is Shembe who communicates with God on behalf of people.

In the light of God's transcendence and in a sense, to the Zulu amaNazaretha adherent, his absence, it becomes clear why . . .

> God is in the background while Shembe himself takes precedence, maintaining that the Zulus were once told of a God who cannot see. . . . "But Isaiah Shembe showed you a God who walks on feet and who heals with his hands, and who can be known by men, a God who loves and who has compassion." Isaiah Shembe brought the distant God into their midst.[33]

---

32. James 5:14 reads, "Is any one of you sick? He should call the elders of the church to pray over him and anoint him with oil in the name of the Lord."

33. Oosthuizen, "Isaiah Shembe and the Zulu Worldview," 7.

Based on the above testimonies and research findings, it is Shembe who mediates healing for the amaNazaretha follower. Jesus plays no part in the healing rituals in the church. The amaNazaretha believe that the power to heal invested in Isaiah Shembe now resides in the present leader, Vimbeni Shembe. The use of water, Vaseline, and other aids such as soap are a carryover from Zulu traditional and cultural beliefs fused with biblical methods of healing, such as Jesus' miraculous healing of the blind man in John 9.

Sabbath Services

During field research I observed the amaNazaretha Church worship services convened at the church's epicenter, Ebuhleni, in the province of KwaZulu-Natal. Sermons were recorded, and the hymns sung in the services were noted. These observations assisted in bringing the amaNazaretha adherents' beliefs (as articulated in interviews) and practices (what they did in their services) into one consistent whole.

Hymns and Sermons

It was anticipated that the hymns that were recorded at the amaNazaretha Church Sabbath services would tell more about the role of Jesus Christ in the church and especially in the worship experience of the members. However, all of the hymns sung during my visits to the Sabbath services did not relate to the person and work of Christ. Rather, they related more to the consciousness of the members regarding Isaiah Shembe, his work, and the reasons for gathering at Ekuphakameni. Ancestors also featured in many of the hymns. For example, in Hymn 184, Isaiah Shembe states the following:

> They have been called out of their graves;
> They are already out, we have seen them,
> They have entered the holy city
> May Jehova be praised.[34]

This one stanza refers to the ancestors who are invited to join the living community at the amaNazaretha worship center. Isaiah Shembe is present as head and leader of both the living-dead and the worshippers.[35]

From analysis of the sermons, the following conclusions were drawn. First, the content of the sermons reveals that ethical issues, Sabbath ob-

---

34. Shembe, *Izihlabelelo ZamaNazaretha*, 184.
35. Oosthuizen, "The Theology of Londa Shembe," 35.

servances, and motivation for upright and exemplary living dominate the preachers' messages. Stories relating to the deeds of Isaiah Shembe, J. G. Shembe, and Amos Shembe are introduced into the sermon content even though the text bears no relevance to such stories. On some occasions, a biblical text was not used at any time in the sermon delivery. I noted that stories relating to Isaiah Shembe dominated the sermons more than any other topic.

In this regard my observation was that Shembe became the primary source of the sermon exposition, and the biblical text took second place. Thus, in the amaNazaretha Church, the words and deeds of Shembe (Isaiah, J. G., Amos, and Vimbeni) function as the enscripturated word. In other words, the words and works of Shembe are regarded as authoritative and form the narrative that preachers recall from memory. In speaking of memory as a moral exercise for Christian ethics, Stanley Hauerwas speaks of the coalescence of scripture and personal story. This kind of fusion of biblical and personal story is evident in the amaNazaretha preaching. Hauerwas contends the following:

> To remember, we require not only historical-critical skills, but examples of people whose lives have been formed by that memory. The authority of Scripture is mediated through the lives of the saints identified by our community as most representing what we are about.[36]

For the amaNazaretha Church, telling stories about Shembe motivates the believers to live after the example of their leaders, so much so that the person and work of Jesus Christ recede into the background. Evangelist Mpanza, in a group discussion, said that while the amaNazaretha accept the Old and the New Testament teachings, the Jews do not relate to the New Testament. Thus, if the amaNazaretha Church were to produce a third testament, it would not be accepted by the Christians. He believed that Shembe's words and works are authoritative beyond the Christian canon of scripture because Jesus promised that Shembe the Holy Spirit would follow him.

One of the theories used to evaluate Shembe's sermons is Loubser's "The Oral Christ of Shembe: Believing in Jesus in Oral and Literate Societies." Loubser argues for an implicit Christology operating in the amaNazaretha Church on the basis of his analysis of some sermons preached in the early 1990s. Loubser says, "The implicit soteriological significance of the founder-evangelist, Isaiah Shembe, becomes clear when

---

36. Hauerwas, *The Peaceable Kingdom*, 70.

considering the Christological language in which his deeds are narrated."[37] For example, among others, Loubser cites stories narrated in the Shembe preaching about Shembe's birth that resemble the birth of Jesus and John the Baptist.[38] In a similar vein, he shows how, through the sermons, Shembe's preachers fuse stories regarding Shembe's birth, early life, and calling with that of the biblical narratives of Christ. The result is that oral listeners see Shembe as the one who succeeds Jesus, or at best that both are equal. While Loubser is sympathetic in his evaluation of the amaNazaretha theology, he does raise open-ended questions regarding the role of Christ: "Does the Shembe Christ liberate man from sin by grace? Is He the ultimate statement of God's love, enabling humanity to live in hope, faith and love?"[39] Loubser does not, however, come to a firm conclusion regarding how salvation is effected in the amaNazaretha Church.

Based on observation and study of the sermons delivered by the amaNazaretha preachers and Vimbeni Shembe, foremost in the minds and hearts of the amaNazaretha congregants when they come to worship on the Sabbath is Shembe. Shembe's entrance into the worship arena, the "pillow ceremony," the hymns sung, and the sermon preached all center around Shembe's words and works. In the many occasions when I participated in the worship services, the name of Jesus Christ was rarely mentioned. In such a setting the mediatorial role of Shembe cannot be missed when one participates in the Sabbath worship.

Shembe the Forgiver of Sins

The research findings delineated in ch. 5 demonstrate that the amaNazaretha adherents enjoy a reciprocal relationship with the living-dead, their ancestors. Respondents (67 of 68) believed that their ancestors call on the living when they, the ancestors, are in need. One reason that obligated the living to respond to their ancestors' needs was that until the ancestors received assistance from the living, the ancestors were rendered helpless to intervene in the affairs of the living. Interviewees stated that since the ancestors were in "jail," the living should endeavor to extricate them from such a position. The process by which this liberation was achieved was that the living relative approached Shembe with an offering, *nikela*, and Shembe would then free the ancestor. Some respondents stated that they also had the option to purchase a "release ticket" from the church office.

---

37. Loubser, "The Oral Christ of Shembe," 72.
38. Ibid.
39. Ibid., 77.

When the ticket was presented to Shembe, he would order the release of the ancestor. The concept of "jail" is likened to the Roman Catholic doctrine of purgatory in medieval times. Kuiper says the following:

> According to the Church at that time and the Roman Catholic Church today, purgatory is a place to which those who are to enter heaven are assigned for a period of cleansing by fire before they are fit for entrance. The more faithfully the believer went through the rites and ceremonies on earth, the shorter would be his time of suffering in purgatory.[40]

For the amaNazaretha member there are several reasons why one's ancestor would be confined to purgatory, as my research findings show. Because the ancestor was unable to make restitution for the wrongs committed while on earth, he or she has the option to call on the living to assist by making a payment of money for his or her release. In the Roman Catholic Church in medieval times, such practice, the purchase of a papal ticket, an indulgence, was common.[41]

A close study of the system as is operative in the amaNazaretha Church shows that Shembe possesses power and authority to forgive sins of the dead. It was earlier stated that Shembe is considered to be above the ancestors in the Zulu hierarchical structure of divinities. If Shembe has the power to forgive sins of the dead, my research has shown that according to the majority of interviewees, he also has the power to forgive sins of the living. Most interviewees, as the data indicates, also believed that since Shembe has the power to forgive sins, he himself does not possess sin. Some interviewees suggested that Shembe perhaps did have sin before he became the leader of the church. It is at this point that members of the amaNazaretha Church would view Shembe as apotheosized.[42] From a biblical perspective Christians believe it is only through the death and resurrection of Jesus Christ and one's belief in the finished work of Christ that one receives salvation. Hence, in Shembe Christology, while the amaNazaretha accept the incarnation of Christ, there is "complete absence of any theology of the cross."[43] Thus, Shembe functions as mediator of salvation for the amaNazaretha.

---

40. Kuiper, *The Church in History*, 158.
41. Ibid., 159.
42. This is the error that says that a person can be deified, becoming God.
43. Loubser, "The Oral Christ of Shembe," 78.

Mediation: Ancestors or Christ?

A study of the literature (ch. 1) on the status and role of ancestors in the Zulu cosmological structure shows that ancestors are intimately connected to the everyday lives of their living descendants. This connection also became evident from the results of interviews and participant observation (chs. 5 and 6), where it was again confirmed that ancestors do occupy a strategic place in the lives of the amaNazaretha, both in their cultural and religious beliefs and practices. Stated earlier is the fact that illness in the Zulu context cannot be defined too narrowly. In African culture generally and Zulu culture specifically, illness may be defined as the result of "a disturbance of the balance between man [humans] and spiritual or mystical forces."[44] The goal in such instances "is to restore the equilibrium."[45] One recourse for the living is that they may approach the ancestors, who both diagnose the problem and offer treatment toward a solution. Buhrmann confirms what interviewees articulated when he states the following:

> To restore this balance, communication and communion with the Ancestors through the performance of rites, rituals, ceremonies and sacrifices are required. There is a large variety of such rites forming a complicated fabric of behavior, such as purification to protect against evil, ritual dances to stimulate body function and to invoke the participation of the Ancestors in their healing procedures.[46]

In describing ancestors Buhrmann further articulates the sentiments expressed by many of the amaNazaretha who were interviewed:

> The Ancestors, the deceased forebears . . . are experienced as not visible, but very human and living with their kind in and around the homestead. The relationship is natural and usually friendly. They can feel cold, hungry, neglected, annoyed and happy. They are conceived of as being omnipresent and nearly omniscient and they normally function as wise guides and protectors, but when annoyed their roles can be reversed and they may either expose one to the power of witches or themselves cause all kinds of illness and misfortune.[47]

---

44. Buhrmann, "Religion and Healing," 30.
45. Ibid.
46. Ibid.
47. Ibid.

When illness and disturbances do not receive any positive results from ancestors, the living relatives consult traditional healers and diviners (*sangomas*) for assistance. In the Zulu tradition *sangomas* are believed to possess the necessary power to approach the ancestors to diagnose the patient's problem and prescribe the necessary treatment to alleviate the problem of their patients.[48]

Research in August 2002 revealed that one of J. G. Shembe's daughters assists people who need communication with their ancestors when their own efforts in that direction have proved futile. Through a friend of Shembe's daughter, I secured an appointment to visit her home, a few miles away from Ebuhleni. Upon arrival visitors were requested to remove our shoes and wait for her. After two hours she emerged from her dwelling and proceeded to a hut especially prepared for receiving people who needed her assistance. The hut was sparsely furnished, with a grass mat on the floor. However, in the hut a grass chair,[49] similar to the one Shembe occupies during the Sabbath service at Ebuhleni, was conspicuously placed. My inquiry revealed that it was there representing the presence of Isaiah Shembe.

Joseph told me that her main function was to invoke the spirits of one's ancestors, and through them she would make prophetic utterances regarding the past, present, and future status of the individual. A man and two women had come to solicit her help. She appeared to fall into a trancelike state and seemed to be outside of her body, communicating with the spirits of the person's ancestors. In the trance she spoke in different voices, perhaps the voices of the ancestors. Some fifteen minutes later she returned to her normal state and advised the person according to her communication with the ancestral spirits. Joseph was next in line to receive her attention. According to Joseph she had told him about some of the situations he was facing at that time. For example, he was intending to take a second wife and was told that the woman he intended taking was not the right person for him. She also told Joseph that the ancestors had inquired about the motor vehicle they had given him. Joseph told her that the vehicle had broken down. She told Joseph that an ancestor needed his help; therefore, he had to buy a white gown and a baptismal certificate for the ancestor so that the ancestor could join the church. Only when Joseph fulfilled the ancestor's request would he be in a position to assist him.

---

48. Ibid., 31.

49. This chair represents the presence of the ancestor who aids the diviner in her work.

Joseph later informed me that apart from foretelling, one of the duties Shembe's sister performed was to cleanse the ancestors[50] so that they could be of benefit to their living descendants. This ceremony is carried out through the payment of a sum of money and a ritual that frees the ancestor from an undesirable state to a position of acceptability among the ancestors. It was later stated by some ministers that this woman functioned as a *sangoma*,[51] and that both the office and the practice are forbidden by the church.[52]

While it is true that the church forbids its members from visiting the *sangoma*, they have indeed replaced the traditional *sangoma* with a functional substitute,[53] Shembe. It is Shembe who now mediates members' needs by approaching the ancestors on their behalf. In this regard, Whiteman's study of "form and meaning" is helpful. He reminds us that "cultural forms are important because of the meaning they convey, and not because there is any intrinsic value in them."[54]

While it is important to bear in mind Hiebert's caution that in a cross-cultural setting "the purpose is to understand old ways not judge them" through phenomenological study of the forms used in Zulu tradition and their attendant meaning,[55] it is Whiteman who cogently characterizes the nature of form and meaning. He says:

> One of the most important areas of culture that contributes to the problem of cross-cultural communication is the relationship between cultural forms and the meanings they convey. Cultural forms are the obvious, observable and audible parts of culture such

---

50. The term *cleanse* refers to the purification rite performed by the family through the living Shembe. The rite releases the ancestor from "jail" or an undesirable place and reunites the ancestor with the company of the living-dead.

51. A *sangoma* is a diviner-healer in the Zulu tradition in South Africa. The *sangoma* derives his or her power from an ancestor and functions as an ancestral spirit. In a consultation the ancestral spirit of the patient speaks through the *sangoma*'s mouth as if the ancestor were present. The ancestral spirit reveals, among other things, imminent death, sickness, the failure to keep vows, and abrogation of taboos.

52. My research assistant, Joseph Mhlongo, reported that this woman claimed to possess the spirit of Isaiah Shembe's mother. This belief is in keeping with the calling or authentication of a *sangoma*, that she or he possesses the spirit of one's ancestor. Joseph also told me that any member of the church who visited the *sangoma* for spiritual assistance, if found out, would have to pay a penalty and be cleansed before engaging in any spiritual activity in the church.

53. See Nida, *Message and Mission*, 25–27, for examples of functional substitutes in the early church.

54. Whiteman, *Melanesians and Missionaries*, 435.

55. Hiebert, *Anthropological Reflections*, 89.

as material artifacts, behavior, ceremonies, words, etc. and they are always culture specific. That is, they do not convey any universal meaning, but are related to a specific meaning which is determined by the cultural context in which they are employed.[56]

While displaying zest for and commitment to the Old Testament biblical faith and Jewish practices, the amaNazaretha have not totally abandoned Zulu cultural beliefs and practices. This holding on to Zulu beliefs is evident in that they have identified a functional substitute for the office of the *sangoma*. Interviews and participant observation reveal that the amaNazaretha, in the absence of the *sangoma*, appeal to Vimbeni Shembe, believing that he possesses power to influence the decisions made by ancestors on behalf of the congregants. They have substituted a new *form* but retained the old *meaning*. Kraft states by way of two diagrams that a form may have a variety of meanings and also that there may be a variety of forms attached to one single meaning:[57]

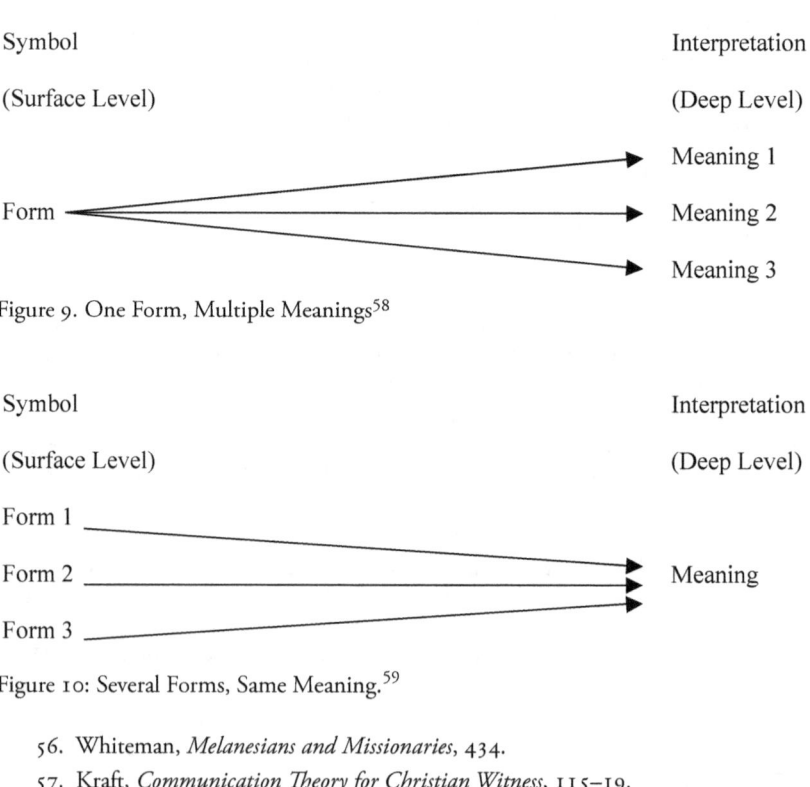

Figure 9. One Form, Multiple Meanings[58]

Figure 10: Several Forms, Same Meaning.[59]

56. Whiteman, *Melanesians and Missionaries*, 434.
57. Kraft, *Communication Theory for Christian Witness*, 115–19.
58. Ibid., 117
59. Ibid.

Theology and Christology in the amaNazaretha Church

It is evident that the amaNazaretha, in making a conscious move away from Zulu traditional religion, resist the temptation of visiting the *sangoma* (the old form) and now appeal to Shembe (the new form) as one who mediates between the living and the ancestors. Nida suggests that change in religion may be experienced in four ways: "deletion, addition, substitution, and coalescence."[60] He argues that "more often than not, change in religion means some form of substitution, a combination of addition and deletion" that results in coalescence rather than mere addition or substitution.[61] Nida's argument fits the case of the amaNazaretha's move away from the *sangoma* yet gravitating to Shembe, who fills the old function. Nevertheless, the meaning has not changed in that ancestors are still central in the existential life of the amaNazaretha.

Since we know that for the African all of life's activities are viewed through religious eyes, so much so that "religion penetrates and propels all of life,"[62] the traditional Zulu customs and biblical (Old Testament) beliefs coalesce to the point that even after almost one hundred years the amaNazaretha do not differentiate between the religious and the secular cultural dynamics. The Zulu worldview with the ancestor as central takes precedence over Christian teaching regarding mediation, and thus the person and work of Christ is diminished, if not overlooked altogether.

The strategic role that ancestors have in the Zulu worldview and the amaNazaretha Church harks back to the belief in "life force," as has been explained earlier in chs. 2 and 4. The "life force" or power that animates and perpetuates life for both the individual and the community is derived from the ancestor.[63] Thus, ancestors in their mediatorial role are indispensable in the religiocultural life of the amaNazaretha adherents. This fact becomes evident when, in the diminishing of "vital force" and in the experience of illness, misfortune, or even death, Zulus believe that such loss is attributed to the ancestor who has withheld the flow of life power, and the living consequently become subject and vulnerable to the forces of evil.[64]

---

60. Nida, "New Religions for Old," 244.
61. Ibid., 245.
62. Wendland, "Traditional Central African Religion," 19.
63. Beyerhaus, "The Christian Encounter," 79–80.
64. It should be noted that "vital force" or power, according to African traditionalists, may also be obtained through "magical practices" (Oosthuizen, "Isaiah Shembe and the Zulu Worldview," 5). According to Zahniser, "Magic consists of symbolic and ritual procedures designed to control and manipulate real, imaginary, or symbolic powers. These powers become the sources of benefit and guidance when it comes to the intimate issues of life. They take the place God wants to occupy, and that is idolatry" (*Symbol and Ceremony*, 172).

The neglected ancestors have to be appeased through ritual sacrificial offerings before the living experience a reversal in their situation.[65]

The above narrative of the persons who approached Shembe's sister, the *sangoma*, argues for the entrenched belief that ancestors are the key to survival of the living in a hostile world and, consequently, they must be involved in the affairs of the living. While the amaNazaretha believe that God exists, "God is somehow far away and yet near, and the only real link is vouchsafed through the ancestors in an eternally active life-principle."[66] Therefore, it is the ancestor and not Jesus Christ who serves as a link or mediates between the living and God.

Several prayers offer a clue as to the function and role of ancestors in the religious life of amaNazaretha members. The prayers I recorded were spontaneous, and they expressed the everyday life situations that people were experiencing at the time. Heiler differentiates between what he calls "primary" and "secondary" prayers. The former refers to prayers that are spontaneous, and the latter to prayers that are more formal.[67] Primary-type prayers are "closer to the real life experience of individuals," and they reveal the heartfelt desires and emotions of the worshipper.[68]

In terms of Shorter's typology,[69] research shows that amaNazaretha prayers are directed to God, the Supreme Being, but through ancestors or Shembe, thus interfacing with what Shorter calls "symmetrical mediation" (Fig. 5 above applies in this instance as well).

In this model ancestors are "distinct intermediaries, acting not only as vehicles for [humankind's] worship of the Supreme Being, but actually mediating [humankind's] experience of him and the gift of life itself."[70]

The question at this point in the discussion is "How does ancestral mediation affect the mediatorial role of Jesus Christ?" The universal scope of God's salvific work on behalf of a lost humanity is in and through Jesus Christ. It is central to the Christian faith. First Timothy 2:5–6 reads, "For there is one God and one mediator between God and men, the man Christ Jesus, who gave himself as a ransom. . . ." In his discussion of these verses, Gordon D. Fee discerns three fundamental tenets of the Christian faith as being "the unity of God, Christ as mediator, and Christ's death as securing

---

65. Beyerhaus, "The Christian Encounter," 82.
66. Oosthuizen, "Isaiah Shembe and the Zulu Worldview," 7.
67. Heiler, *Prayer*, 3.
68. Shorter, *Prayer in the Religious Traditions of Africa*, 9.
69. See ch. 1 above for his typology.
70. Shorter, *Prayer*, 11.

redemption."[71] The following discussion aims to show how these three aspects (unity of God, Christ as mediator, and Christ's death as redemption) are understood or feature in the amaNazaretha beliefs and practices.

First, my research reveals that traditional Zulus believe in the existence of a Supreme Being followed by lesser intermediaries, and not least among them are ancestors. The religiocultural belief in the role of ancestors is carried over when traditional Zulus join the amaNazaretha Church. The amaNazaretha, who place greater emphasis on the teachings of the Old Testament rather than the New Testament, believe that the God of the Old Testament is *the one* and *only* God, yet transcendent and removed from the existential daily lives of people. Their belief in the one God is reflected in the Sabbath liturgy, the hymns, and the sermons. The amaNazaretha hold to a theology that is *theocentric*—that the God of the Old Testament is still their God, and thus there exists only one God who is God of the universe and all people. However, access to the Supreme Being comes through ancestors. Consequently, the person and work of Christ has little meaning for them.

The early Christians also had to live with the tension regarding their identity as monotheistic Jews and followers of Christ at the same time. Bosch argues that in the immediate post-Resurrection era believers in Christ "had not yet understood themselves as being members of a separate religion over against Judaism but primarily as a renewal movement within it."[72] Thus, Matthew, in his Gospel, while affirming continuity with the Old Testament—that the God of the Old Testament is still the God of the New Testament—is also careful to show that Jesus is Lord and the promised Messiah, God's final revelation to humankind. Matthew does so through the various allusions and quotations he uses from the Old Testament to sustain his argument of both promise and fulfillment.

Study of the amaNazaretha Church shows that members have not moved beyond the Old Testament in their beliefs and practices. Although they do appropriate Old Testament prophecies and promises, their interpretations are not consistent with orthodoxy. One interviewee, evangelist Mpanza, speaking on the issue of the religious beliefs of the amaNazaretha Church, said, "[In] the Nazarite Baptist Church, Isaiah Shembe took the laws of God as they are found in the Old Testament, and he took the ethical teachings of the New Testament, and then he coupled these with the customs, African customs, and he made it one thing" (RF1: August 2002). He went on to say that the amaNazaretha believe on the teachings of Jesus

---

71. Fee, *1 and 2 Timothy, Titus*, 65.
72. Bosch, *Transforming Mission*, 58.

Christ, but qualified his statement by referring to Christ's teachings on love, honesty, and humility (RF1: August 2002). Evangelist Mpanza went on to affirm that the Old Testament Jewish practices were not foreign to Zulu culture. He offered examples such as animal sacrifices, purification rites, and rituals regarding the dead (RF1: August, 2002).

Second, my research shows that Christ's mediatorial role in the amaNazaretha Church's beliefs and practices is mitigated in the light of the prominent role of ancestors as mediators. The Christian scriptures declare unequivocally that "there is a single mediator between God and humankind."[73] Lea asserts the following in his commentary on 1 Timothy 2:5:

> As the God-man, Christ is uniquely qualified to serve as a go-between who can bring sinful people into God's family. The reference to Jesus as the one mediator between God and humanity rules out any understanding that angels (Dan. 6:22; Gal. 3:19) served as mediators. It also excludes the Gnostic idea that intermediary deities stand between God and humanity.[74]

The writer of the Epistle, in asserting that "the one God has provided one mediator between himself and humans who is himself human, namely Christ Jesus,"[75] also emphasizes that the one mediator excludes all other mediators. In the early church it is likely that both angels and other intermediaries were believed to stand between God and humans[76]

Third, on the basis of the Christian belief in the scriptures, tradition, and experience, Christ's mediatorial function becomes a reality for Christians in terms of his atoning work (1 Tim 2:6), intercession, and future return. My research has shown that ancestors, not Jesus Christ, mediate between the amaNazaretha and the Supreme Being. The question of Christ's salvific work, his death, resurrection, ascension, and return has no consequence for the amaNazaretha.

The Status and Role of Christ in the amaNazaretha Church

The taxonomy used to interpret the data regarding the status and role of Christ in the amaNazaretha Church is Nyamiti's *Christ as our Ancestor*. In this work, Nyamiti demonstrates how ancestors may be incorporated

---

73. Lea and Griffin, *1, 2 Timothy, Titus*, 90
74. Ibid.
75. Knight, *Commentary on the Pastoral Epistles*, 121.
76. Lea and Griffin, *1, 2 Timothy, Titus*, 90.

into the existential life of Africans without obfuscating the person and work of Christ. Nyamiti goes at length to show that Christ supersedes ancestors, thus becoming "brother" to Christians. He clearly defines the differences between the African ancestor and Christ as brother-ancestor. Nyamiti explains:

> A far more profound difference lies in the fact that Christ is God-man. For it is in virtue of His hypostatic union that He has been established as our Brother and Mediator. The implication is that His Brotherhood to us is rooted not only in consanguineous ties but in the mystery of the Trinity itself. As such it transcends not only family, clanic, or racial boundaries, but any consanguineous limitations whatsoever. This means that thanks to His theandric condition Christ is potentially the Brother and Mediator of any human being whether he be of Adamite origin or not.[77]

Nyamiti shows how Christ may be related to the ancestor, but goes further to show the major theological difference when he juxtaposes the divinity of Christ with his humanity. Nyamiti is also careful to point, to the perichoresis, that the interpenetration of the three members of the Trinity with each other is unique to Christian theology. However, this kind of interpenetration may also be the pattern for human relationships with ancestors.

While Nyamiti's work is helpful in moving people beyond ancestor dependence, or accommodating ancestors in the cultural ethos of African tradition and thus positioning Jesus Christ above them, research has shown that since the amaNazaretha espouse a low Christology, much work has to be done to move them to the place where they would continue to appreciate the role of ancestors yet make room for the person and work of Jesus Christ as sole mediator.

On another front, the popular bumper sticker "Shembe Is the Way" raised the question as to what the sticker meant to amaNazaretha adherents. Most respondents believed that "Shembe is the way to heaven." When the question was posed to Vimbeni Shembe himself, he responded, "Shembe is the way insofar as Jesus said, 'I am the way and the truth. Nobody sees my Father but through me because my Father is in me and I in Him.'"[78] Some respondents went so far as to explain that, in their understanding,

---

77. Nyamiti, *Christ as Our Ancestor*, 21.

78. It is evident that biblical texts are quoted here to indicate that *Shembe* is the way for the amaNazaretha just as Jesus is the way for the Christian.

believing in Shembe will take them to heaven, while others said following Shembe and obeying him would take them to heaven.

The responses to this question indicate that for the amaNazaretha, salvation is mediated by Shembe, and that the finished work of Jesus has no effect today as he lived at a point in time and history for a particular people. Matthew's confession (Matt 16:13–16) that Jesus is the Christ the Son of the living God, a pre-Resurrection confession, and Paul's hymn in Phil 2:5–11, a post-Resurrection affirmation of the finished work of Christ, compel the Christian to consider the life, death, and resurrection of Jesus in order to appropriate salvation, past, present, and future. His past work, present intercession on the believer's behalf, and future coming are considered by the Christian to be necessary for salvation. Research also shows that the amaNazaretha may subscribe to some aspects of Christ's life and times without acknowledging that he is God's final revelation.

Summary

In the final chapter, I offer some missiological implications where I will discuss the two main theories that undergird this study, namely, Hiebert's Bounded and Centered Sets model and Turner's Four-Part Classification of AICs. I will conclude with a response to the main research question: *A Christward movement is one that recognizes that "Jesus is Lord." The amaNazaretha Church could be considered a Christward movement if it affirms, "Jesus is Lord" in the sense that adherents of the Christian faith acknowledge and receive the person and work of Christ on the basis of the past (his work of atonement), present (his mediatorial role and intercession on our behalf), and future (his second coming in glory as our hope).*

I will finally offer some suggestions for how the amaNazaretha Church, after almost one hundred years of existence, may be brought back to orthodox Christianity.

8

Conclusions, Missiological Implications, and Suggestions for Further Study

THIS CHAPTER BRINGS THIS study to a close with some conclusions based on the three main theories that were used to interpret the data from interviews and participant observation. Some missiological implications that derive from the study are offered as generalized principles for missiology. I conclude by suggesting some areas for further research that were beyond the scope of this dissertation.

Conclusions: Shembe, Ancestors, or Christ?

I return to the purpose of this study, namely, that my intention was to discover if the amaNazaretha Church is a Christward movement. I defined a Christward movement as one that recognizes that "Jesus is Lord." I argued throughout this study that the amaNazaretha Church could be considered a Christward movement *if* it affirms, "Jesus is Lord" in the sense that adherents of the Christian faith acknowledge and receive the person and work of Christ on the basis of the past (his work of atonement), present (his mediatorial role and intercession on our behalf), and future (his second coming in glory as our hope). Specifically, we considered the mediatorial role of Christ in the lives of the amaNazaretha from three perspectives: (1) Christ's work of atonement as one who forgives our sins through his finished work on the cross and thus reconciles us with the Father; (2) his work as healer; and (3) his intercession on our behalf in our prayers.

I have thus far shown through my field research with interviews and participant observation that Shembe and ancestors occupy a more dominant role than Jesus Christ, both in the everyday lives of the amaNazaretha people and in their religious activities and observances. This finding brings me to the place where I now apply my theoretical framework to interpret the data and demonstrate that the amaNazaretha espouse a low Christology in their beliefs and practices and therefore do not qualify as a Christward movement.

Hiebert's "Bounded and Centered Sets" Theory

The first of the three main theories is Hiebert's "Bounded and Centered Sets" theory as depicted in Figure 1 below:

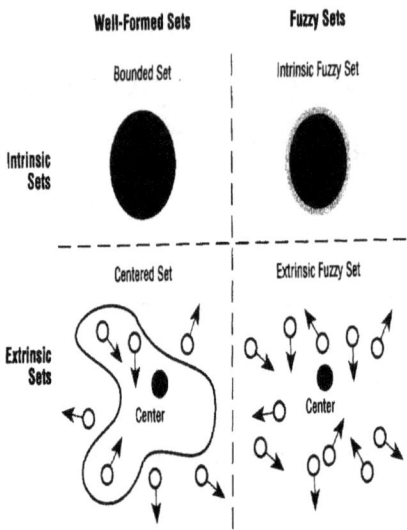

Figure 1. A Typology of Sets.[1]

Chapter 1 discussed Hiebert's taxonomy of Intrinsic Bounded Sets as those that "are formed on the basis of the essential nature of the members themselves—on what they are in and of themselves.... They are all uniform in character."[2] According to Hiebert, the Christian in the category of Bounded Set is determined on the basis of the characteristics that go to make up what is Christian. To be Christian is determined by both orthodoxy (right beliefs) and orthopraxis (right practices). Further, by viewing the Christian category of the Bounded Set, one can draw a sharp distinction between Christians and people of other faiths. If Christianity is perceived as a Bounded Set, the boundary determines where the person is in terms of her or his Christian faith. The boundary separates a Christian from one who is *not* a Christian. The Bounded Set also suggests that all Christians within the set will be considered as equal, irrespective of age differences or the length of time one is part of the Christian tradition. In other words, no distinction is made between experienced Christians and those who are

---

1. Hiebert, *Anthropological Reflections*, 112
2. Ibid, 110.

relatively new to the faith.[3] The critical point in this set is that "conversion is seen as a single, dramatic crossing the boundary between being a non-Christian and being a Christian."[4] Conversion to the Christian faith is discerned by one's faith in Jesus Christ both in word and deed, which the new convert has appropriated. The Bounded Set approach is too restrictive in that it does not allow for conversion to be experienced as a process as one gains maturity in Christian beliefs and practices. It assumes that when one comes to conversion as in the category of the Bounded Set, one is fully Christian immediately in the sense that one has been converted, discipled, and matured as a Christian all at the same time.

The Extrinsic Centered Set is defined by its center and the relationship of people to that center, as the diagram shows. What is critical in the Centered Set is that people "related to the center belong to the set and those not related to the center do not."[5] Hiebert's idea in this model is that, in the case of people who may or may not be considered Christian, the reference point is not the fixed boundary as in the Bounded Set, but it is the movement toward or away from the center. In other words, "Distant members can move toward the center, and those near it can slide back while still headed toward it."[6] However, there is still the boundary; it includes all of those who are making a conscious effort to move in a Christward direction. The conversion experience orients one in the direction of the set though one may not be close to the center. However, those moving away from the center place themselves outside of the boundary and thus are considered non-Christian.

Hiebert uses the language of sanctification to suggest that salvation is a process in which the new convert grows in faith daily.[7] The Centered Set model lends itself to the doctrine of sanctification, where one who has turned in a Christward direction through faith in Jesus Christ conforms (moves toward) more and more to the likeness of Christ every day. The Centered Set emphasizes relationships—how one relates to the center—more than mere cognitive assent and verbal articulation of Christian doctrine.

---

3. Ibid., 115.
4. Ibid.
5. Ibid., 123.
6. Ibid., 124.
7. Ibid., 116.

Sanctification has been interpreted in various ways in Christian history. John Wesley, in his significant contribution to Methodism, namely, the doctrine of Christian perfection, regarded this state as "'pure love reigning alone in the heart and life' and as a real possibility for every Christian who has first been justified by faith."[8] Justification comes by faith in Jesus Christ alone. Sanctification, or to use Wesleyan language, Christian perfection, is incipient in regeneration. It is a process throughout one's Christian journey, transforming the believers more each day to the likeness of Jesus Christ. In the Centered Set model, the new convert acknowledges that she or he has accepted the grace offered by none other than Christ.

In applying this taxonomy to the amaNazaretha Church, one has to ask the question, "Are amaNazaretha members moving *toward* the center because they acknowledge Jesus Christ as sole mediator between God and humankind, irrespective of how defective that knowledge may be articulated both in their beliefs and practices, or have they moved *away* from the center?" To be drawn to the center is to acknowledge Jesus Christ as Lord and God and as the center of one's life both in word and deed.

First, my research has shown that Vimbeni Shembe and the ancestors have displaced Jesus Christ in terms of his mediatorial work since the amaNazaretha members now call on Shembe and the ancestors in their prayers, and Shembe mediates healing to his congregation in the sense that while people believe that God ultimately heals, it is Shembe and not Jesus Christ who mediates between God and people.

Second, in the study of the amaNazaretha preaching, I discovered that the Old Testament was used more, and more centrally, than the New Testament, and that Shembe and his words and works are given greater prominence than Jesus Christ. Harold Turner,[9] from his experience studying the Church of the Lord (Aladura), concurs with Greenslade,[10] who suggested that a movement should be judged, whether it is a church or not, not by what it lacks but by what it possesses. In this regard he was referring to the primacy—both the acceptance and authority—of the Bible. Karl Barth[11] went further to suggest that the question is not just the acceptance or possession of and acknowledging the Bible as the law of the church's faith and order, but more important it is whether the church actually is a witness to Jesus Christ.

---

8. Harvey, *A Handbook of Theological Terms*, 178.
9. Turner, *Profiles Through Preaching*, 11.
10. Greenslade, *Schism in the Early Church*, 214–17.
11. Barth, *Church Dogmatics*, 753.

Conclusions, Missiological Implications, and Suggestions for Further Study

Harold Turner documented sermons preached in the Church of the Lord (Aladura) and came to the conclusion that the New Testament was quoted and used in the sermons more than Old Testament texts. The Gospels featured prominently, where the works and words of Jesus dominate. A comparative study was done concurrently with the Anglican Church in Nigeria, which showed a slightly higher ratio for the New Testament to that of the Church of the Lord. This comparison is made only to suggest that the amaNazaretha have not moved beyond the Old Testament teaching; consequently, Jesus Christ is not central in the beliefs and practices in the church. My research has shown that the words of Isaiah Shembe and his successors dominate the preaching in the church and are given equal status with the Bible.

In terms of Hiebert's model of the Centered Set, Isaiah Shembe, when he seceded from the Wesleyan and Baptist churches and gained his own following, was closer to the center, that is, the orthodox Christian faith, and thus in a Christward direction. However, with time he and his followers moved away from the center—in relation to Jesus Christ—making Shembe the new center. His successors, including Vimbeni Shembe, are accorded similar status to that of the founder. In my interview with Vimbeni Shembe, he stated, "We are not a Christian church, but we are a Nazarite Church." The above two examples, in the light of Hiebert's taxonomy, suggest that the amaNazaretha Church presently may not be considered a Christward movement, as Jesus Christ is not Lord of the church.

Harold Turner's New Religious Movements Typology

The second of the three theories I applied to interpret the data is Harold Turner's New Religious Movements typology.[12] The figure below represents the four categories thus: (a) Neo-primal, (b) Synthesist, (c) Hebraist, and (d) Independent Churches:[13]

---

12. Turner, "A Typology for African Religious Movements," 1–34.
13. I discussed Turner's classification earlier in ch. 4 in greater detail.

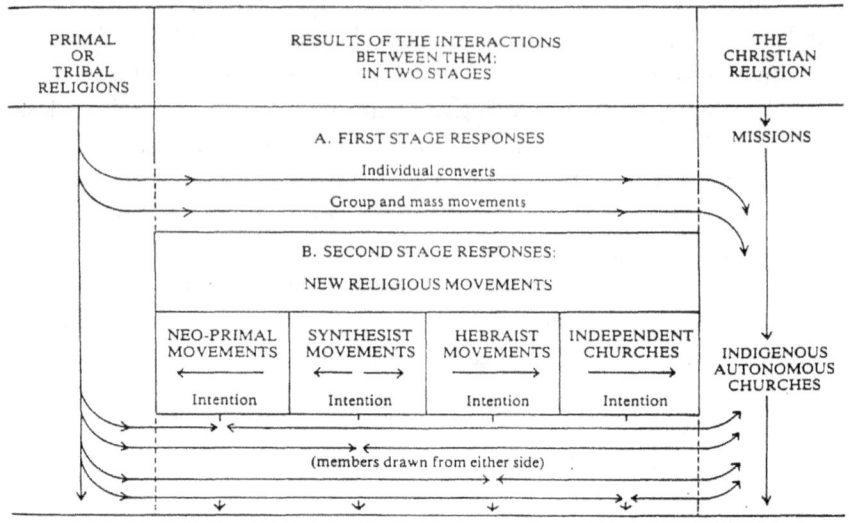

Figure 2. Four-Part Classification of African Independent Churches

People in neo-primal movements are those who, though opposed to Christianity, have rejected the traditional gods and spirits and have accepted the one Supreme God.

The next grouping, Synthesists, identifies with neither the traditionalists nor the Christian movement. They do, however, borrow from both these traditions and consequently constitute a new movement quite different from the original traditional form. Hebraists, on the other hand, make a conscious move away from traditional religions to the world of the Bible. This group places more importance on the Old Testament than the New. Since they reject Christianity, they consequently place very little importance on the New Testament. The last group is the Independent Churches. Having converted from traditional religions, they now follow the teachings of the Bible, both the Old and the New Testaments. According to Turner,

> They use the Scriptures, they make something central of Jesus Christ and especially of the Holy Spirit . . . . They may be described as having been founded in Africa by Africans for Africans to worship God in African ways and to meet African needs as Africans feel them.[14]

---

14. Turner, *Religious Movements in Primal Societies*, 10–11.

Conclusions, Missiological Implications, and Suggestions for Further Study

In their use of the whole Bible, although pneumatology appears to be dominant, the words and works of Jesus Christ are not overlooked but in fact are central to their beliefs and practices.

In terms of Turner's taxonomy, my research suggests that the amaNazaretha most closely fit his Hebraist type, only in the light of their strict adherence to Old Testament teachings. My research findings described in ch. 5 and the participant observation discussed in ch. 6 show that the amaNazaretha Church, while moving away from Zulu Traditional Religion, has gravitated to the Old Testament. In the interview with Vimbeni Shembe, reported above, he affirmed that the amaNazaretha Church is not a Christian church but a Nazarite movement. In the interview with the "theologian" of the church, evangelist Mpanza, it was learned that the amaNazaretha Church is not Christian in that it is a combination of three religious systems: Zulu Traditional Religion and culture, the Old Testament teachings as observed by Jews, and the ethical teachings of the New Testament. Dominant in the religiocultural ethos of the amaNazaretha Church are the Old Testament Nazarite proscriptions and the Old Testament Jewish laws, particularly the Levitical laws and Sabbath prohibitions. In interviews, both members and ministers in the church explained their religious affiliation in response to the questions "How would you characterize your religious affiliation? Are the amaNazaretha Christian?" thusly:

1. "We are different from Christians. We follow our traditional customs and follow the rules of the Bible. Christians do not follow the rules, like shaving, wearing shoes, and the Sabbath." (MR:10)

2. "For example, we worship on the Sabbath as Jesus did. But the Christians do not follow that. Even the Zion Church is different from amaNazaretha." (MR:14)[15]

3. "The amaNazaretha is a combination of Judaism, Christianity, and traditional religion." (EV:1)

4. "The problem is that followers of Jesus do not worship on the Sabbath. They wear shoes when they go to church even though the Christians' principles from God deny that. Most of them shave. So the Christians are anti-practitioners [Christians do not

---

15. This minister went further than other respondents in that he not only discerned differences between Christians and the amaNazaretha, he also saw the amaNazaretha as different from the largest AIC in South Africa, namely, the Zion Christian Church with seven million members, a church that is considered to espouse orthodox Christian beliefs and practices in indigenous forms.

follow of the laws of God as prescribed in the Old Testament]." (YL:3)

5. "I respect Jesus. I am a Nazarite. But I am not a Christian. I do not follow him [Jesus]. I follow the rules as a Nazarite. I have never seen in the Bible where it says that followers of Christ were called Christians." (LP:1)

6. "The Messiah to them [Christians] is still Jesus Christ. We believe Jesus has sent another messiah. God has sent the next messiah, while the Christians are still waiting for the next messiah. We believe that the next messiah has come." (LP:31)

The above responses confirm that dominant in the beliefs and practices of the amaNazaretha are early Jewish teachings as found in the Old Testament. Turner's Hebraist typology fits closest to the amaNazaretha profile, where they have moved from Zulu Traditional Religion, yet they have not yet moved from the Old Testament to a New Testament position in terms of their beliefs and practices. From the review of the literature on this score, I learned how the amaNazaretha make the connection between the Old Testament and Zulu tradition. Oosthuizen, citing an interview with Londa Shembe, the son of J. G. Shembe and the grandson of Isaiah Shembe, wrote:

> He [Londa Shembe] firmly believed that his grandfather had a special place in the celestial sphere. For him, Isaiah Shembe was a messianic figure who had been a messiah to eight other people, before he was incarnated into the Zulu people.[16] Thus, Londa Shembe saw Isaiah Shembe as a global figure who was born into the Zulu nation at a special stage of their history to be their messiah . . . . Londa Shembe maintained that his grandfather, Isaiah Shembe, continued the essence of Jewish religion in his own teachings. He taught that the biblical prophet Jeremiah referred to the Zulu people, whom he believed were descended from the Jews.[17]

My field research, study of the literature, and the above statements attributed to Londa Shembe suggest that Turner's taxonomy of Hebraist movements places the amaNazaretha Church in this category, without even considering other aspects of the amaNazaretha beliefs and practices I discovered through my research. As is the case with those who espouse Judaism, the New Testament and its teaching on the person and work of

---

16. Sibisi, Shembe's aide, made this statement in an interview.
17. Oosthuizen, "The Theology of Londa Shembe," 24.

Conclusions, Missiological Implications, and Suggestions for Further Study

Christ bear little relevance for the amaNazaretha, except that it is their belief that Shembe replaced Jesus and it is he who promised Shembe's coming to the Zulu nation. Given this development, Turner's typology does not account for this third component in the amaNazaretha beliefs and practices, namely, that Shembe has replaced Christ. Consequently, I argue (later in the chapter) for a new typology that shows the amaNazaretha to be a post-Christian movement, thus going beyond Turner's Hebraist model but not in the direction of indigenous Christianity.

N. T. Wright: Christological Interpretation

For a theological and Christological interpretation of the data, I studied the writings of N. T. Wright. Wright's work *What Saint Paul Really Said* and his article "Paul's Gospel and Caesar's Empire" are two sources that I use to interpret the data and thus offer a response to the main research question, "Is the amaNazaretha Church a Christward movement?"

In his chapter "Herald of the King," Wright argues for Paul's use of the term *gospel* in the New Testament. Wright lifts two passages from Isaiah (40:9; 52:7) that predate Israel's return from exile to show the proleptic nature of the Old Testament passages as good news and the arrival of a herald who will vindicate Israel and liberate her from bondage. He argues that this Jewish background is the context for the New Testament understanding of the term *gospel*.[18] He says the following:

> When their God, YHWH, acted within history to deliver his people, the spurious gods of the heathen would be defeated. If and when YHWH set up his own king as true ruler, his true earthly representative, all other kingdoms would be confronted with their rightful overlord. . . . To announce that YHWH was king was to announce that Caesar was not. This was the "good news" that Isaiah's herald was called to proclaim.[19]

Isaiah's message is thus seen as a prolepsis. It is a message from God about God that relates to the message concerning his Son, and this message God imparted to the prophet. In other words, the gospel of the Old Testament anticipates the death and resurrection of Jesus Christ. In Wright's words,

18. Wright, *What Saint Paul Really Said*, 43. The passages in Isaiah read as follows: "Get you up to a high mountain, O Zion, herald of good tidings; lift up your voice with strength, O Jerusalem, herald of good tidings; lift it up; do not fear; say to the cities of Judah, 'Here is your God!'" (40:9 NKJV); "How beautiful upon the mountains are the feet of the messenger who announces peace, who brings good news, who announces salvation, who says to Zion, 'Your God reigns'" (52:7 NKJV).

19. Ibid., 44.

"Jesus, the crucified and risen Messiah, is Lord."[20] This was the fulfilled promise that God gave through Abraham for all the nations of the world, that evil will be finally eradicated. The promise reaches its climax when Paul says in Galatians 6:15 that "Neither circumcision or uncircumcision means anything; what counts is a new creation." The fact of a new creation and Christ's role in it is again affirmed by Paul in 2 Corinthians 5:17: "Therefore, if anyone is in Christ, he is a new creation; the old has gone, the new has come!" It is in Christ that humankind undergoes a radical transformation resulting in an entirely new person.

Wright argues that the prophetic utterances in the Old Testament, in this instance the Isaianic servant songs passages, had a futuristic event in view, which culminates in the death of Jesus Christ. Thus, the God of the Old Testament is also the God of the New Testament, who finally reveals himself in the person of Jesus Christ. This revelation is Paul's "good news" that "the Messiah died for our sins according to the scriptures" (cf. 1 Cor 15:3).

My research has shown that the amaNazaretha believe and call upon the name of the God of the Old Testament, Jehovah. However, their belief is that Jesus did die and rise again, but that he had come to this earth specifically for the Jews at a particular time in history. Consequently, his death upon the cross has little relevance for them. Bosch argues, in his study of Matthew's Gospel,[21] that the Jewish community in his (Matthew's) day also needed counsel regarding the person and work of Christ and their own position as part of the Jewish tradition. Bosch says, "The purpose of the so-called formula quotations is to prove that Jesus is the Messiah and as such the fulfillment of Old Testament promises."[22] According to Senior, Matthew, in his endeavor to refute the way Jewish theologians use scripture, uses the Old Testament as witness against them by casting "the aura of fulfillment to practically every dimension of Jesus life."[23]

The amaNazaretha, however, are yet to be convinced that Jesus Christ is the fulfillment and God's final revelation of the entire biblical story, culminating in his lordship through his death, resurrection, and enthronement. Paul's "gospel" is the good news that the covenant God of the Old Testament does finally reveal himself to the world in the person of Jesus Christ.

20. Ibid., 46.
21. Bosch, *Transforming Mission*, 1991.
22. Ibid., 59.
23. Senior and Stuhlmueller, *The Biblical Foundations for Mission*, 241.

Conclusions, Missiological Implications, and Suggestions for Further Study

In Wright's study of the Philippians passage (2:5–8),[24] he states:

> The truth about God is revealed, for Paul, supremely on the cross. As he says in Romans, "God commends his love for us in that while we were yet sinners, Christ died for us." The sentence, we should note, only makes sense if, somehow, God is fully and personally involved in the death of Jesus Christ.[25]

Wright argues again that it is in fulfillment of the covenant God of Abraham, Isaac, and Jacob that God demonstrates his "deep, utterly self-giving, utterly trustworthy love" to Paul,[26] the once-persecuting Saul, and not only to Paul but also to a lost humanity. In an interview with a senior minister in the amaNazaretha Church, I inquired as to whether I could participate in the yearly sacrament service. When I was politely refused admittance to the sacrament service, I engaged the minister in conversation about the significance of the communion service in the amaNazaretha Church. I raised the question "Do you believe that Christ died for the sins of the world?" Minister Ngidi responded:

> If I sin now, is it forgiven because someone died two thousand years ago? If I sin now, I go to Shembe and ask for forgiveness, because at this point in time Shembe is here. If I ask for atonement of sins, how will I know that Christ will forgive me? I believe Shembe because he replies to me when I ask for forgiveness. (MR:8)

From my discussion with minister Ngidi and other members, I received similar responses, as my interviews have shown. The amaNazaretha Church does not accept the atoning work of Jesus Christ as the fulfillment of the scriptures, both Old and New Testaments. Rather, it is their belief that it was Jesus himself who promised the coming of Shembe when he was about to depart. Minister Ngidi responds:

> Shembe in his own words said when I came out of heaven (Christ: John 16) he [Jesus] is bidding [me] goodbye. Christ said he would ask the Comforter to come. In the very same way Shembe said that Christ sent him. It is Christ who asks for the Comforter to come to the earth. The Nazarites are the true Christians[27] because what we practice is what Christ told his Apostles. (MR:8)

---

24. Verse 8 of the passage reads, "And being found in appearance as a man, he humbled himself and became obedient to death—even death on a cross!"

25. Wright, *What Saint Paul Really Said*, 68.

26. Ibid.

27. The minister was articulating the fact that the amaNazaretha are "true Christians" in that Jesus was a Nazarite who obeyed all the Old Testament prohibitions, Sabbath, and

My research shows that Shembe has displaced Jesus Christ. As noted above, the amaNazaretha Church believes that it is recorded in the Bible (New Testament) that Jesus would send the Comforter, who is interpreted by the amaNazaretha to be Shembe.

In N. T. Wright's third essay, "Paul's Gospel and Caesar's Empire," the author juxtaposes the Greco-Roman slogan "Caesar is Lord" with Paul's proclamation that "Jesus is Lord." Wright's exegetical work on Phil 2:5–11 brings him to affirm that Jesus Christ is the risen Lord while implicitly counteracting the claims of the political and religious lord of the day, Caesar.

Wright argues:

> For Paul "the gospel" is the announcement that the crucified and risen Jesus of Nazareth is Israel's Messiah and the world's Lord. It is in other words, the thoroughly Jewish, and indeed Isaianic, message which challenges the royal and imperial messages in Paul's world.[28]

Hence, when Paul writes in Phil 2:10 that "at the name of Jesus every knee should bow," he is suggesting that what God had claimed for God's self in Isaiah is now shared with Jesus. In Isaiah 45:23 YHWH declares, "Before me every knee will bow; by me every tongue will swear." Wright adds:

> Paul was announcing that Jesus was the true King of Israel and hence the true Lord of the world, at exactly the time in history, and over exactly the geographical spread, where the Roman emperor was being proclaimed, in what styled itself a "gospel," in very similar terms.[29]

Paul's assertion puts in bold relief the question of loyalty—loyalty to the empire of Rome in the person of Caesar, or loyalty to the crucified Lord now exalted and hailed as *Kyrios*, Lord. In my participant observation at the amaNazaretha worship Sabbath services, I noted with much interest the reverence and aura with which Vimbeni Shembe is introduced into the worship space upon his appearance. Young maidens untie his shoes so that he may enter the sacred tabernacle, worshippers bow on their knees, and as he approaches they chant, "*Ameni, Oyingcwele!*" meaning "Amen, he is holy." Chapter 6 described the pillow ceremony, where worshippers go down on their knees when the pillow is brought into the

---

Levitical laws, whereas Christians have abrogated the said laws.

28. Wright, "Paul's Gospel and Caesar's Empire," 3.

29. Ibid., 5.

Conclusions, Missiological Implications, and Suggestions for Further Study

temple arena. The pillow is said to represent Isaiah Shembe and his presence in the temple. Further, the bumper stickers "Shembe Is the Way" and "Shembe Is the Black Messiah" are slogans that carry strong sentiments for the amaNazaretha adherents. Like Caesar, Shembe is apotheosized by the worshippers. In such an environment, the lordship of Jesus Christ recedes into the background; Jesus is not Lord for the amaNazaretha, as Shembe becomes the focus of praise, adoration, and respect.

The enthronement passage in Eph 1:20–21 places Jesus Christ at the right hand of God, "far above all authority, power and dominion, and every title that can be given, not only in the present age but also in the age to come." E. K. Simpson, in his commentary on Ephesians, states:

> Not only has the Redeemer been released from the icy grip of death, the most tenacious of all turnkeys, but God has set Him at His own right hand, robed in mediatorial sovereignty, upraised triumphantly above all the heavenly hierarchies and given Him a name loftier than every other name however preeminent of whatsoever dynasty or dominion, present or to come.[30]

However, Andrew T. Lincoln, in his commentary on Ephesians, suggests that Ps 110, which is employed in the Ephesians enthronement pericope, was used as an enthronement psalm for the king in the Old Testament. He adds:

> Its terminology of a session at the right hand had parallels in the ancient Near East world where the king was often represented as seated next to the tutelary deity of a particular city or nation. Occupying a place on the god's right hand meant that the ruler exercised power on behalf of the god and held a position of favor (Psalm 80:18; Jeremiah 22:24).[31]

From my interviews I gathered that the slogan "Shembe Is the Way" meant that it is Shembe, not Jesus Christ, who sits at heaven's gate admitting the amaNazaretha member. At best, members of the church suggested that Jesus, if present, would only be responsible for his own people, the Jews. The enthronement passage in Ephesians, which exalts Jesus to the position at the right hand of God as mediator for all who confess him, is obfuscated by Shembe in the amaNazaretha Church.

From my field research, both my interviews and participant observation, and my study of the literature, and in the light of the above discus-

---

30. Simpson, *Commentary on the Epistle to the Ephesians and the Colossians*, 41.
31. Lincoln, *Ephesians*, 79.

sion on Christology, I conclude that the amaNazaretha Church does not qualify to be a Christward movement as Jesus Christ is not Lord of their lives. It is Shembe who has succeeded Jesus Christ and thus occupies the central place in their lives.

Missiological Implications

There are four implications emanating from this study that may be applied to future missiological studies: (1) a revision of Turner's "Four-Part Classification" of AICs; (2) a discipleship program that would bring AICs that are on the fringes of the Christian Church back to orthodox faith; (3) an observation that when churches move beyond ethnic, language, and cultural barriers, they are more likely to gravitate to biblical norms rather than to cultural norms; and (4) a reconsideration of Turner's view that "when AICs get the Bible in their own language it functions as a magnet to draw them closer to orthodox beliefs and practices."[32]

A Revision of Turner's Typology

First referred to is Harold Turner's "Four-Part Classification" of the various interactions between Christianity and tribal religions.[33] We are indeed indebted to Turner for his pioneering work in the field of religious studies, which with acute insight and diligence he began in 1957 in order to study the phenomenon called New Religious Movements (NRMS). The original study of the genesis, rise, nomenclature, typology, and descriptions of each type is indeed the monumental achievement of Turner. While Turner has engaged in the study of various New Religious Movements, he is particularly known for his work among the African Independent Churches, more so in the Church of the Lord (Aladura) in Nigeria.

Turner's "Four-Part Classification" (see typology above) of African Independent Churches depicts both the first and second stage responses to the Christian gospel. In the first stage, people move from primal or tribal religions to what he terms *mission churches*; the second stage depicts four groups, namely, Neo-primal movements, Synthesist movements, Hebraist movements, and Independent Churches. The first movement, Neo-primal, is most likely in the second stage to move back to primal or tribal religions; the second group, the Synthesist movements, can move in either direction, that is, back to tribal religions or forward to indig-

---

32. This statement was quoted by Darrell Whiteman from a seminar conducted by Harold Turner on NRMs held at Pyramid, Irian Jaya, Indonesia, in 1981.

33. Turner, "Religious Movement," 49.

Conclusions, Missiological Implications, and Suggestions for Further Study

enous autonomous churches; the third group, the Hebraists, are more likely to move forward to indigenous autonomous churches; and, finally, Independent Churches are more likely to move in a forward direction to indigenous autonomous churches.

My research has shown that according to Turner's taxonomy, the amaNazaretha *could* fall into the Hebraist category given the fact that they resonate with the Old Testament. I have also shown that a revival of Zulu culture and a strong emphasis on the Old Testament Jewish laws and some use of the New Testament coalesced to the point that the amaNazaretha Church in the final years of Isaiah Shembe's life had already gravitated to a position somewhere between the Synthesist movement and the Hebraist movement positions. Whereas Turner's diagram depicts the Hebraists as having the potential to move in a Christward direction rather than back to a Synthesist position, I argue that the amaNazaretha Church *could* also fall into a category between the Hebraists and the Synthesists. Yet, Turner's taxonomy does not allow for a position where the leader, Shembe, has replaced Christ and the Holy Trinity, thus going beyond a Christian orthodox position. A new category needs to be created to accommodate this new phenomenon in African religious movements in Turner's typology—a post-Christian movement. My sketch below shows where I place the amaNazaretha Church in a revised typology:

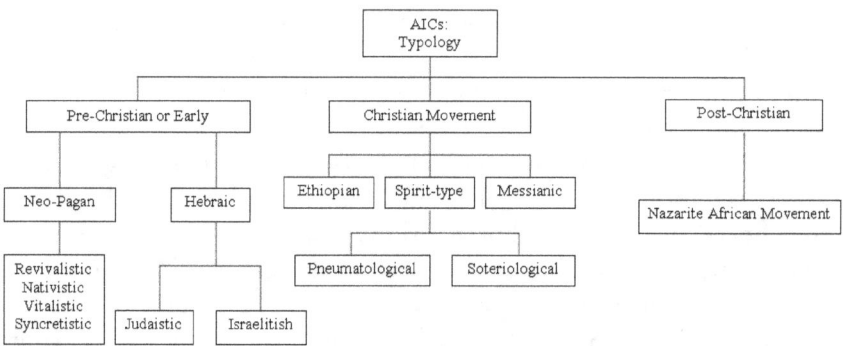

Figure 11. A Revision of Turner's Four-Part Classification of New Religious Movements that Accommodates the Category of Post-Christian Groups

The creation of this post-Christian category is necessary in light of the research and interviews where three religious systems are at work in the amaNazaretha Church. As evangelist Mpanza stated, "The Nazarite Baptist Church of Isaiah Shembe took the laws of God as they are found in the Old Testament. He took the ethical teachings of the New Testament, and then he coupled these with African customs and he made them one thing."[34] A close aide of Vimbeni Shembe, preacher Sibisi, said in an informal conversation that the amaNazaretha Church is not a Christian church but a new religious movement. He did not, however, elaborate. Based on my observations and field research, I believe that Turner's taxonomy would need to be expanded to accommodate groups that may imbibe more than two systems and consequently move beyond a Christian position. While Oosthuizen is convinced that the amaNazaretha Church "is not a Sabbatarian Christian sect but is a definite nativistic messianic movement,"[35] I see the amaNazaretha as a post-Christian Judeo-Zuluized religious movement with the potential to move back to an indigenous Christian orthodox position. Presently, I would place the amaNazaretha beyond Turner's indigenous autonomous church position to a new position, namely, post-Christian.

An Indigenous Discipleship Program

Second, a discipleship program that would bring AICs that are on the fringes of the Christian Church back to orthodox faith could and should be developed. Schreiter raises a caution that applies to the amaNazaretha Church. He asks, "Is a local church willing to stand under the judgment of other churches in the matter of its Christian performance or does it close itself off, assured of its own truth?"[36] Historically, we know that before Isaiah Shembe seceded from the Wesleyan Church, and later the African Baptist Church, he had received some catechetical instruction and also had the opportunity to lead the Wesleyan service on occasion. However, when he seceded from these churches and gained his own following, whether he received formal Bible training is not known. We know that he planted churches everywhere he had preached the gospel, prayed for the sick, and counseled people. Local leadership developed from faithful followers and disciples. The movement grew to be what it is today, some two million people throughout South Africa and in the surrounding African countries. They have been in existence now for almost one hundred years with no outside influence or ecumenical fellowship. Leaders in the church, including ministers, evangelists, and preachers, are awarded position in the

---

34. Evangelist Mpanza explained in the same conversation that "most of the laws of God which are found in the Old Testament and in the Torah are similar to all African customs."

35. Oosthuizen, "Isaiah Shembe and the Zulu Worldview," 28.

36. Schreiter, *Constructing Local Theologies*, 120.

Conclusions, Missiological Implications, and Suggestions for Further Study

church on the criteria of faithful membership over a long and protracted period of time; leaders from other churches who have joined the amaNazaretha Church are awarded positions on the basis of their office held in their former churches; and some leaders are selected on the basis of their superior education and professional status. From my research, I discovered that none of the ministers, evangelists, or preachers had had any Bible instruction or formal theological education. Vimbeni Shembe himself, who studied to become a teacher but never taught a class, herded his father's cattle before he was called to leadership upon the death of his father.

Schreiter's caution is pertinent to the case of the amaNazaretha Church, which has not opened itself to the test of the larger church community and today has moved significantly away from a Christian orthodox position.

A follow-up principle would be to introduce a discipleship program that may be taught by trained indigenous leadership. The larger church whose expatriate missionaries are on the field may be involved in the training and implementation of the discipleship program, with a preplanned exit strategy. The exit strategy will foster and perpetuate the preparation of new indigenous leadership over time. An alternate strategy may be to select one or more individuals for scholarships and grants to travel to first-world countries where they may receive their education and return to train new leaders. In this way the older churches in the North Atlantic community have the opportunity to partner with younger churches in the South and thus create a positive ecumenical environment that augers well for the larger church.

This experiment is similar to the life and times of Saint Patrick. Hunter writes that Patrick "trained for the priesthood perhaps in Rome, or in Gaul, more likely in England. His training immersed his mind in the scriptures, and grounded him in the basic orthodox theology that prevailed in the Western Church of that time."[37] When Patrick received his "Macedonian Call" to take the gospel back to his captors, he was ordained and appointed to Ireland as a missionary bishop.[38] Patrick's ministry in Ireland was fruitful because he had learned the culture from an *emic* perspective, as an insider, although under captivity. The principle here is that an indigenous leader trained in a Western seminary or Bible college could be an effective discipler in his or her own context like Patrick, who knew the culture of Ireland.

---

37. Hunter, *The Celtic Way of Evangelism*, 15.
38. Ibid.

With an oral culture like the amaNazaretha Church, a discipleship program that meets the needs of nonliterate and semiliterate people will be the key for effective discipleship. Several programs may be recommended. One may be the Chronological Bible Story method, which uses selected stories from the Bible that are told in chronological order, with dialog and discussion after the story is told. This method allows the storyteller to ask relevant questions that will guide the listener to discover the important facets of the story and thus discover the meaning conveyed in the biblical story.

In the amaNazaretha Church, stories are told to communicate faith, and these stories operate in tandem with the Bible. The preacher, though illiterate, recalls Bible verses from memory. The chronological method of storying takes the person or congregation from the Old Testament into the New Testament and thus presents Jesus Christ as the final revelation from God. Where people in some religious movements have not moved beyond the Old Testament, the chronological story method reduces such a possibility significantly. The amaNazaretha Church is one example of a church that has not moved beyond the Old Testament teachings and consequently espouses a low Christology.

Nussbaum, who claims that the "Mennonites [have] placed more personnel in more countries than any other groups working with independents,"[39] argues for a dialogical approach to discipleship developed by Mennonite pioneers Edwin and Irene Weaver. The Weavers' approach was one of learning from the indigenous people, while teaching them through "inductive, small-group Bible studies."[40] In his study, Nussbaum endorses the Weavers' approach, suggesting that it "has significant bearing on both the understanding and the communication of the Gospel of Jesus Christ."[41]

The chronological approach to studying the Bible with a dialogical approach as adopted by the Mennonites will resonate with the amaNazaretha Church and other churches that have not as yet come to fully embrace Jesus Christ as God's full and final revelation for all of creation.

As stated earlier (ch. 1), this study of the amaNazaretha will open new vistas of opportunity for evangelicals who have hitherto brushed aside the African Initiated Churches as aberrant and at the margins of orthodoxy. Hopefully, this study will be a catalyst to initiate dialogue and discussion between the AICs and other churches. Further, those who are passionate

---

39. Nussbaum, *Toward Theological Dialogue*, 8
40. Ibid.
41. Ibid.

about kingdom work will find innovative ways to work alongside indigenous Africans in discipleship programs. Where previously held caricatures and stereotypes existed, they could be transformed into greater appreciation for the AICs, as they too belong to the household of God.

Biblical and Cultural Considerations

Third, is an observation that when churches move beyond ethnic, language, and cultural barriers, they are more likely to gravitate to biblical norms rather than to cultural norms if they have access to the Bible in their own language. The amaNazaretha Church is predominantly a Zulu ethnic movement; consequently, the Zulu culture and traditions predominate in the church. The seven-million member Zion Christian Church, on the other hand, the largest AIC in South Africa, consists of various ethnic, cultural, and linguistic groups. The result is that it is not possible to gravitate to one cultural or linguistic expression in the church. The ZCC is much closer to Christian orthodoxy because it appeals to the Bible as their common source rather than to only one cultural and linguistic expression. In contrast, for the amaNazaretha Church, cultural norms take precedence over biblical norms.

The Bible and Orthodoxy

Fourth, is a consideration of Turner's view that "when AICs receive the Bible in their own language it functions as a magnet to draw them closer to orthodox beliefs and practices."[42] While this conclusion comes through Turner's experience from his study of the AICs, my research has shown that the amaNazaretha have had the Bible in their own Zulu language for almost one hundred years but have not moved toward a Christward position. On the contrary, as already intimated, they have moved away from an orthodox Christian position. In his discussion of the "linguistic drift," linguist Edward Sapir demonstrated that built into the structure of every language is a prefigured linguistic pattern that causes the language to change over time in a predetermined way.[43] In other words, languages have a tendency to change over time in a prescribed pattern. Similarly, V. F. Calverton argues that cultural compulsives in a society shape how a people perceive truth and reality. Anytime Christianity confronts a culture, it

---

42. This statement was quoted by Darrell Whiteman from a seminar conducted by Harold Turner on NRMs held at Pyramid, Irian Jaya, Indonesia, in 1981.

43. Sapir, *Language*, 147–70.

comes into contact with that society's cultural compulsives.[44] Hence, from Sapir's *linguistic drift* and Calverton's *cultural compulsives*, one can see how the Zulu culture has shaped the amaNazaretha Church's experience and expression of Christianity. Consequently, without interacting with other Christians, their religious patterns have taken on more Zulu traditional practices than Christian characteristics. This tendency for culture to dominate Christian faith underscores the critical importance of discipleship and interaction at the indigenous level with biblical norms so that indigenous groups may come closer to an orthodox Christian position.

The above four missiological implications have potential to be applied to other situations that bear similar characteristics to those of the amaNazaretha Church in Durban, South Africa.

Suggestions for Further Study

My research findings have opened new vistas of inquiry for further study in the amaNazaretha Church. However, among them were some areas that I had anticipated to cover in my research that did not materialize. I shall begin with these first.

I had anticipated that I would have the opportunity to observe funeral services and rituals. My attempt to gain access to the funerals, which were few and far between, was denied to me. People whose relatives had passed on were not familiar with me, so I had not gained sufficient trust to be part of the services and grave ceremonies. I did, however, attend one memorial service where the member, an elderly woman, had died the previous week. My minister friend Gcwenza invited me to attend the service. To ascertain beliefs about the afterlife beyond the interviews, it will be necessary to be a participant observer at these services and grave rituals.

One of the new areas for study that I stumbled upon during my research was the administration of the sacrament. The communion service is held once every year at Ebuhleni and at other large temple services that Vimbeni Shembe visits during the course of the calendar year. From my conversations with some ministers of the church, I gathered that the sacrament service was a very sacred ritual and only a few members were admitted to it. It is usually held at night. My research assistant, Joseph Mhlongo, confirmed that he had not been invited to one as yet, and he is a long-standing member who was raised in the church. Research in this area will further confirm what role Shembe, ancestors, and Christ have in the ceremony.

---

44. Calverton, "Modern Anthropology," 1–37.

Conclusions, Missiological Implications, and Suggestions for Further Study

My research has also shown that the amaNazaretha have a vague, yet unorthodox understanding of the Trinity. They believe in the God of the Old Testament, God the Father; that Jesus is the Son of God and that God has many sons; and further that the Shembes are successors of Christ whom Christ promised before he departed as recorded in the Bible. Then, the person of the Holy Spirit is most confused in the amaNazaretha Church as both members and ministers believe that Shembe is more than a surname; Shembe is also *the* Holy Spirit, or Shembe *possesses* the Holy Spirit. This area needs to be researched, as I have learned from the literature and subsequently from my own research that AICs appear to portray a more overt pneumatology and a deficient Christology in their religious beliefs and practices. The amaNazaretha Church displays a greater affinity to the work of the Holy Spirit than they do to Jesus Christ.

Epilogue

I BEGAN MY STUDY of the amaNazaretha Church with a preconception that the church had come under unfair and harsh criticism regarding its beliefs and practices. Earlier studies, especially those done by Oosthuizen, were regarded as being insensitive to the amaNazaretha Church tradition. I believed that after almost one hundred years of existence, the church would be closer to an orthodox Christian position. However, my research shows that the amaNazaretha today cannot be called a Christward movement as Jesus Christ is not central to the life world of the people. Yet, I believe that given time and the introduction of orthodox Christian beliefs and practices through indigenous discipleship and training, the amaNazaretha Church could become a Christward movement again.

If the history of the church has any hope for us, I recall that the early church grappled with similar issues that the amaNazaretha Church encounters today. For example, the Council of Nicaea (AD 325) had as its main agenda the question whether Christ, the son of God, was truly and fully God as the Father. The Council of Constantinople (AD 381) came to the conclusion that the Holy Spirit is God. Later, in AD 451, the Council of Chalcedon affirmed that Jesus Christ was fully human and fully God.

The amaNazaretha Church has on its side some two thousand years of Christian tradition and thus could become a Christward movement as it struggles with its understanding of the person and work of Christ and the role of the Holy Trinity in its beliefs and practices. If the amaNazaretha Church becomes a Christward movement, its members will discover that they can be thoroughly Zulu and completely Christian at the same time. In other words, a truly indigenous Christian church will take root in the Zulu soil of South Africa.

Appendix

Statistical Data of Interviewees

CP	IN	Name	G	Age	Y of Mb	Pre/Rel	EB	WS
MR	1	M.M	M	56	28	EthiopC	Std4	DTr
MR	2	M.M	M	56	Birth	N/A	--	--
MR	3	M.M	M	62	Birth	N/A	--	--
MR	4	-.M	M	59	Birth	N/A	--	--
MR	5	-.M	M	61	Birth	N/A	--	--
MR	6	-.K	M	62	Birth	N/A	--	--
MR	7	M.C	M	45	Birth	N/A	--	--
MR	8	-N	M	52	Birth	N/A	DIP.T	ST
MR	9	M.G	M	47	Birth	N/A	--	FW
MR	10	-.K	M	47	Birth	N/A	--	--
MR	11	-.M	M	67	Birth	N/A	--	--
MR	12	A.N	M	51	Birth	N/A	--	--
MR	13	E.N	M	57	Birth	N/A	--	--
MR	14	-.M	M	67	57	N/A	--	--
MR	15	W.S	M	54	12	ZCC	--	--
EV	1	M.M	M	50	Birth	N/A	BJur.	G.Of
EV	2	-.M	M	83	Birth	N/A	--	Fm.
EV*	3	-.M	M	43	Birth	N/A	--	HAdm
EV	4	N.N	M	65	23	StJAFM	--	--
EV	5	A.N	M	63	55	N/A	--	--
EV	6	D.N	M	44	16	S.Army	--	--
EV	7	M.M	M	64	Birth	N/A	--	--
EV	8	M.D	M	47	Birth	N/A	--	CF
PR	1	S.N	M	82	Birth	N/A	N.Lit	Fm.
PR	2	J.G	M	82	Birth	N/A	--	--
PR	3	-.N	M	60	25	N/A	--	--
PR	4	-.M	M	58	30	ATR	--	--
PR	5	-.X	M	54	27	RCC	--	--
PR	6	-.M	M	56	Birth	N/A	--	--
YL	1	C.D	M	33	Birth	N/A	BPS	TU

Appendix

CP	IN	Name	G	Age	Y of Mb	Pre/Rel	EB	WS
YL	2	P.Z	M	26	10	Ang.	--	--
YL	3	Z.G	M	28	Birth	N/A	--	Clerk
YL	4	V.Z	M	34	Birth	N/A	--	ST*
UK	1	S.M	F	--	Birth	N/A	--	HW
UK	2	M.B	F	--	Birth	--	--	CV
LP	1	J.M	M	44	Birth	N/A	Std8	FW
LP	2	M.M	M		14	ATR	--	FW
LP	3	M.N	F	88	Birth	N/A	N.Lit	Fm.
LP	4	D.P	M	74	Birth	N/A	N.Lit	Fm.
LP	5	S.M	M	70	2	ZCC	N.Lit	--
LP	6	M.M	M	41	12	ATR	--	--
LP	7	N.M	M	--	44	ATR	--	--
LP	8	Z.D	M	--	37	ATR	--	SEmp
LP	9	S.D	M	88	Birth	N/A	N.Lit	--
LP	10	-.D	M	--	7	RCC	--	--
LP	11	P.M	M	--	7	ZCongC	--	--
LP	12	M.N	M	42	Birth	N/A	--	--
LP	13	W.-	M	81	63	ATR	--	Ret.
LP	14	M.M	M	--	16	ZCongC	--	--
LP	15	I.M	M	54	6	ZCC*	--	FW
LP	16	B.M	M	50	6	ACC*	--	MD
LP	17	T.N	M	38	Birth	N/A	--	GSO
LP	18	M.M	M	30	20	ZCC	--	--
LP	19	-.N	M	--	Birth	N/A	--	--
LP	20	M.M	F	--	6	ATR	--	--
LP	21	B.D	M	51	15	Meth.	--	--
LP	22	-.H	M	58	Birth	N/A	--	--
LP	23	C.M	M	22	Birth	N/A	--	UEm
LP	24	-.M	M	--	8	ATR	--	--
LP	25	T.M	M	26	Birth	N/A	Mat.	UEm
LP	26	S.N	F	33	12	RCC	Std8	FW
LP	27	-.H	F	--	2	ZCC	--	CV
LP	28	P.S	F	64	40	ATR	--	CV
LP	29	T.M	F	--	Birth	N/A	--	--
LP*	30	L.S	F	33	Birth	N/A	--	Clerk
LP	31	M.C	F	30	Ad.*	AFM	--	Nur.
LP	32	P.M	F	40	Birth	N/A	--	LE
LP	33	K.C	F	34	8	ZCC	--	Nur

Statistical Data of Interviewees

Meaning of Abbreviations

CP: Church Position:
MR—Minister; EV—Evangelist; PR—Preacher; YL—Youth Leader; UK—Women's leader; LP—Layperson

IN: Interview Number

Name: Name of Interviewee (Initials Only)

G: Gender: M—Male; F—Female

Age: Age of Interviewee

Y of Mb: Years of Membership

Pre/Rel: Previous Religious Affiliation/Church:
ZCC—Zion Christian Church; ATR—African Traditional Religion; RCC—Roman Catholic Church; ZCC—Zulu Congregational Church; ACC—African Congregational Church; Ang.—Anglican Church; Meth.—Methodist Church; AFM—Apostolic Faith Mission; StJAFM—St. John's Apostolic Faith Mission; S.Army—Salvation Army; EthiopC—Ethiopian Church

EB: Educational Background:
BPS—Bachelor of Arts-Political Science; Std 4—Standard 4 (grade 6); Std8—Standard 8 (grade 10); N.Lit—Nonliterate; Mat.—Matriculation (grade 12); BJur—Bachelor of Law

WS: Work Status:
UEm—Unemployed; TU—Trade Union; FW—Factory Worker; Fm.—Farmer; SEmp.—Self-employed; Ret.—Retired; MD—Medical Doctor; CF—Chief of a Zulu clan; GSO—Grocery Store Owner; Clerk—Office Worker; ST—Schoolteacher; HW—Housewife; CV—Curio Vender; Nur.—Nurse; LE—Law Enforcement; G.Of—Government Official; HAdm—Hospital Administrator; DTr—Director of Public Transport (KZN Province)

APPENDIX

Statistical Analyses

Total Number of Interviews:	68	100%
Laypersons	33	48% (10 female and 23 males)
Youth Leaders	4	6%
Umkhokheli (women's leaders)	2	3%
Preachers	6	9%
Evangelists	8	12%
Ministers	15	22%
TOTAL	**68**	**100%**
Female-to-Male Ratio:	12:56	18%:82%

Church Affiliation

Raised in the Church:	38	56%
Conversion from ATR	9	13%
Conversion from ZCC	10	15%
Conversion from RCC	4	6%
Conversion from Others	7	10%
TOTAL	**68**	**100%**

Average Age of Ministers:	(15)	56 yrs
Average Age of Evangelists:	(8)	57 yrs
Average Age of Preachers:	(6)	65 yrs
Average Age of Youth Leaders:	(4)	30 yrs

(No stats for women and laypersons)

Bibliography

Abanuka, Bartholomew. "Ancestors and the Idea of Ultimate Reality and Meaning in the Igbo Worldview: A Further Contribution to Uram Igbo Studies." *Ultimate Reality and Meaning* 13, no. 3 (2000) 134–44.
Adeyemo, Tokunboh. "Towards an Evangelical African Theology." *Evangelical Review of Theology* 7, no. 1 (1983) 147–54.
Aigbe, Sunday Agbons. "Phenomenon of Prayer in African Traditional Religions." PhD diss., Fuller Theological Seminary, 1992.
All Africa Church Conference. *The Crisis in the Christian Ministry in Africa*. Kitwe, Northern Rhodesia, 1964.
Allison, Norman E. "Make Sure You're Getting Through." *Evangelical Missions Quarterly* 20, no. 2 (1984) 165–70.
Anderson, Allan. *African Reformation: African Initiated Christianity in the 20th Century*. Trenton, NJ: African World, 2001.
———. "The Hermeneutical Processes of Pentecostal-Type African Initiated Churches in South Africa." *Missionalia* 24, no. 2 (1996) 171–85.
———. *Tumelo: The Faith of African Pentecostals in South Africa*. Pretoria: University of South Africa Press, 1993.
———. *Zion and Pentecost: The Spirituality and Experience of Pentecostal and Zionist/Apostolic Churches in South Africa*. Pretoria: University of South Africa Press, 2000.
Arnold, Clinton E. *The Colossian Syncretism: The Interface between Christianity and Folk Belief at Colossae*. Grand Rapids: Baker, 1995.
Awolalu, J. Omosade. "Sin and Its Removal in African Traditional Religion." *Journal of the American Academy of Religion* 44 (1976) 275–87.
Baer, G. F. A. "Missionary Endeavor in Pondoland." *International Review of Missions* 42, no. 168 (1953) 413–20.
Baeta, C. G. *Christianity in Tropical Africa: Studies Presented and Discussed at the Seventh International African Seminar, University of Ghana, April, 1965*. London: Oxford University Press, 1968.
Balia, Daryl M. *Black Methodists and White Supremacy in South Africa*. Durban, South Africa: Madiba, 1991.
Barrett, David B. *Schism and Renewal in Africa: An Analysis of Six Thousand Contemporary Religious Movements*. Nairobi, Kenya: Oxford University Press, 1968.
Barrett, David B., George Kurian, and Todd M. Johnson, eds. *World Christian Encyclopedia: Comparative Study of Churches and Religions in the Modern World*. 2nd ed. Vols. 1–2. New York: Oxford University Press, 2001.
Barth, Karl. *Church Dogmatics*. Vol. 4. Edinburgh: T. & T. Clark, 1956.
Bate, Stuart C., ed. *Inculturation and Healing*. Pietermaritzburg, South Africa: Cluster, 1995.
———. *Human Life is Cultural: Introducing Anthropology*. Pietermaritzburg, South Africa: Cluster, 2002.

Bibliography

———. *Serving Humanity: A Sabbath Reflection: The Pastoral Plan of the Catholic Church in Southern Africa After Seven Years.* Pietermaritzburg, South Africa: Cluster, 1996.
Baur, John. *2000 Years of Christianity in Africa.* Nairobi, Kenya: Publications Africa, 1994.
Bavinck, Herman. *An Introduction to the Science of Missions.* Philadelphia: Presbyterian and Reformed, 1960.
Beane, Wendell C., and William G. Doty, eds. *Myths, Rites, Symbols: A Mircea Eliade Reader.* New York: Harper & Row, 1975.
Beattie, John. "Aspects of Nyoro Symbolism." *Africa* 38 (1968) 413–42.
Beck, Roger B. *The History of South Africa.* London: Greenwood, 2000.
Becken, Hans-Jürgen. "African Independent Churches as Healing Communities." In *Afro-Christian Religion and Healing in Southern Africa,* edited by G. C. Oosthuizen, S. D. Edwards, W. H. Wessels, and Irving Hexham, 227–40. Lewiston, NY: Mellen, 1989.
———. "The Deeds of Shembe as Described by His Eyewitnesses." In *Afro-Christian Religion at the Grassroots in Southern Africa,* edited by G. C. Oosthuizen and Irving Hexham, 151–63. African Studies 19. Lewiston, NY: Mellen, 1991.
———. "Ekuphakameni Revisited: Recent Developments within the Nazaretha Church in South Africa." *Journal of Religion in Africa/Religion en Afrique* 9, no. 3 (1978) 161–72.
———. "Narrative Church History as Proclamation of the Gospel Message [Research Project on Oral History of Nazareth Baptist Church of Shembe]." *Mission Studies* 7, no. 2 (1990) 172–88.
———. "Nazarene's Hymns with Sabbath Liturgy and Morning and Evening Prayers." No publishing data.
———. "The Nazareth Baptist Church of Isaiah Shembe." In *Our Approach to the Independent Church Movement in South Africa,* edited by Hans-Jurgen Becken, 101–14. Natal, South Africa: Lutheran Theological College, 1965.
———. "On the Holy Mountain: A Visit to the New Year's Festival of the Nazaretha Church on Mount Nhlangakazi, 14 January 1967." *Journal of Religion in Africa/Religion en Afrique* 1, no. 2 (1967) 138–49.
Beckford, J. A. "Explaining Religious Movements." *International Social Science Journal* 29, no. 2 (1976) 235–49.
Bediako, Kwame. "Biblical Christologies in the Context of African Traditional Religions." In *Sharing Jesus in the Two-Thirds World: Evangelical Christologies from the Contexts of Poverty, Powerlessness, and Religious Pluralism,* edited by Vinay Samuel and Christopher Sugden, 35–42. Grand Rapids: Eerdmans, 1983.
———. *Christianity in Africa: The Renewal of a Non-Western Religion (Studies in World Christianity).* Edinburgh: Edinburgh University Press, 1995.
———. *Jesus and the Gospel in Africa: History and Experience.* Theology in Africa Series. Maryknoll, NY: Orbis, 2004.
———. *Theology and Identity: The Impact of Culture upon Christian Thought in the Second Century and Modern Africa.* Oxford: Regnum, 1992.
———. "Understanding African Theology in the 20th Century." *An International Bulletin for Theological and Religious Studies Students* 20, no. 1 (1994) 14–20.
Bedwell, H. K. *Black Gold: The Story of the International Holiness Mission in South Africa.* Cape Town, South Africa: Cape Times, 1936.
Beemer, Hilda. "The Swazi Rain Ceremony: Critical Comments on P. J. Schoeman's Article." *Bantu Studies* 9 (1935) 273–81.
Beetham, T. A. *Christianity and the New Africa.* New York: Praeger, 1967.

Bibliography

Beidelman, T. O. "Pig: (Guluwe) An Essay on Ngulu Sexual Symbolism and Ceremony." *South-western Journal of Anthropology* 20 (1964) 359–92.

———. "Right and Left Among the Kaguru: A Note on Symbolic Classification." *Africa* 31 (1961) 250–57.

———. "Three Tales of the Living and the Dead: The Ideology of Karugu Ancestral Propitiation." *Journal of the Royal Anthropological Institute of Great Britain and Ireland* 94, no. 2 (1964) 109–37.

Benedict, Ruth. *Patterns of Culture*. Boston: Houghton Mifflin, 1934.

Bentsen, Cheryl. *Maasai Days*. New York: Doubleday, 1989.

Benz, Ernst. *Dreams, Hallucinations, Visions*. Translated by Tomas H. Spiers. New York: Swedenborg Foundation, 1968.

Berglund, Axel-Ivar. "Communion with the Shades in Traditional Zulu Society." *Missionalia* 1, no. 2 (1973) 39–41.

———. "Heaven-Herds: A Study in Zulu Symbolism." In *Religion and Social Change in Southern Africa*, edited by Michael G. Whisson and Martin West, 34–47. Cape Town, South Africa: David Philip, 1975.

———. *Zulu Thought-Patterns and Symbolism*. New York: Africana, 1976.

Bettenson, Henry, ed. *Documents of the Christian Church*. 2nd ed. London: Oxford University Press, 1963.

Bevans, Stephen B. *Models of Contextual Theology: Faith and Cultures*. Maryknoll, NY: Orbis, 2003.

Bews, J. W. "List of Zulu Plant Names." *Annals of the Natal Museum* 4 (1922) 455–67.

Beyerhaus, Peter. "Begegnung mit messianishen Bewegungen: Zur Kennzeichung der Mission-wissenschaft als theologischer Disziplin." *Zeitschrift für Theologie und Kirche* 64 (1967) 496–518.

———. "The Christian Encounter with Afro-Messianic Movements." In *Christopaganism or Indigenous Christianity?*, edited by Tetsunao Yamamori and Charles R. Taber, 77–95. Pasadena, CA: William Carey Library, 1975.

Beyerhaus, Peter and Carl F. Hallengreutz, eds. *The Church Crossing Frontiers: Essays on the Nature of Mission. In Honor of Bengt Sundkler*. Studia Missionalia Upsaliensia 11. Lund, Sweden: Gleerup, 1969.

Blomberg, Craig L. *Matthew*. New American Commentary 22. Nashville: Broadman, 1991.

Bodenstein, W., and O. F. Raum. "A Present Day Zulu Philosopher." *Africa* 30 (1960) 166–81.

Bond, George, Walton Johnson, and Sheila S. Walker, eds. *African Christianity: Patterns of Religious Continuity*. New York: Academic, 1979.

Boot, Frans H. "Religious Pluralism in a Zulu Chiefdom." In *Afro-Christian Religion at the Grassroots in Southern Africa*, edited by G. C. Oosthuizen and Irving Hexham, 115–50. African Studies 19. Lewiston, NY: Mellen, 1991.

Booth, Newell S., Jr. "An Approach to African Religions." In *African Religions: A Symposium*, edited by Newell S. Booth, 1–12. New York: Nok, 1977.

Booth, Wayne C., Gregory G. Colomb, and Joseph M. Williams. *The Craft of Research*. Chicago: University of Chicago Press, 1995.

Bosch, David J. *Church and Culture Change in Africa*. Pretoria, South Africa: N. G. Kerk-Boekhandel, 1971.

———. *Transforming Mission: Paradigm Shifts in Theology of Mission*. Maryknoll, NY: Orbis, 1991.

Bibliography

Bourguignon, Erica. "The Effectiveness of Religious Healing Movements: A Review of Recent Literature." *Transitional Psychiatric Research Review* 13 (1976) 5–21.

Brown, Kenneth I. "The African Christian in His African Culture." *Religion in Life* 33 (1964) 106–15.

Brownlee, Charles. "A Fragment on Xhosa Religious Beliefs." *African Studies* 14 (1955) 37–41.

Bryant, A. T. "The Zulu Cult of the Dead." *Man* 17 (1917) 140–45.

Buhrmann, M. V. "Religion and Healing: The African Experience." In *Afro-Christian Religion and Healing in Southern Africa*, edited by G. C. Oosthuizen, S. D. Edwards, W. H. Wessels, and Irving Hexham, 25–34. African Studies 8. Lewiston, NY: Mellen, 1989.

Bujo, Benezet. *African Theology in Its Social Context*. Translated by John O'Donohue. Maryknoll, NY: Orbis, 1992.

———. "Toward an African Ecclesiology." *Theology Digest* 42, no. 1 (1995) 3–8.

Burnett, David. *Clash of Worlds: A Christian's Handbook on Cultures, World Religions, and Evangelism*. Nashville: Nelson, 1990.

Buthelezi, Mangosuthu G. "The Early History of the Buthelezi Clan." In *Social System and Tradition in Southern Africa*, edited by John Argyle and Eleanor Preston-Whyte, 1–78. Cape Town, South Africa: Oxford University Press, 1978.

Callaway, H. *The Religious System of the AmaZulu*. Cape Town, South Africa: C. Struik, 1970.

———. *The Religious System of the AmaZulu, Izinyanga Zokubula; Or, Divination, as Existing Among the AmaZulu in Their Own Words*. Natal, South Africa: Adams, 1870.

Calverton, V. F. "Modern Anthropology and the Theory of Cultural Compulsives" In *The Making of Man: An Outline of Anthropology*, edited by V. F. Calverton 1–37. New York: The Modern Library, 1931.

Campion, Nardi R. *Ann the Word: The Life of Mother Ann Lee, Founder of the Shakers*. Boston: Little, Brown, 1976,

Carbutt, Hugh Lancaster. "Some Minor Superstitions and Customs of the Zulus Connected with Children." *Folk-lore Journal* 2 (1880) 10–13.

Carmoday, Brendan. "Towards an African Notion of Divinity." *African Ecclesial Review* 23 (June 1981) 142–47.

Casalis, Eugene. *My Life in Basuto Land: A Story of Missionary Enterprise in South Africa*. Translated by J. Brierley. Piccadilly, UK: Religious Tract Society, 1889.

Cassidy, Michael, and Gottfried Osei-Mensah. *Together in One Place: The Story of PACLA*. Nairobi, Kenya: Evangel, 1978.

Cassidy, Michael, and Luc Verlinden, eds. *Facing the New Challenges: The Message of PACLA*. Nairobi, Kenya: Evangel, 1978.

Chidester, David. *Religions of South Africa*. London: Routledge, 1992.

Chiu, Andrew. "Is There Ancestor Worship in the Old Testament?" *Evangelical Review of Theology* 8, no. 2 (1984) 217–24.

Chiu, Peter Chung-Hang. "An Historical Study of Nestorian Christianity in the T'ang Dynasty between A.D. 635–845." PhD diss., Southwestern Baptist Theological Seminary, 1987.

Cochrane, J. R., J. W. de Gruchy, and R. Petersen. *In Word and In Deed: Towards a Practical Theology for Social Transformation*. Pietermaritzburg, South Africa: Cluster, 1991.

Coe, Shoki. "Contextualizing Theology." In *Mission Trends*, no. 3, edited by Gerald H. Anderson and Thomas F. Stranskey, 21–22. Grand Rapids: Eerdmans, 1976.

Coleman, Will. "Tribal Talk: Black Theology in Postmodern Configurations." *Theology Today* 50 (1993) 68–77.
Comaroff, John L., and Jean Comaroff. *Of Revelation and Revolution: Christianity, Colonialism, and Consciousness in South Africa*. Vol. 1. Chicago: University of Chicago Press, 1991.
———. *Of Revelation and Revolution: The Dialectics of Modernity on a South Africa Frontier*. Vol. 2. Chicago: University of Chicago Press, 1997.
Combrink, Johannes Jacob. "Christian Origins and Growth in South Africa: A Dutch Reformed and Charismatic Church Case Study." PhD diss., Fuller Theological Seminary, 1990.
Cone, James H. *Speaking the Truth: Ecumenism, Liberation, and Black Theology*. Maryknoll, NY: Orbis, 1999.
Congdon, G. Dal. "An Investigation into the Current Zulu Worldview and Its Relevance to Missionary Work." *Evangelical Missions Quarterly* 21 (1985) 296–99.
Cope, Nicholas. *To Bind the Nation: Solomon kaDinuzulu and Zulu Nationalism: 1913–1933*. Pietermaritzburg, South Africa: University of Natal Press, 1993.
Covar, P. R. "Brief Communications and Research Notes." *Philippine Sociological Review* 21 (1973) 283–89.
Cox, James L. "Ancestors, the Sacred and God: Reflections on the Meaning of the Sacred in Zimbabwean Death Rituals." *Religion* 25 (1994) 339–55.
Crane, William H. "Indigenization in the African Church." *International Review of Missions* 53, no. 212 (1964) 408–22.
Cullmann, Oscar. *Christ and Time: The Primitive Christian Conception of Time and History*. Translated by Floyd V. Filson. Philadelphia: Westminster, 1963.
———. *The Christology of the New Testament*. 8th ed. Translated by Shirley C. Guthrie and Charles A. M. Hall. Philadelphia: Westminster, 1975.
———. *Salvation in History*. London: SCM, 1967.
Cuthbertson, Greg, et al. *Frontiers of African Christianity Essays in Honour of Inus Daneel*. Pretoria, South Africa: University of South Africa Press, 2003.
Dalfovo, A. T. "The Divinity among the Lugbara." *Journal of Religion in Africa* 28 (1996) 468–93.
Dammann, Ernst. "Das Christusverständnis in nachchristlichen Kirchen und Sekten Afrikas." In *Messianische Kirchen, Sekten und Bewegungen im heutigen Afrika*, edited by Ernst Benz, 1–21. Beiheft der Zeitschrift für Religions- und Geistesgeschichte 10. Leiden: Brill, 1965.
———. "Tentative Philological Typology of Some African High Deities." *Journal of Religion in Africa* 2 (1969) 81–95.
Daneel, M. L. *African Earthkeepers: Interfaith Mission in Earth-Care*. Vol. 1. Pretoria, South Africa: University of South Africa, 1996.
———. *The Background and Rise of Southern Shona Independent Churches*. Amsterdam: Mouton, 1971.
———. "Black Messianism: Corruption or Contextualism?" *Theologia Evangelica* 17, no. 1 (1984) 40–77.
———. "The Christian Gospel and the Ancestor Cult." *Missionalia* 1, no. 2 (1973) 46–73.
———. *Old and New in Southern Shona Independent Churches*. Vol. 1. *Church Growth-Causative Factors and Recruitment Techniques*. Change and Continuity in Africa. Amsterdam: Mouton, 1971.

Bibliography

———. *Old and New in Southern Shona Independent Churches.* Vol. 2. *Background and Rise of the Major Movements.* Change and Continuity in Africa. The Hague: Mouton, 1974.

———. *Quest for Belonging: An Introduction to a Study of African Independent Churches.* Gwere, Harare: Mambo, 1987.

———. "Towards a Sacramental Theology of the Environment in African Independent Churches." *Theologica Evangelica* 24, no. 1 (1991) 2–26.

Daneel, M. L., and J. N. J. Kritzinger. *Mission as Liberation: Third World Theologies.* Pretoria, South Africa: University of South Africa, 1983.

Davis, J., ed. *Religious Organization and Religious Experience.* London: Academic, 1982.

D'Costa, Gavin. *Christian Uniqueness Reconsidered: The Myth of a Pluralistic Theology of Religions.* Faith Meets Faith Series. Maryknoll, NY: Orbis, 1990.

de Gruchy, John W. *Christianity and Democracy: A Theology for a Just World Order.* Cape Town, South Africa: David Philip, 1995.

———. *Church Struggle in South Africa.* Grand Rapids: Eerdmans, 1976.

de Kock, Leon. *Christianizing Barbarians.* Johannesburg, South Africa: Witwatersrand University Press, 1999.

———. *Civilizing Barbarians: Missionary Narrative and African Textual Response in Nineteenth Century South Africa.* Johannesburg, South Africa: Witwatersrand University Press, 1996.

de Lacey, D. R. "Jesus as Mediator." *Journal for the Study of the New Testament* 29 (1987) 101–21.

Denis, Philippe, ed. "From Church History to Religious History: Strengths and Weaknesses of South African Religious Historiography." *Journal of Theology for Southern Africa* 99 (November 1996) 84–93.

———. *The Making of an Indigenous Clergy in South Africa.* Pietermaritzburg, South Africa: Cluster, 1994.

———. *Orality, Memory, and the Past: Listening to the Voices of Black Clergy under Colonialism and Apartheid.* Pietermaritzburg, South Africa: Cluster, 2000.

Dickson, Kwesi A., and Paul Ellingworth. *Biblical Revelation and African Beliefs.* Maryknoll, NY: Orbis, 1969.

Dinnerstein, Myra. "The American Zulu Mission in the Nineteenth Century: Clash Over Customs." *Church History* 45 (1976) 235–46.

Dodds, Glen Lyndon. *The Zulus and Matabele: Warrior Nations.* London: Arms and Armour, 1998.

Doke, C. M., et al. *English Zulu Dictionary: English-Zulu, Zulu English.* Johannesburg, South Africa: Witwatersrand University Press, 1990.

Douglas, Kelly Brown. *The Black Christ.* The Bishop Henry McNeal Turner Studies in North American Black Religion 9. Maryknoll, NY: Orbis, 1994.

Douglas, Mary. "Animals in Lele Religious Symbolism." *Africa* 27 (1957) 46–58.

Dovlo, Elom. "Ancestors and Soteriology in African and Japanese Religions." *Studies in Interreligious Dialogue* 33, no. 1 (1991) 48–56.

Drewal, Margaret Thompson. *Yoruba Ritual: Performers, Play, Agency.* African Systems of Thought. Bloomington: Indiana University Press, 1992.

Du Plessis, J. *A History of Christian Missions in South Africa.* Cape Town, South Africa: Struik, 1965.

Dubb, Allie A. *Community of the Saved: An African Revivalist Church in the East Cape.* Johannesburg, South Africa: Witwatersrand University Press, 1976.

Dube, John. *The Biography of Isaiah Shembe*. Edited by G. C. Oosthuizen. Translated by Hans-Jürgen Becken. Pietermaritzburg, South Africa: Shorter and Shooter, 1936.
Dube, Musa W. *Other Ways of Reading: African Women and the Bible*. Atlanta: Society of Biblical Literature, 2001.
Dzobo, Noah K. "African Ancestor Cult: The Theological Appraisal." *Reformed World* 38, no. 6 (1985) 333–40.
Eichrodt, Walther. *Theology of the Old Testament*. Vol. 1. Translated by J. A. Baker. Old Testament Library. Philadelphia: Westminster, 1961.
Eiselen, W. M. "Art of Divination as Practiced by the Bamasasemala." *Bantu Studies* 6 (1932) 251–63.
Eister, Allan W., ed. *Changing Perspectives in the Scientific Study of Religion*. New York: Wiley, 1973.
Ela, Jean-Marc. "Ancestors and the Christian Faith: An African Problem." In *Liturgy and Cultural Religious Traditions*, edited by Herman Schmidt and David Powers, 41–50. New York: Seabury, 1977.
Elphick, Richard, and Rodney Davenport, eds. *Christianity in South Africa: A Political, Social and Cultural History*. Oxford: Currey, 1996.
Emerson, Robert M., Rachel I. Fretz, and Linda L. Shaw. *Writing Ethnographic Fieldnotes*. Chicago: University of Chicago Press, 1995.
Ezeanya, Stephen N. "God, Spirits and the Spirit World." In *Biblical Revelation and African Beliefs*, edited by Kwesi A. Dickson and Paul Ellingworth, 30–46. Maryknoll, NY: Orbis, 1969.
Fabella, Virginia, and Sergio Torres, eds. *Doing Theology in a Divided World*. Maryknoll, NY: Orbis, 1985.
Fabian, Dapila N. "The Need for Indigenization of Bible Translations for African Christians." *AFER* 40 (1998) 21–43.
Farisani, Tshenuwani Simon. *In Transit: Between the Image of God and the Image of Man*. Grand Rapids: Eerdmans, 1990.
Fashole-Luke, Edward, Richard Gray, Adrian Hastings, and Godwin Tasie, eds. *Christianity in Independent Africa*. Bloomington: Indiana University Press, 1978.
Fee, Gordon D. *1 and 2 Timothy, Titus*. New International Biblical Commentary 13. Peabody, MA: Hendrickson, 1988.
Ferguson, Everett, ed. *Studies in Early Christianity: A Collection of Scholarly Essays*. New York: Garland, 1991.
Fernandez, James W. "African Religious Movements: Types and Dynamics." *Journal of Modern African Studies* 2, no. 4 (1963) 531–49.
———. "Location and Direction in African Religious Movements: Some Deictic Contours of Religious Conversion." *History of Religions* 25, no. 4 (1986) 352–67.
———. "Politics and Prophecy: African Religious Movements." *Practical Anthropology* 12, no. 2 (1963) 71–75.
———. "Precincts of the Prophet: A Day With Johannes Galilee Shembe." *Journal of Religion in Africa* 5, no. 1 (1973) 32–53.
Fiawoo, D. K. "Ancestral Worship Among the Ewe-Speaking People of Southern Ghana: A Study in Religious Change." *Ghana Journal of Sociology* 5, no. 2 (1969) 18–21.
Fischer, Alan, and Michael Albedas, eds. *A Question of Survival: Conversations with Key South Africans*. Johannesburg, South Africa: Jonathan Ball, 1987.
Flanagan, Finbarr. "African Independent Churches with Special Reference to Isaiah Shembe's Zulu Union." *African Eccesial Review* 23 (1981) 206–14.

Bibliography

Forson, Mathias Kwesi. "Split-Level Christianity in Africa: A Study of the Persistence of Traditional Religious Beliefs and Practices among the Akan Methodists of Ghana." PhD diss., Asbury Theological Seminary, 1993.

Fortes, M. "Some Reflections on Ancestor Worship in Africa." In *African Systems of Thought*, edited by G. Dieterlen and M. Fortes, 122–44. London: Oxford University Press, 1965.

Fredrickson, George M. *Black Liberation: A Comparative History of Black Ideologies in the United States and South Africa*. New York: Oxford University Press, 1995.

Frend, W. H. C. *Saints and Sinners in the Early Church: Differing and Conflicting Traditions in the First Six Centuries*. Theology and Life 2. Wilmington, DE: Glazier, 1985.

Friesen, J. Stanley. *Missionary Responses to Tribal Religions at Edinburgh, 1910*. Studies in Church History 1. New York: Lang, 1996.

———. "Origins of the Spiritual Healing Church in Botswana." *Mission Focus Annual Review* 1 (1993) 53–63.

Fuze, Magema M. *The Black People and Whence They Came: A Zulu View*. Translated by H. C. Lugg. Edited by A. T. Cope. Translation Series (Killie Campbell African Library) 1. Pietermaritzburg, South Africa: University of Natal Press, 1979.

Gable, Eric. "Women, Ancestors, and Alterity among the Manjaco of Guinea-Bassau." *Journal of Religion in Africa/Religion en Afrique* 26 (1996) 104–21.

Gaebelein, Arno C. *The Gospel of Matthew: An Exposition*. Neptune, NJ: Loizeaux, 1961.

Gall, Timothy L., ed. *Worldmark Encyclopedia of Cultures and Daily Life: Africa*. Vol. 1. Detroit: Gale Research, 1996.

Geertz, Clifford. *The Interpretation of Cultures: Selected Essays by Clifford Geertz*. New York: Basic, 1973.

Geffre, Claude, and Bertrand Luneau, eds. *The Churches of Africa: Future Prospects*. New York: Seabury, 1977.

Gefland, Michael. *Shona Religion With Special Reference to the Makorekore*. Cape Town, South Africa: Juta and Company, 1962.

Gehman, Richard J. *African Traditional Religion in Biblical Perspective*. Kijabi, Kenya: Kijabi Printing, 1987.

Gibbs, Henry. *Background to Bitterness: The Story of South Africa 1652–1954*. London: Muller, 1954.

Gibellini, Rosino, ed. *Paths of African Theology*. Maryknoll, NY: Orbis, 1994.

Gifford, Paul. *The Christian Churches and the Democratization of Africa*. Leiden: Brill, 1995.

Giles, Bridget. *Peoples of Southern Africa*. New York: The Diagram Group, 1997.

Gilliland, Dean S. "How Christian Are African Independent Churches?" *Missiology* 14 (1986) 259–72.

———. "Phenomenology as Mission Method." *Missiology* 7 (1979) 451–59.

———. "Principles of the Christian Approach to an African-Based Islamic Society." *Missiology* 25 (1996) 5–13.

Githieya, Francis Kimani. *The Freedom of the Spirit: African Indigenous Churches in Kenya*. American Academy of Religion Academy Series 94. Atlanta: Scholars, 1997.

Glasswell, Mark E., and Edward W. Fashole-Luke, eds. *New Testament Christianity for Africa and the World: Essays in Honour of Harry Sawyer*. London: SPCK, 1974.

Global Mapping. Colorado Springs: Global Mapping International, 1995.

Glock, Charles Y., and Rodney Stark. *Religion and Society in Tension*. Chicago: Rand McNally, 1965.

Gluckmann, Max. "Mortuary Customs Among the Southeastern Bantu." *Bantu Studies and General South African Anthropology* 11 (1937) 117–36.

Bibliography

———. "Social Aspects of First Fruit Ceremonies among the South-Eastern Bantu." *Africa* 11 (1938) 25–41.
———. "Some Processes of Social Change Illustrated from Zululand." *African Studies* 1 (1942) 243–60.
———. "Zulu Women in Hoecultural Ritual." *Bantu Studies and General South African Anthropology* 9 (1935) 255–71.
Goba, Bonganjalo. "Towards a Black Ecclesiology: Insights from the Society of Knowledge." *Missionalia* 9 (1981) 47–65.
Goody, Jack. *Succession to High Office*. Cambridge: Cambridge University Press, 1966.
Greenslade, S. L. *Schism in the Early Church*. London: SCM, 1953.
Gregg, Robert C., and Dennis E. Groh. *Early Arianism: A View of Salvation*. Philadelphia: Fortress, 1973.
Grillmeier, Aloys, SJ. *Christ in Christian Tradition: From the Apostolic Age to Chalcedon*. Vol. 1. Atlanta: John Knox, 1975.
Grimes, Ronald L. *Beginnings in Ritual Studies*. Columbia, SC: University of South Carolina Press, 1955.
Groves, C. P. *The Planting of Christianity in Africa*. 4 vols. London: Lutterworth, 1948–58.
Gunner, Elizabeth. *The Man of Heaven and the Beautiful Ones of God*. Boston: Brill, 2002.
———. "Power House, Prison House: An Oral Genre and Its Use in Isaiah Shembe's Nazareth Baptist Church." *Journal of Southern Africa Studies* 14, no. 2 (1988) 204–27.
———. "Testimonies of Dispossession and Repossession: Writing About the South African Prophet Isaiah Shembe." *Bulletin of the John Rylands University Library of Manchster* 73, no. 3 (1991) 93–103.
Hagner, Donald A. *Matthew 14–28*. Word Biblical Commentary 33b. Dallas: Word, 1995.
Hammond-Tooke, W. D. "Do the Southern Eastern Bantu Worship Their Ancestors?" In *Social System and Tradition in Southern Africa*, edited by J. Argyle and Preston-Whyte, 134–49. Cape Town, South Africa: Oxford University Press, 1978.
———. "The Initiation of a Baca Isangoma Diviner." *African Studies* 14 (1955) 17–21.
———. "Some Bhaca Religious Categories." *African Studies* 19, no. 1 (1960) 1–13.
Hanson, R. P. C. *The Search for the Christian Doctrine of God: The Arian Controversy* 318–31. Edinburgh: T. & T. Clark, 1988.
Hanretta, Sean. "Women, Marginality and the Zulu State: Women's Institutions and Power in the Early Nineteenth Century." *Journal of African History* 39 (1998) 389–415.
Harries, Patrick. "Imagery, Symbolism, and Tradition in a South African Bantustan: Mangosuthu Buthelezi, Inkatha, and Zulu History." Cape Town, South Africa: University of Cape Town, 105–25.
Harvey, Van A. *A Handbook of Theological Terms*. New York: Collier, 1964.
Hastings, Adrian. *The Church in Africa 1450–1950*. Oxford: Claredon, 1994.
———. *Church and Mission in Modern Africa*. Bronx: Fordham University Press, 1967.
———. *A History of African Christianity 1950–1975*. New York: Cambridge University Press, 1979.
Hauerwas, Stanley. *The Peaceable Kingdom: A Primer in Christian Ethics*. Notre Dame, IN: University of Notre Dame Press, 1983.
Hayward, Victor E. "African Independent Church Movements." *International Review of Missions* 52, no. 206 (1963) 163–72.
Healey, Joseph, and Donald Sybertz. *Towards an African Narrative Theology*. Faith and Cultures Series. Maryknoll, NY: Orbis, 1996.

Bibliography

Heidenman, Eugene S. "Syncretism, Contextualization, Orthodoxy, and Heresy." *Missiology* 25 (1996) 37–49.

Heiler, Friedrich. *Prayer: A Study in the History and Psychology of Religion.* New York: Oxford University Press, 1932.

Hening, E. F. *History of the African Mission of the Protestant Episcopal Church in the United States, with Memoirs of Deceased Missionaries and Notices of Native Customs.* New York: Stanford and Swords, 1850.

Hesselgrave, David J. *Communicating Christ Cross-Culturally: An Introduction to Missionary Communication.* 2nd ed. Grand Rapids: Zondervan, 1991.

———. *Dynamic Religious Movements.* Grand Rapids: Baker, 1997.

Hesselgrave, David J., and Edward Rommen. *Contextualization: Meaning, Methods and Models.* Grand Rapids: Baker, 1989.

Hexham, Irving. "African Religions: Recent and Lesser Known Works." *Religion* 20 (1989) 361–72.

———. *G. C. Oosthuisen on Isaiah Shembe and the AmaNazarites.* Calgary: University of Calgary Press, 1993.

———. "Isaiah Shembe, Zulu Religious Leader (African Traditional Religion or New Religious Movement)." *Religion* 27 (1997) 361–73.

———. "Lord of the Sky, King of the Earth: Zulu Traditional Religion and Belief in the Sky God." *Studies in Religion* 10 (1981) 273–85.

———. *The Scriptures of the amaNazaretha of EkuphaKameni: Selected Writings of the Zulu Prophets Isaiah and Londa Shembe.* Edited by Irving Hexam, et al. Translated by Londa Shembe and Hans-Jürgen Becken. Calgary: University of Calgary Press, 1994.

———. "The Scriptures of the amaNazaretha of EkuphaKameni: Selected Writings of the Zulu Prophets Isaiah and Londa Shembe." *Journal of African History* 37 (1996) 332–34.

———. "Survey Article: African Religions: Some Recent and Lesser Known Works." *Religion* 20 (1990) 361–72.

———. *Texts on Zulu Religion: Traditional Zulu Ideas About God.* African Studies 6. Lewiston, NY: Mellen, 1987.

———. "Zulu Spiritual Leader Murdered." *Christianity Today* 33, no. 65 (1989) 16.

Hexham, Irving, and G. C. Oosthuizen, eds. *The Story of Isaiah Shembe: The History and Traditions Centered on Ekuphakameni and Mount Nhlangakazi.* Sacred History and Traditions of the AmaNazaretha 1. Translated by Hans-Jurgen Becken. Lewiston, NY: Mellen, 1996.

———. *The Story of Isaiah Shembe: Early Regional Traditions of the Acts of the Nazarites.* Sacred History and Traditions of the AmaNazaretha 2. Lewiston, NY: Mellen, 1999.

———. *The Story of Isaiah Shembe: The Continuing Story of the Sun and the Moon: Oral Testimony and the Sacred History of the Ama-Nazarites Under the Leadership Traditions of the AmaNazaretha.* Sacred History and Traditions of the AmaNazaretha 3. Translated by Hans-Jurgen Becken. Lewiston, NY: Mellen, 2001.

Hexham, Irving, and Karla Poewe. *New Religions as Global Cultures: Making the Human Sacred.* Boulder, CO: Westview, 1997.

Hiebert, Paul G. *Anthropological Insights for Missionaries.* Grand Rapids: Baker, 1985.

———. *Anthropological Reflections on Missiological Issues.* Grand Rapids: Baker, 1994.

———. "Critical Contextualization." *International Bulletin of Missionary Research* 11, no. 3 (1987) 104–12.

———. *Cultural Anthropology.* 2nd ed. Grand Rapids: Baker, 1983.

———. *Missiological Implications of Epistemological Shifts: Affirming Truth in a Modern/Postmodern World.* Harrisburg, PA: Trinity, 1999.
Hiebert, Paul G., and Eloise Hiebert Meneses. *Incarnational Ministry: Planting Churches in Band, Tribal, Peasant, and Urban Societies.* Grand Rapids: Baker, 1995.
Hiebert, Paul G., R. Daniel Shaw, and Tite Tienou, eds. *Understanding Folk Religion: A Christian Response to Popular Beliefs and Practices.* Grand Rapids: Baker, 1999.
Hinchliff, Peter. *The Church in South Africa: Church History Outlines.* London: SPCK, 1968.
Hollenweger, Walter J. "Charismatic Renewal in the Third World: Implication for Mission." *Occasional Bulletin of Missionary Research* 4, no. 2 (1980) 68–76.
Hood, Robert E. *Begrimed and Black: Christian Traditions on Blacks and Blackness.* Minneapolis: Fortress, 1994.
———. *Contemporary Political Orders and Christ: Karl Barth's Christology and Political Praxis.* Pittsburgh Theological Monograph Series 14. Allison Park, PA: Pickwick, 1985.
———. *Must God Remain Greek? Afro Culture and God-Talk.* Minneapolis: Fortress, 1990.
———. "Role of Black Religion in Political Change: The Haitian Revolution and Voodoo." *Journal of the Interdenominational Theological Center* 9, no. 1 (1981) 45–69.
———. "A Theological Framework for an Afro-Anglican Communion." *Journal of Religious Thought* 44 (1987) 61–63.
Hope, Marjorie, and James Young. *The South African Churches in a Revolutionary Situation.* 2nd ed. Maryknoll, NY: Orbis, 1983.
Hostetter, Darrel M. "Disarming the Emadloti: The Ancestors." In *Empirical Studies of African Independent Churches,* edited by G. C. Oosthuizen and Irving Hexham, 111–27. Lewiston, NY: Mellen, 1991.
———. "Stories of Faith Among the Zionists." In *Afro-Christianity at the Grassroots,* edited by G. C. Oosthuizen, M. C. Kitshoff, and S. W. D. Dube, 246–58. Leiden: Brill, 1994.
Hunter, George G., III. *The Celtic Way of Evangelism: How Christianity Can Reach the West Again.* Nashville: Abingdon, 2000.
Hutchinson, Bertram. "Some Social Consequences of Missionary Activity among South African Bantu." *Practical Anthropology* 6 (1959) 67–77.
Idowu, E. Bolaji. *African Traditional Religion: A Definition.* London: SCM, 1991.
Isichei, Elizabeth. *A History of Christianity in Africa: From Antiquity to the Present.* Grand Rapids: Eerdmans, 1995.
Jackel, Theodor G. "The Zion Christian Church: A Christian Church with African Characteristics, or an African Church with Christian Characteristics?" PhD diss. University of Natal, Pietermaritzburg.
Jafta, Lizo Doda. "African Independent Churches in Dialogue with Schleiermacher." In *Empirical Studies of African Independent Churches,* edited by G.C. Oosthuizen and Irving Hexham, 141–56. Lewiston, NY: Mellen, 1992.
———. "One, the Other, the Divine, the Many in Zulu Traditional Religion of Southern Africa." *Dialogue and Alliance: Journal of the International Religions Foundation* 6, no. 2 (1992) 79–90.
Jasper, David, and T. R. Wright, eds. *The Critical Spirit and the Will to Believe: Essays in Nineteenth-Century Literature and Religion.* New York: St. Martin's, 1989.
Jenkins, Philip. *The Next Christendom: The Coming of Global Christianity.* Oxford: Oxford University Press, 2002.
Jeffreys, M. D. W. "Confessions by Africans." *The Eastern Anthropologist* 6 (1952) 42–57.

Bibliography

Johnson, Walton, George Bond, and Shelia Walker, eds. *African Christianity: Patterns of Religious Continuity.* New York: Academic, 1979.
Johnstone, Patrick. *Operation World.* Grand Rapids: Zondervan, 1994.
Kabasele, Francois. "Christ as Ancestor and Elder Brother." In *Faces of Jesus in Africa*, edited by Robert J. Schreiter, 116–27. Faith and Culture Series. Maryknoll, NY: Orbis, 1995.
Kaiser, Walter C., Jr. *Toward an Exegetical Theology: Biblical Exegesis for Preachers and Teachers.* Grand Rapids: Baker, 1981.
———. *Mission in the Old Testament.* Grand Rapids: Baker, 2000.
Kalu, Ogbu U., ed. *The History of Christianity in West Africa.* London: Longman, 1980.
Karenga, M. Kwanzaa. *A Celebration of Family, Community and Culture.* Los Angeles: University of Sankore Press, 1997.
Karotemprel, Sebastian, ed. *Following Christ in Mission: A Foundational Course in Missiology.* Nairobi, Kenya: Pauline Publications Africa, 1995.
Kelly, J. N. D. *Early Christian Doctrine.* 2nd ed. New York: Harper and Brothers, 1960.
Kendrim, Protus O. "Towards Inclusiveness for Women in the African Churches." *Mission Studies* 12 (1995) 71–77.
Kiernan, J. P. "The African Independent Churches." In *Living Faiths in South Africa*, edited by Martin Prozesky and Jon de Gruchy, 116–28. Cape Town, South Africa: David Philips, 1995.
———. "The Canticles of Zion: Song as Word and Action in Zulu Zionist Discourse." *Journal of Religion in Africa* 20, no. 2 (1990) 188–204.
———. "The Role of the Adversary in Zulu Zionist Churches." *Religion in Southern Africa* 8 (1987) 3–13.
———. *The Production and Management of Therapeutic Power in Zionist Churches Within a Zulu City: Studies in African Health and Medicine.* Vol. 4. Lewiston, NY: Mellen, 1990.
———. "Wear 'N' Tear and Repair: The Colour Coding of Mystical Mendig in Zulu Zionist Churches." *Africa* 61, no. 1 (1991) 26–39.
———. "The Weapons of Zion." *Journal of Religion in Africa* 10, no. 1 (1979) 13–21.
King, Fergus J. "Angels and Ancestors: A Basis for Christology?" *Mission Studies* 11 (1994) 10–26.
King, Nicholas, SJ. *Setting the Gospel Free.* Pietermaritzburg, South Africa: Cluster, 1995.
King, Noel Q. *Religions of Africa: A Pilgrimage Into Traditional Religions.* New York: Harper & Row, 1970.
———. *Religions of Africa.* New York: Harper & Row, 1969.
Kirwen, Michael C. *The Missionary and the Diviner: Contending Theologies of Christian and African Religions.* Maryknoll, NY: Orbis, 1987.
Kitshoff, M. C. *African Independent Churches Today: Kaleidoscope of Afro-Christianity.* Vol. 44 of *African Studies.* Lewiston, NY: Mellen, 1996.
———. "Exorcism as Healing Ministry in the African Independent/Indigenous Churches." *Studia Historiae Ecclesiasticae* 20, no. 1 (1994) 30–50.
———. "From Veneration to Deification of Isaiah Shembe: Reflections on an Oral History." In *African Independent Churches Today: Kaleidoscope of Afro-Christianity*, edted by M. C. Kitshoff, 282–98. African Studies 44. Lewiston, NY: Mellen, 1996.
———. "Isaiah Shembe's Views on the Ancestors in Biblical Perspective." *Journal of Theology of Southern Africa* 95 (July 1996) 23–36.
Knight, George W. *Commentary on the Pastoral Epistles.* New International Greek Testament Commentary. Grand Rapids: Eerdmans, 1992.

Bibliography

Kolie, Cece. "Jesus as Healer." In *Faces of Jesus in Africa*, edited by Robert J. Schreiter, 128–50. Faith and Culture Series. Maryknoll, NY: Orbis, 1997.
Kopytoff, Igor. "Ancestors as Elders in Africa." *Africa* 41 (1979) 129–42.
Kraft, Charles H. *Appropriate Christianity*. Pasadena, CA: William Cary Library, 2005.
———. *Christianity in Culture: A Study in Dynamic Biblical Theologizing in Cross-Cultural Perspective*. Maryknoll, NY: Orbis, 1979.
———. *Communication Theory for Christian Witness*. Nashville: Abingdon, 1983.
———. "The Contextualization of Theology." *Evangelical Missions Quarterly* 14 (1978) 31–46.
Kretzschmar, Louise. *The Voice of Black Theology in South Africa*. Johannesburg, South Africa: Ravan, 1986.
Krige, Eileen. "Girls' Puberty Songs and Their Relation to Fertility, Health." *Africa* 38 (1968) 173–98.
Kristensen, W. Brede. *The Meaning of Religion: Lectures in the Phenomenology of Religion*. Translated by John B. Carmen. The Hague: Nijhoff, 1960.
Kritzinger, J. N. J., and W. A. Saayman, eds. *Mission in Creative Tension: A Dialogue with David Bosch*. Pretoria, South Africa: Missiological Society, 1989.
Kuiper, B. K. *The Church in History*. Grand Rapids: Eerdmans, 1982.
Kunnie, Julian. *Models of Black Theology: Issues in Class, Culture and Gender*. Valley Forge, PA: Trinity, 1994.
Kurtz, Lester. *Gods in the Global Village: The World's Religions in Sociological Perspective*. Thousand Oaks, CA: Pine Forge, 1995.
Kuster, Volker. *The Many Faces of Jesus Christ: Intercultural Christology*. Maryknoll, NY: Orbis, 1999.
Lalouvière, Paul la Hausse de. *Restless Identities: Signatures of Nationalism, Zulu Ethnicity and History in the Lives of Petros Lamula (c. 1881–1948) and Lymon Maling (1889–c.1936)*. Pietermaritzburg, South Africa: University of Natal Press, 2000.
Landau, Paul Stuart. *The Realm of the World: Language, Gender, and Christianity in a Southern African Kingdom*. Portsmouth: Heinemann, 1995.
Langley, J. Ayo. *Ideologies of Liberation in Black Africa, 1856–1970*. London: Rex Collins, 1979.
Larom, Margaret S., ed. *Claiming the Promise: African Churches Speak*. New York: Friendship, 1994.
Lawson, E. Thomas. *Religions of Transformation: Traditions in Transformation*. San Francisco: Harper & Row, 1985.
Lea, Thomas D., and Hayne P. Griffin. *1, 2 Timothy, Titus*. The New American Commentary 34. Nashville: Broadman, 1992.
Lee, S. G. "Social Influences in Zulu Dreaming." *The Journal of Social Psychology* 47 (1958) 265–83.
Legrand, Lucien. *The Bible on Culture: Belonging or Dissenting?* Faith and Culture Series. Maryknoll, NY: Orbis, 2000.
Lessa, William A., and Evon Z. Vogt, eds. *Reader in Comparative Religion: An Anthropological Approach*. 4th ed. New York: Harper & Row, 1979.
Levine, Donald N. "The Flexibility of Traditional Culture." *Journal of Social Issues* 24, no. 4 (1968) 129–41.
Lewis, Gavin. *Between the Wire and the Wall: A History of South African "Coloured" Politics*. Cape Town, South Africa, David Phillips, 1987.
Lincoln, Andrew T. *Ephesians*. Word Biblical Commentary 42. Dallas: Word, 1990.

Bibliography

Lingenfelter, Sherwood. *Agents of Transformation: A Guide for Effective Cross-Cultural Ministry.* Grand Rapids: Baker, 1996.

———. *Transforming Culture: A Challenge for Christian Mission.* Grand Rapids: Baker, 1992.

Linton, Ralph. *The Study of Man.* Madison, WI: Appleton-Century, 1936.

Loewen, Jacob A. "Mission Churches, Independent Churches, and Felt Needs in Africa." *Missiology* 4 (1976) 405–25.

Long, Charles H. "The West African High God: History and Religious Experiences." *History of Religions* 3 (1963) 328–42.

Loubser, J. A. *A Critical Review of Racial Theology in South Africa: The Apartheid Bible.* Texts and Studies in Religion 53. Lewiston, NY: Mellen, 1987.

———. "The Oral Christ of Shembe: Believing in Jesus in Oral and Literate Societies." *Scriptura* 12 (1993) 70–80.

Lukhaimane, E. K. "The St. Engenas Zion Christian Church." In *Afro-Christian Religion at the Grassroots in Southern Africa*, edited by G. C. Oosthuizen and Irving Hexham, 227–43. Lewiston, NY: Mellen, 1991.

Lumbala, F. Kabasele. *Celebrating Jesus in Africa: Liturgy and Inculturation.* Maryknoll, NY: Orbis, 1998.

Luzbetak, Louis J. *The Church and Cultures: New Perspectives in Missiological Anthropology.* Maryknoll, NY: Orbis, 1988.

Lwandle, Protus Sipho. "Concepts of Christ in Africa as Reflected in the Shembe Church." Master's thesis, University of South Africa, 1996.

MacCulloch, J. A. "Abode of the Blest." In vol. 2 of *Encyclopedia of Religion and Ethics*, edited by James Hastings, 680–87. New York: Scribners, 1955.

———. "Door." In vol. 4 of *Encyclopedia of Religion and Ethics*, edited by James Hastings, 846–52. New York: Scribners, 1955

———. "State of the Dead." In *Encyclopedia of Religion and Ethics*, edited by James Hastings, 11:817–28. New York: Scribners, 1955.

Macdonald, James. "Manners, Customs, Superstitions, and Religions of South African Tribes." *Journal of the Anthropological Institute of Great Britain and Ireland* 19 (1890) 264–96.

Magesa, Laurenti. *African Religion: The Moral Traditions of Abundant Life.* Maryknoll, NY: Orbis, 1997.

Mahdi, Louise Carus, Steven Foster, and Meredith Little, eds. *Betwixt and Between: Patterns of Masculine and Feminine Initiation.* La Salle, IL: Open Court, 1987.

Makhathini, D. L. "Ancestors, Umoya, Angels." In *Our Approach to the Independent Church Movement in South Africa*, edited by Hans-Jürgen Becken, 154–59. Mapumulo, South Africa: Missiological Institute, Lutheran Theological College, 1965.

Makhubu, Paul. *Who Are the Independent Churches?* Johannesburg, South Africa: Skotaville, 1991.

Maluleke, Tinyiko Sam. "Black and African Theologies in the New World Order: A Time to Drink From Our Own Wells." *Journal of Theology for Southern Africa* 96 (1997) 3–17.

———. "Do I, With My Excellent PhD, Still Need Affirmative Action? The Contribution of Black Theology to the Debate." *Missionalia* 24 (1996) 303–21.

———. "Half a Century of African Christian Theologies: Elements of the Emerging Agenda for the Twenty-First Century." *Journal of Theology for Southern Africa* 90 (1997) 4–23.

Bibliography

Mana, Kä. *Christians and Churches of Africa*. Theology in Africa Series. Maryknoll, NY: Orbis, 2004.
Manus, Ukachukwu Chris. *Christ, the African King: New Testament Christology*. New York: Peter Lang, 1993.
Markus, Robert. *The End of Ancient Christianity*. Cambridge: Cambridge University Press, 1990.
Marquard, Leo. *The Story of South Africa*. London: Faber & Faber, 1963.
Marsh, John. *The Gospel of Saint John*. London: Penguin, 1988.
Martey, Emmanuel. *African Theology: Inculturation and Liberation*. Maryknoll, NY: Orbis, 1993.
Masuku, Tobias. "African Initiated Churches: Christian Partners or Antagonists? Reflecting on the Unisa Dictionary Project with AICs." *Missionalia* 24 (1996) 441–55.
Maylam, Paul. *A History of the African People of South Africa: From the Early Iron Age to the 1970s*. London: Croom Helm, 1986.
Mayr, Rev. Father. "The Zulu Kafirs of Natal." *Anthropos* 1 (1906) 453–72.
Mbiti, John S. *African Religions and Philosophy*. New York: Praeger, 1969.
———. *African Religions and Philosophy*. 2nd ed. Portsmouth: Heinemann Education, 1990.
———. "African Tradition and the Christian God [Review]." *International Review of Missionary Research* 5 (1981) 41–42.
———. *Concepts of God in Africa*. London: SPCK, 1970.
———. "The Encounter of Christian Faith and African Religion." *Christian Century* 98, no. 9 (1981) 817–20.
———. *Introduction to African Religion*. New York: Praeger, 1975.
———. *The Prayers of African Religion*. Maryknoll, NY: Orbis, 1975,
———. "Response to John Kinney." *Occasional Bulletin of Missionary Research* 3, no. 2 (1976) 68.
McCabe, Joseph. *The Social Record of Christianity*. London: Watts, 1935.
McCall, Daniel F., and Edna G. Bay. *African Images: Essays in African Iconology*. Boston University Papers on Africa 6. New York: Africana, 1975.
McGeveran, William A. *The World Almanac and Book of Facts*. New York: World Almanac Books, 2003
McKenzie, Peter. *The Christians: Their Beliefs and Practices*. London: SPCK, 1988.
McVeigh, Malcolm J. *God in Africa: Conceptions of God in African Traditional Religion and Christianity*. Cape Cod, MA: Stark, 1974.
Mendosa, Eugene L. "Journey of the Soul in Sisala Cosmology." *Journal of Religion in Africa/Religion en Afrique* 7 (1975) 62–70.
Mitchell, Henry. *Black Church Beginnings: The Long-Hidden Realities of the First Years*. Grand Rapids: Eerdmans, 2004.
Mitchell, R. C., and H. W. Turner. *A Comprehensive Bibliography of Modern African Religious Movements*. Evanston, IL: Northwestern University Press, 1967.
Moila, M. P. "The Effect of Belief in the Living Dead in the Church's Mission in South Africa." *Africa Theological Journal* 18 (1989) 140–50.
Moore, Basil, ed. *The Challenge of Black Theology in South Africa*. Atlanta: John Knox, 1973.
Moripe, Simon. "Indigenous Clergy in the Zion Christian Church." In *The Making of an Indigenous Clergy in Southern Africa*, edited by Philippe Denis, 103–22. Pietermaritzburg, South Africa: Cluster, 1995.

Bibliography

Morris, Donald R. *The Washing of the Spears: The Rise and Fall of the Zulu Nation.* New York: Simon and Schuster, 1965.
Morris, Leon. *The Gospel According to John.* New International Commentary on the New Testament. Grand Rapids: Eerdmans, 1971.
Mosala, Itumeleng J. *Biblical Hermeneutics and Black Theology in South Africa.* Grand Rapids: Eerdmans, 1989.
Mpanza, Mthembeni. "The Biography of Isaiah Shembe." No publishing data.

M'Passou, Denis. "The Continuing Tension Between Christianity and Rites of Passage in Swaziland." In *Rites of Passage in Contemporary Africa: Interaction Between Christian and African Traditional Religions*, edited by James L. Cox, 15–33. Cardiff, Wales: Cardiff Academic, 1998.
Mthethwa, B. N. "Music and Dance as Therapy in African Traditional Societies with Special Reference to the iBlanda amaNazaretha ('the Church of the Nazarites')." In *Afro-Christian Religion and Healing in Southern Africa*, edited by G. C. Oosthuizen, S. D. Edwards, W. H. Wessels, and Irving Hexham, 241–56. African Studies 8. Lewiston, NY: Mellen, 1989.
Mugabe, Henry Johannes. "Christology in an African Context." *Review and Expositor* 88 (1991) 343–56.
Mugambi, J. N. K. *African Heritage and Contemporary Christianity.* Nairobi, Kenya: Longman Kenya, 1989.
———. *The Church in African Christianity: Innovative Essays in Ecclesiology.* Nairobi, Kenya: Initiatives, 1990
Mugambi, J. N. K. and Laurenti Magesa, eds. *Jesus in African Christianity: Experimentation and Diversity in African Christology.* 2nd ed. Nairobi, Kenya: Initiatives, 1998.
Muller, Carol. *Rituals of Fertility and the Sacrifice of Desire: Nazarite Women's Performance in South Africa.* Chicago: University of Chicago Press, 1999.
———. "Written into the Book of Life: Nazarite Women's Performance Inscribed as Spiritual Text in *Ibandla lamaNazaretha.*" *Research in African Literatures* 28, no. 1 (1997) 3–14.
Murray, Colin. *Families Divided.* Johannesburg, South Africa: Ravan Press, 1981.
Murray, G. W. "The Northern Beja." *Journal of the Royal Anthropological Institute of Great Britain and Ireland* 57 (1927) 39–53.
Muzibuko, B. A. *Missiology: Mission as African Initiative: African Initiated Churches, Nisa Study Guide.* Pretoria, South Africa: University of South Africa, 1989.
Muzorewa, Gwinyai H. "Christ as Our Ancestor: Christology from an African Perspective: A Review Essay." *African Theological Journal* 17 (1988) 255–64.
———. *The Origins and Development of African Theology.* Maryknoll, NY: Orbis, 1985.
Nash, Ronald H. "The Notion of Mediator in Alexandrian Judaism and the Epistle to the Hebrews." *Westminster Theological Journal* 40 (Fall 1977) 89–115.
Naude, Piet. The Zionist Christian Church In South Africa: A Case-Study in Oral Theology. Lewiston, NY: Mellen, 1995.
Neill, Stephen. *A History of Christian Missions.* Harmondsworth, UK: Penguin, 1964.
———. *Jesus through Many Eyes: Introduction to the Theology of the New Testament.* Philadelphia: Fortress, 1976.
Neimark, Philip J. *The Way of Orisa: Empowering Your Life through the Ancient African Religion of Ifa.* San Francisco: Harper, 1993.
Ngada, N. H., and K. E. Mofokeng. *African Christian Witness: African Indigenous Churches.* Pietermaritzburg, South Africa: Cluster, 2001.

Ngubane, J. B. "The Role of Amadlozi/Amathongo as Seen in the Writing of W. B. Vilakazi." *Religion in Southern Africa* 5, no. 2 (1984) 55–75.
Ngubane, H. *Body and Mind in Zulu Medicine: An Ethnography for Health and Disease in Nyuswa-Zulu Thought and Practice.* London: Academic, 1977.
Nichols, Bruce J. "Theological Education and Evangelization." In *Let the Earth Hear His Voice*, edited by J. D. Douglas, 647. Minneapolis: World Wide, 1975.
Nida, Eugene A. *Customs and Cultures: Anthropology for Christian Missions.* New York: Harper & Row, 1953.
———. *Message and Mission: The Communication of the Christian Faith.* New York: Harper & Row, 1959.
———. "New Religions for Old: A Study of Culture Change." *Practical Anthropology* 18, no. 6 (1971) 241–53.
———. *Religion Across Cultures: A Study in the Communication of the Christian Faith.* Pasadena, CA: William Carey Library, 1968.
———. "Religion: Communication with the Supernatural." *Practical Anthropology* 7, no. 3 (1958) 97–112.
———. "Some Comments Made During Discussion Sessions." In *Church and Culture Change in Africa: Lux Mundi* 3, edited by David Bosch, 94–99. Pretoria, South Africa: N. G. Kerk-Boekhandel, 1971.
Nkurunziza, Deusdedit R. K. *Bantu Philosophy of Life in the Light of the Christian Message: A Basis for an African Vitalistic Theology.* Frankfurt: Lang, 1989.
Norris, Richard A., Jr., ed. *The Christological Controversy.* Philadelphia: Fortress, 1980.
Northcott, Cecil. *Christianity in Africa.* Philadelphia: Westminster, 1963.
Nussbaum, Stan. "Toward Theological Dialogue: A Study of Five Congregants in Lesotho." PhD thesis, University of South Africa, 1986.
Nxumalo, Jabulani A. "Christ and Ancestors in the African World: A Pastoral Consideration." *Journal of Theology for Southern Africa* 32 (1980) 3–21.
Nyamiti, Charles. "African Ancestral Ecclesiology: Its Relevance for African Local Churches." In *How Local Is the Local Church?* edited by A. Radoli, 36–56. Gweru, Harare: Mambo, 1993.
———. "The African Sense of God's Motherhood in the Light of Chrsitian Faith." *AFER* 23, no. 5 (1981) 269–74.
———. *African Theology: Its Nature, Problems, and Methods.* Kampala, Uganda: Gaba, 1973.
———. *Christ as Our Ancestor: Christology from an African Perspective.* Gweru, Harare: Mambo, 1984.
———. "Contemporary African Christologies: Assessment and Practical Suggestions." In *Paths of African Theology*, edited by Rosini Gibellini, 62–77. Maryknoll, NY: Orbis, 1994.
———. "Contemporary Liberation Theologies in the Light of the African Traditional Conception of Evil." *Studia Missionalia* 45 (1996) 237–65.
———. *The Scope of African Theology.* Kampala, Uganda: Gaba, 1973.
Oduyoye, Mercy Amba. *Beads and Strands: Reflections of an African Woman on Christianity in Africa.* Theology in Africa Series. Maryknoll, NY: Orbis, 2004.
Oduyoye, Mercy Amba, and Musimbi R.A. Kanyoro, eds. *The Will To Arise: Women, Tradition and the Church in Africa.* Maryknoll, NY: Orbis, 1992.
Ogden, Graham S. "Ancestors and the Present: An OT View and Some Implications." *Taiwan Journal of Theology* 2 (1980) 132–43

Bibliography

Okeke, George E. "Ancestor Worship Among the Igbo." *Communio Viatorum* 27, no. 3 (1984) 137–52.

Okolo, Chukwudum B. "Christ is Black." In *African Christian Spirituality*, edited by Aylward Shorter, 68–71. Maryknoll, NY: Orbis, 1978.

Okurre, Teresa. "Conversion, Commitment: An African Perspective." *Mission Studies* 10 (1993) 109–33.

Oladipo, Caleb Oluremi. *The Development of the Doctrine of the Holy Spirit in the Yoruba (African) Indigenous Christian Movement*. Theology and Religion, 185 New York: Lang, 1996.

Olupona, Jacob K. *African Traditional Religions in Contemporary Society*. St. Paul: Paragon, 1991.

Olupona, Jacob K., and Sulayman S. Nyang, eds. *Religious Plurality in Africa: Essays in Honour of John S. Mbiti*. Religion and Society 32. Berlin: Mouton De Gruyter, 1993.

Ong, Walter. *Orality and Literacy*. New York: Routlege, 2002.

Oosthuizen, G. C. *Afro-Christian Religions*. Leiden: Brill, 1979.

———. *African Independent Churches and Small Businesses: Spiritual Support for Secular Empowerment*. Pretoria, South Africa: HSRC Publishers, 1997.

———. "Baptism in the Context of the African Independent Churches." In *Afro-Christian Religion and Healing in Southern Africa*, edited by G. C. Oosthuizen, S. D. Edwards, W. H. Wessels, and Irving Hexham, 137–88. African Studies 8. Lewiston, NY: Mellen, 1989.

———. *The Healer-Prophet in Afro-Christian Churches*. New York: Brill, 1992.

———. "Indigenous Christianity and the Future of the Church in South Africa." *International Bulletin of Missionary Research* 21, no. 1 (1997) 8–12.

———. "Interpretation of Demonic Powers in Southern African Independent Churches." *Missiology* 16 (1988) 3–22.

———. "Isaiah Shembe and the Zulu Worldview." In *Our Approach to the Independent Church Movement*, 115–53. Mapumulo, South Africa: Missiological Institute.

———. "Isaiah Shembe and the Zulu Worldview." *History of Religions* 8 (1968) 1–30.

———. "Leadership Struggle within the Church of the Nazarites: Ibandla lamaNazaretha." *Religion in Southern Africa* 2, no. 2 (1981) 12–24.

———. *Post-Christianity in Africa: A Theological and Anthropological Study*. Grand Rapids: Eerdmans, 1968.

———. *Studies on the Nazareth Baptist Church/Ibandla Lamanazaretha*. Translated by Hans-Jurgen Becken. Natal, South Africa: Shuter and Shooter, 1993.

———. "The Theology of Londa Shembe." In *The Scriptures of the AmaNazaretha of Ekuphakameni*, edited by Irving Hexham, 23–49. Calgary: University of Calgary Press, 1994.

———. *The Theology of a South African Messiah: An Analysis of "The Hymnal of the Church of the Nazarites."* Leiden: Brill, 1976.

Oosthuizen, G. C., S. D. Edwards, W. H. Wessels, and Irving Hexham, eds. *Afro-Christian Religion and Healing in Southern Africa*. African Studies 8. Lewiston, NY: Mellen, 1989.

Oosthuizen, G. C., and Irving Hexham. *Afro-Christian Religion at the Grassroots in Southern Africa*. African Studies 19. Lewiston, NY: Mellen, 1991.

———. *Empirical Studies of African Independent/Indigenous Churches*. Lewiston, NY: Mellen, 1992.

Bibliography

———. "Diviner-Prophet Parallels in the African Independent and Traditional Churches and Traditional Religion." In *Empirical Studies of African Independent/Indigenous Churches*, edited by Irving Hexham, 163–94. Lewiston, NY: Mellen, 1992.

———. *Studies of the Nazareth Baptist Church Ibandla LamaNazaretha*. Vol. 1 of *The Story of Isaiah Shembe*. Lewiston, NY: Mellen, 1994.i

Oosthuizen, G. C., M. C. Kitshoff, and S. W. D. Dube, eds. *Afro-Christianity at the Grassroots: Its Dynamics and Strategies*. Studies of Religion in Africa 9. Leiden: Brill, 1994.

Osovo, Onibere S. G. A. "Christian Reactions to Indigenous Religion in Nigeria: The Ancestor Factor as a Case-in-point." *Bulletin de Theologie Africaine* 3, no. 5 (1980) 53–59.

Paden, John N., and Edward W. Soja. *The African Experience: Essays*. Evanston, IL: Northwestern University Press, 1970.

Paden, William E. *Interpreting the Sacred: Ways of Viewing Religion*. Boston: Beacon, 1992.

Papini, Robert. "Carl Faye's Transcript of Isaiah Shembe's Testimony of His Early Life and Calling." *Journal of Religion in Africa* 29 (1999) 243–84.

Papini, Robert, and Irving Hexham, eds. *The Catechism of the Nazarites and Related Writings*. Vol. 4. Lewiston, NY: Mellen, 2002.

Parratt, John, ed. *The Practice of Presence: Shorter Writings of Harry Sawyer*. Grand Rapids: Eerdmans, 1994.

———. *A Reader in African Christian Theology*. London: SPCK, 1988.

Parrinder, Geoffrey. *Africa's Three Religions*. 2nd ed. London: Sheldon, 1976.

———. *African Traditional Religion*. 2nd ed. London: SPCK, 1962.

———. "Learning from Other Faiths: VI. African Religion." *The Expository Times* 133, no. 11 (1972) 324–28.

Partain, Jack. "Christians and Their Ancestors: a Dilemma of African Theology." *Christian Century* 103, no. 36 (1986) 1066–69.

Paton, Alan. *Hope for South Africa*. New York: Praeger, 1959.

Pauw, B. A. *Religion in a Tswana Chiefdom*. Westport, CT: Greenwood, 1960.

P'Bitek, Okot. *African Religions in Western Scholarship*. Kampala, Uganda: East African Literature Bureau, 1970.

Pelikan, Jaroslav. *The Christian Tradition: A History of the Development of Doctrine: The Emergence of the Catholic Tradition (100–600)*. Chicago: University of Chicago Press, 1971.

Pillay, J. G., and J. W. Hofmeyer, eds. *Perspectives on Church History: An Introduction for South African Readers*. Pretoria, South Africa: Haum, 1991.

Platvoet, Jan, James Cox, and Jacob Olupona, eds. *The Study of Religions in Africa Past, Present and Prospects*. Cambridge: Roots and Branches, 1996.

Pobee, J. S., ed. *Religion in a Pluralistic Society*. Leiden: Brill, 1976.

Pobee John S., and Gabriel Ositelu, II. *African Initiatives in Christianity: The Growth, Gifts, and Diversities of Indigenous African Churches: A Challenge to the Ecumenical Movement*. Geneva: WCC, 1998.

———. "Aspects of African Traditional Religion." *Sociological Analysis* 37 (spring 1976) 1–18.

———. *Toward an African Theology*. Nashville: Abingdon, 1979.

Poewe, Karla. *Charismatic Christianity as a Global Culture*. Columbia: University of South Carolina, 1994.

———. *Religion, Kinship, and Economy in Luapula, Zambia*. African Studies 9. Lewiston, NY: Mellen, 1989.

Bibliography

Pope-Levison, Priscilla, and John R. Levison. *Jesus in Global Contexts*. Louisville: Westminster, 1992.
Prestige, G. L. *God in Patristic Thought*. London: SPCK, 1952.
Pretorius, Hennie, and Lizo Jafta. "A Branch Springs Out: African Initiated Churches." In *Christianity in South Africa: A Political, Social and Cultural History*, edited by Richard Elphick and Rodney Davenport, 211–26. Cape Town, South Africa: David Philips, 1997.
Prozesky, Martin, and John de Gruchy, eds. *Living Faiths in South Africa*. New York: St. Martin's, 1995.
Race, Alan. *Christians and Religious Pluralism*. London: SCM, 1983.
Randrianasolo, Joseph. "Christ and Ancestors in the African Context: A Lutheran Perspective." PhD diss., Lutheran School of Theology, 1991.
Ranger, T.O., and I. N. Kimambo, eds. *The Historical Study of African Religions*. Berkeley, CA: University of California Press, 1972.
Ranger, T. O., and John Weller, eds. *Themes in the Christian History of Central Africa*. Berkeley, CA: University of California Press, 1975.
Rasmussen, Anne Marie Bak. *Modern African Spirituality: The Independent Holy Spirit Churches in East Africa, 1902—1976*. London: British Academic, 1996.
Rattray, R. S. *Ashanti*. New York: Negro University Press, 1969.
Raum, O. F. "The Interpretation of the Nguni First Fruit Ceremony." *Paideuma; Mitteilungen zur Kulturkunde* 13 (1967) 148–63.
Ray, Benjamin C. *African Religions: Symbol, Ritual, and Community*. Englewood Cliffs, NJ: Prentice-Hall, 2000.
Reyburn, William D. "Conflicts and Contradictions in African Christianity." *Practical Anthropology* 4 (1957) 161–69.
Reyher, Rebecca Hourwich. *Zulu Woman*. New York: Columbia University Press, 1948.
Rigby, Peter. "Dual Symbolic Classification Among the Gogo of Central Tanzania." *Africa* 36, no. 1 (1966) 1–17.
Roberts, Esther L. *Shembe: The Man and His Work*. Edited by Robert Papini. Pretoria, South Africa: University of South Africa, 1963
Robertson, Roland, ed. *Sociology of Religion: Selected Readings*. Harmondsworth, UK: Penguin, 1969.
Rose, Brian A. "African and European Magic: A First Comparative Study of African Administration, Cultures, and Languages." *African Studies* 23, no. 1 (1964) 1–9.
Rynkiewich, Michael, A. "The Ossification of Local Politics: The Impact of Colonialism on a Marshall Islands Atoll." In *Political Development in Micronesia*, edited by Daniel T. Hughes and Sherwood Lingenfelter, 144–65. Columbus: Ohio State University Press, 1974.
Saayman, Willem, and Klippies Kritzinger, eds. *Mission in Bold Humility*. Maryknoll, NY: Orbis, 1996..
Samuelson, L. M. "Some Zulu Customs." *Journal of the African Society* 10 (1910) 191–99.
Sanders, E. P. *The Historical Figure of Jesus*. London: Allen Lane, 1993.
Sanneh, Lamin. *West African Christianity: The Religious Impact*. Maryknoll, NY: Orbis, 1997.
Sapir, Edward. *Language: An Introduction to the Study of Speech*. New York: Harcourt, Brace and World, 1921.
Schapera, Isaac. "Society and Witchcraft in Bechuanaland." *African Affairs* 41 (1952) 41–52.

Schrag, Rhoda M. "Kimbanguist Beliefs Taught in Zambia: Law, Jesus Christ, Simon Kimbangu: A Study of the Lusaka Congregation." *Mission Focus Annual Review* 2 (1994) 105–21.
Schreiter, Robert J. *Constructing Local Theologies*. Maryknoll, NY: Orbis, 1985.
———. *Faces of Jesus in Africa*. Faith and Culture Series. Maryknoll, NY: Orbis, 1991.
———. *Mission in the Third Millennium*. Maryknoll Press, NY: Orbis, 2001.
Schwarz, Hans. *Christology*. Grand Rapids: Eerdmans, 1999.
Scotch, N. A. "Magic, Sorcery, and Football Among Urban Zulu: A Case of Reinterpretation Under Acculturation." *The Journal of Conflict Resolution* 5, no. 1 (1961) 70–74.
Senior, Donald, and Carroll Stuhlmueller. *The Biblical Foundations for Mission*. Maryknoll, NY: Orbis, 1983.
Setiloane, Gabriel M., and Ivan H. M. Peden, eds. *Pangs of Growth: A Dialogue on Church Growth in Southern Africa*. Braamfontein, South Africa: Skotaville, 1988.
Shairp, J. C. *Culture and Religion: In Some of Their Relations*. Boston: Houghton, Mifflin, 1890.
Shank, David A., ed. *Ministry of Missions to African Independent Churches*. Elkhart, IN: Mennonite Board of Mission, 1987.
———. *Ministry in Partnership with African Independent Churches*. Elkhart, IN: Mennonite Board of Missions, 1991.
Sheils, Dean. "The Great Ancestors Are Watching: A Cross-Cultural Study of Superior Ancestral Religion." *Sociological Analysis* 41 (1980) 247–57.
Shembe, J. Galilee. *Izihlabelelo ZamaNazaretha*. Ekuphakameni, South Africa: n.p. 1940.
Shembe, Isaiah, Londa Shemba, and Irving Hexham, eds. "The Scriptures of the Ama-Nazaretha of EkuphaKameni." Translated by Hans-Jurgen. *Journal of African History* 37 (1993) 332–34.
———. *The Scriptures of the amaNazaretha of EkuphaKameni*. Calgary: University of Calgary Press, 1995.
Shenk, David W. *Global Gods: Exploring the Role of Religions in Modern Societies*. Scottdale, PA: Herald, 1996.
Shenk, Wilbert R. *Changing Frontiers of Mission*. American Society of Missiology Series 28. Maryknoll, NY: Orbis, 1999.
Shooter, J. *The Kafirs of Natal and the Zulu Country*. London: Stanford, 1857.
Shorten, Richard. "An Anglican Renewal Movement in Relation to Its Zulu Context." *Journal of Theology for Southern Africa* 58, no. 1 (2001) 32–40.
Shorter, Aylward, ed. *African Christian Spirituality*. Maryknoll, NY: Orbis, 1980.
———. *African Christian Theology: Adaptation or Incarnation?* London: Chapman, 1975.
———. *African Culture and the Christian Church: An Introduction to Social and Pastoral Anthropology*. London: Geoffrey Chapman, 1973.
———. *Prayer in the Religious Traditions of Africa*. Nairobi, Kenya: Oxford University Press, 1973.
———. *Priest in the Village: Experiences of African Community*. London: Chapman, 1979.
———. "Theology in a Multi-Cultural Church." *AFER* 20 (June 1978) 164–68.
Shropshire, Denys. "Bantu Conception of the Supra-Mundane World." *Journal of the African Society* 30 (1931) 58–68.
Sibisi, Harriet. "The Place of Spirit Possession in Zulu Cosmology." In *Religion and Social Change in Southern Africa*, edited by Michael G. Whisson and Martin West, 48–57. Cape Town, South Africa: David Philip, 1975.

Bibliography

Simbandumwe, Samuel S. *A Socio-Religious and Political Analysis of the Judeo-Christian Concept of Prophetism and Modern Bakongo and Zulu African Prophet Movements.* African Studies 28. Lewiston, NY: Mellen, 1992.

Simpson, E. K. *Commentary on the Epistle to the Ephesians and the Colossians.* New International Commentary on the New Testament. Grand Rapids: Eerdmans, 1957.

Smart, Ninian. *The Religious Experience of Mankind.* New York: Scribner, 1969.

Smith, Edwin W. *African Ideas of God: A Symposium.* London: Edinburgh House, 1966.

———. *The Christian Mission in Africa: A Study Based on the Work of the International Conference at Le Zoute, Belgium, September 14th to 21st, 1926.* Edinburgh: International Missionary Council, 1926

Snyder, Howard A. *Models of the Kingdom.* Nashville: Abingdon, 1991.

"Social Status." *Encyclopedia Britannica* [database online]. Available from *http://search.eb.com/article?eu*=70236; Internet; accessed 14 January 2004.

Spielberg, Fana, and Stuart Dauermann. "Contextualization: Witness and Reflection." *Missiology* 25 (1997) 15–35.

Spilhaus, M. Whiting. *South Africa in the Making 1652—1806.* Cape Town, South Africa: Juta, 1963.

Spradley, James P. *Participant Observation.* Fort Worth: Holt, Rinehart, and Winston, 1980.

Stanley, Brain. *Missions, Nationalism, and the End of Empire.* Grand Rapids: Eerdmans, 2003.

Stark, Rodney, and William Sims Bainbridge. *The Future of Religion: Secularization, Revival and Cult Formation.* Berkeley: University of California Press, 1985.

Stark, Rodney, and Roger Finke. *Acts of Faith: Explaining the Human Side of Religion.* Berkeley: University of California Press, 2000.

Stevenson, J., ed. *Creeds, Councils, and Controversies: Documents Illustrative of the History of the Church A.D. 337–461.* London: SPCK, 1966.

Stewart, Charles J., William B. Cash, Jr. *Interviewing: Principles and Practices.* 4th ed. Dubuque, IA: Brown, 1985.

Stine, Philip C., and Ernst R. Wendland, eds. *Bridging the Gap: African Traditional Religion and the Bible.* Reading, UK: IBS Monograph, 1990.

Stott, John, ed. *Making Christ Known: Historic Mission Documents from the Lausanne Movement, 1974–1989.* Grand Rapids: Eerdmans, 1996.

Strommen, Merton P. *Five Cries of Youth.* Rev. ed. San Francisco: Harper & Row, 1988.

Sundkler, B. G. M. *Bantu Prophets in South Africa.* 2nd ed. Oxford: Oxford University Press, 1961.

———. *The Christian Ministry in Africa.* Uppsala, Sweden: Almquist & Wiksells, 1959.

———. *Zulu Zion and Some Swazi Zionists.* London: Oxford University Press, 1976.

Swart, Morrell F. *The Call of Africa: The Reformed Church in America Mission in the Sub-Sahara, 1958–1998.* Grand Rapids: Eerdmans, 1998.

Swidler, Leonard, and Paul Mojzes. *The Uniqueness of Jesus: A Dialogue with Paul F. Knitter.* Faith Meets Faith. Maryknoll, NY: Orbis, 1997.

Taber, Charles R. "The Limits of Indigenization in Theology." *Missiology* 6 (1978) 53–79.

Tanner, Ralph E. S. *Transition in African Beliefs: Traditional Religion and Christian Change: A Study in Sukumaland, Tanzania, East Africa.* Maryknoll, NY: Maryknoll, 1967.

Taryor, Nya Kwiawon. *Impact of the African Tradition on African Christianity.* Chicago: The Strugglers' Community, 1984.

Taylor, John V. *The Primal Vision: Christian Presence Amid African Religion.* London: SCM, 1963.

———. *Process of Growth in an African Church*: I. M. C. Research Pamphlets, no. 6. London: SCM, 1958.
Temples, Placide. *Bantu Philosophy*. Translated by Colin King. Paris: Presence Africaine, 1959.
Theissen, Gerd. *The First Followers of Jesus: A Sociological Analysis of the Earliest Christianity*. Translated by John Bowden. London: SCM, 1978.
———. *Social Reality and the Early Christians: Theology, Ethics, and the World of the New Testament*. Translated by Margaret Kohl. Minneapolis: Fortress, 1991.
Thiselton, Anthony C. *New Horizons in Hermeneutics*. Grand Rapids: Zondervan, 1992.
Thomas, Linda E. *Under the Canopy: Ritual Process and Spiritual Resilience in South Africa*. Columbia: University of South Carolina, 1999.
Thomas, Norman E. "Images of Church and Mission in African Independent Churches." *Missiology* 23 (1995) 17–29.
Thompson, Jack. "Shembe Mismanaged? A Study of the Varying Interpretations of the Ibandla lamaNazaretha." *Bulletin of the John Rylands University Library of Manchester* 70 (Autumn 1988) 185–96.
Thompson, William M. "The Cosmic Christ in a Transcultural Perspective." *SLJT* 21, no. 1 (1978) 26–42.
Thorpe, S. A. *African Traditional Religions: An Introduction*. Pretoria: University of South Africa, 1991.
———. "The Call of the 'Shaman' in South-East Africa." *Journal for the Study of Religion* 20 (1990) 49–64.
Tomlinson, Richard, and Mark Addleson, eds. *Regional Restructuring Under Apartheid: Urban and Regional Policies in Contemporary South Africa*. Johannesburg, South Africa: Raven, 1987
Torres, Sergio, and Virginia Fabella, eds. *Emergent Gospel: Theology from the Underside of History*. Maryknoll, NY: Orbis, 1978.
Tracey, Hugh. "What are Mashaw Spirits?" *NADA: the Southern Rhodesia Native Affairs Department Annual* 12 (1934) 39–52.
Tshabala, M. Z. "Shembe's Hymn Book Reconsidered: Its Sources and Significance." MA thesis, Aberdeen University, 1983.
Turnbull, Colin. *The Lonely African*. New York: Simon & Schuster, 1962.
———. *Man in Africa*. Garden City, NY: Doubleday, 1976.
Turner, Edith. *Experiencing Ritual: A New Interpretation of African Healing*. Philadelphia: University of Pennsylvania Press, 1991.
Turner, Harold W. *African Independent Church*. Vol. 2. London: Oxford University Press, 1968.
———. *African Independent Church: The Life and Faith of the Church of the Lord (Aladura)*. Oxford: Claredon, 1967.
———. "African Prophet Movements." *The Hibbert Journal* 61, no. 242 (1963) 112–16.
———. "Bibliography of Modern African Religious Movements." *Journal of Religion in Africa* 7 (1967) 3.
———. *Bibliography on New Religious Movements in Primal Societies*. Boston: Hall, 1977.
———. "The Approach to Africa's Religious Movements." *African Perspectives* 2 (1976) 13–23.
———. *From Temple to House Meeting*. The Hague: Mouton, 1979.
———. *History of an African Independent Church: The Church of the Lord (Aladura)*. Oxford: Clarendon, 1967.

Bibliography

———. "Humanity's Common Religious Heritage: The Primal Religion of Tribal People." Speech given at the Assembly of the World's Religions, McAfee, NJ, November 15–21 1985.
———. *Living Tribal Religions*. London: Ward Lock Educational, 1968.
———. *Living Tribal Religions: An Introductory Survey of the Religious Life of Tribal Societies on a Thematic Basis*. London: Ward Lock Educational, 1971.
———. "A New Field in the History of Religions." *Religion: Journal of Religion and Religions* 1 (1971) 15–23.
———. "Pagan Features in West African Independnent Churches." *Practical Anthropology* 12, no. 4 (1965) 145–51.
———. *Profiles Through Preaching*. London: Edinburgh House, 1965.
———. *Religious Innovation in Africa: Collected Essays on New Religious Movements*. Boston: Hall, 1979.
———. *Religious Movements in Primal Societies*. Elkhart, IN: Mission Focus, 1989.
———. "Religious Movement in Primal (or Tribal) Societies." *Mission Focus* 9, no. 3 (1981) 45–55.
———. "The Religious Reactions of Primal Societies to Higher Cultures: A New Field in the History of Religions." Seminar on Christianity in the Non-Western World at the University of Aberdeen, Aberdeen, Scotland, 1970.
———. "Tribal Religious Movements, New." In *Encyclopedia Britannica*, 18:697–705. Chicago: Benton, 1976.
———. "A Typology for African Religious Movements." *Journal of Religion in Africa* 1, no. 1 (1967) 1–34.
———. "The Way Forward in the Religious Study of African Primal Religions." Center for the Study of New Religious Movements in Primal Religions, Birmingham, UK, 1990.
Turner, Victor. *Schism and Continuity in an African Society: A Study of Ndembu Village Life*. Manchester: Manchester University Press, 1971.
Twesigye, Emmanuel. *African Religion, Philosophy, and Christianity in Logos-Christ: Common Ground Revisited*. Theology and Religion 188. New York: Lang, 1996.
———. *Common Ground: Christianity, African Religion, and Philosophy*. Theology and Religion 25. New York: Lang, 1987.
Tyler, Josiah. *Forty Years Among the Zulus*. Boston: Congregational Sunday School and Publishing Society, 1891.
Ubah, C. N. "Religious Change Among the Igbo During the Colonial Period." *Journal of Religion in Africa/Religion en Afrique* 18, no. 1 (1988) 71–91.
United Nations Children's Fund. Available from *http://www.unicef.org*; Internet; accessed 2001.
Uzukwu, Elochuukwu Eugene. "The God of Our Ancestors and African Unity." *AFER* 23, no. 6 (1979) 344–52.
———. *A Listening Church: Autonomy and Communion in African Churches*. Maryknoll, NY: Orbis, 1976.
Van den Berghe, Pierre. *South Africa: A Study in Conflict*. Berkeley: University of California Press, 1963.
Van der Raaij, M. "An African Doctrine of God and Images of Christ." *Evangelical Review of Theology* 20 (1996) 233–39.
Van der Spuy, Roelie. "The Sickness of the Spirit: A White (South) African Perspective." *Journal of Theology for Southern Africa* 97 (1997) 62–67.

Bibliography

Vilakazi, Absolom, et. al. "Isonto LamaNazaretha: The Church of the Nazarites." Hartford Theological Seminary, 1954.

———. *Shembe: The Revitalization of African Society.* Johannesburg, South Africa: Skotaville, 1986.

Villa-Vicencio, Charles, and John W. De Gruchy. *Resistance and Hope: South African Essays in Honour of Beyers Naude.* Grand Rapids: Eerdmans, 1994.

Vorster, W. S., ed. *Building a New Nation: The Quest for a New South Africa.* Pretoria, South Africa: University of South Africa, 1991.

Waardenburg, Jacques. *Classical Approaches to the Study of Religion: Aims, Methods and Theories of Research: Introduction and Anthology.* New York: de Gruyter, 1999.

Wach, Joachim. *Sociology of Religion.* Chicago: University of Chicago Press, 1944

Walker, Eric A. *A History of Southern Africa.* London: Longmans, 1968.

Walker, Williston. *The History of the Christian Church.* 3d ed. Revised by Robert T. Handy. New York: Scribner, 1970.

Wallace, Anthony. "Revitalization Movements." *American Anthropologist* 58 (1956) 264–81

Walls, Andrew. "Bibliography of the Society for African Church History—I." *Journal of Religion in Africa* 1, no. 1 (1963) 46–94.

———. *The Missionary Movement in Christian History: Studies in the Transmission of Faith.* Maryknoll, NY: Orbis, 1996.

———. "Towards Understanding Africa's Place in Christian History." In *Religion in a Pluralistic Society*, edited by J. S. Pobee, 18–33. Lieden, The Netherlands: Brill, 1976.

Walshe, Peter. *Church Versus State in South Africa: The Case of the Christian Institute.* Maryknoll, NY: Orbis, 1983..

———. *Prophetic Christianity and the Liberation Movement in South Africa.* Pietermaritzburg, South Africa: Cluster, 1994.

Wambuta, Daniel N. "An African Christian Looks at Christian Missions in Africa." *Practical Anthropology* 17 (1970) 169–76.

Wan-Tatah, Victor. *Emancipation in African Theology: An Inquiry on the Relevance of Latin American Liberation Theology in Africa.* Theology and Religion 14. New York: Lang, 1989.

Watt, J. M., and N. J. V. Warmelo. "Medicines and Practices of a Sotho Doctor." *Bantu Studies* 4 (1930) 47–63.

Weber, Max. *The Sociology of Religion.* Translated by Ephraim Fischoff. Boston: Beacon, 1964.

Webster's New Collegiate Dictionary. Boston: Merriam, 1973.

Wendland, Ernst R. "Traditional Central African Religion." In *Bridging the Gap: African Traditional Religion and Bible Translation*, edited by Philip Stine and Ernst Wendland, 1–129. New York: United Bible Societies, 1990.

West, Martin. "The Shades Come to Town: Ancestors and Urban Independent Churches." In *Religion and Social Change in Southern Africa*, edited by Michael G. Whisson and Martin West, 185–206. Cape Town, South Africa: David Philip, 1975.

Westerlund, David. *African Religion in African Scholarship: A Preliminary Study of the Religious and Political Background.* Stockholm: Institute of Comparative Religion, 1984.

Westermann, Diedrich. *Africa and Christianity.* London: Oxford University Press, 1935.

———. *The African To-Day.* London: Oxford University Press, 1932.

Whisson, Michael G., and Martin West, eds. *Religion and Social Change in Southern Africa.* Cape Town, South Africa: David Philip, 1975.

Bibliography

Whiteman, Darrell L. "Contextualization: The Theory, the Gap, the Challenge." *International Bulletin of Missionary Research* 21, no. 1 (1997) 3–7.

———. "Contextualizing the Gospel." *Missiology* 25, no. 1 (1997) 3–4.

———. "The Cultural Dynamics of Religious Movements." In *Religious Movements in Melanesia Today*, edited by Wendy Flannery, 3. Goroka, Papua New Guinea: The Melanesian Institute for Pastoral and Socio-Economic Service, 1984.

———. *Melanesians and Missionaries: An Ethnohistorical Study of Social and Religious Change in the Southwest Pacific*. Pasadena, CA: William Carey Library, 1983.

———, ed. *Missionaries, Anthropologists, and Cultural Change: Studies in Third World Societies*. No. 25. Williamsburg, VA: Department of Anthropology, College of William and Mary, 1985.

Wild, Emma. "Is it Witchcraft? Is it Satan? It is a Miracle. Mai-mai Soldiers and Christian Concepts of Evil in North-east Congo." *Journal of Religion in Africa* 28 (1998) 450–67.

Willis, Geoffrey Grimshaw. *Saint Augustine and the Donatist Controversy*. London: SPCK, 1950.

Willoughby, W. C. *The Soul of the Bantu: A Sympathetic Study of the Magico-Religious Practices and Beliefs of the Bantu Tribes of Africa*. Garden City, NY: Doubleday, 1928.

Wilson, William J., ed. *The Church in Africa: Christian Mission in a Context of Change*. World Horizon Books. Maryknoll, NY: Maryknoll, 1963.

World Almanac and Book of Facts. New York: Simon & Schuster, 2003.

"Worship." *Encyclopedia Britannica* [database online]. Available from http://search.eb.com/eb/article?eu=117411; Internet; accessed 17 February 2004.

Wright, N. T. "Paul's Gospel and Caesar's Empire." In *Center of Theological Inquiry*, edited by Richard A. Horsley, 1–13. Harrisburg, PA: Trinity, 2000.

———. *What Saint Paul Really Said: Was Paul of Tarsus the Real Founder of Christianity?* Grand Rapids: Eerdmans, 1997.

Young, Josephine Peyton. "Boy Talk Critical Literacy and Masculinities." *Reading Research Quarterly* 35 (2000) 312–37.

Young, Josiah U. *African Theology: A Critical Analysis and Annotated Bibliography*. Westport, CT: Greenwood, 1993.

Zahniser, A. H. Mathias. "Islam and Judaism." Class notes from fall 1997 at Asbury Theological Seminary, Wilmore, KY.

———. *Symbol and Ceremony: Making Disciples Across Cultures*. Monrovia, CA: MARC, 1997.

Zeusse, Evan M. "Divination and Deity in African Religions." *History of Religions* 15 (1975) 158–82.

Zulu, A. H. "The South African Church in the Light of Ibadan, 1958." *The International Review of Missions* 67, no. 188 (1957) 377–85.

Zvarevashe, Ignatius M. "The Problem of Ancestors and Inculturation." *African Ecclesial Review* 29 (1984) 242–51.

———. "Shona Traditional Religion." *African Ecclesial Review* 22 (1979) 294–303.

Index

abavangeli, 90
African Baptist Church, xi, 89, 204
African Independent Churches, ix, xvi, 1, 2, 13, 26, 27, 61, 194, 202
    movement, 24
African Initiated Churches, 71, 79, 84, 95, 206
    movement, 77
AIC. *See* African Independent Churches and African Initiated Churches
African Methodist Episcopal Church, 70, 79
African traditional religion, ix, xii, 5, 23, 27, 28, 29, 30, 31, 34, 35, 36, 37, 39, 43, 45, 95, 215
African Zion Church, 1
Akan, 28, 29, 40, 41
Allen, Richard, 70
Amadhlozi, 51
amafundisi, 90
amaNazaretha Church, xi, xii, xiii, 2, 3, 4, 5, 6, 8, 9, 11, 12, 13, 14, 15, 16, 17, 18, 19, 20, 21, 22, 23, 24, 25, 26, 27, 28, 30, 31, 35, 46, 48, 49, 55, 57, 58, 59, 61, 76, 77, 79, 86, 87, 89, 92, 93, 96, 98, 100, 101, 103, 106, 110, 112, 115, 116, 118, 123, 124, 126, 127, 128, 139, 140, 141, 142, 143, 144, 145, 146, 156, 157, 162, 163, 164, 165, 166, 168, 169, 171, 172, 173, 175, 176, 177, 178, 183, 185, 186, 188, 189, 192, 193, 195, 196, 197, 199, 200, 201, 202, 203, 204, 205, 206, 207, 208, 209, 211
    three phases of, 26
amatonga, 50
ancestor
    as intercessor or mediator, xii, 6, 7, 8, 15, 23, 28, 36, 41, 43, 45, 48, 52, 83, 94, 95, 112, 113, 114, 121, 122, 123, 124, 127, 137, 140, 143, 162, 163, 165, 167, 169, 179, 183, 184, 185, 186, 192
    cult, 5, 41, 43, 44, 45, 52, 55, 93, 96, 116, 127
    role of, xii, 4, 5, 6, 8, 11, 15, 16, 17, 21, 22, 27, 28, 41, 42, 45, 48, 51, 52, 83, 93, 103, 104, 105, 106, 110, 112, 121, 122, 126, 139, 140, 142, 143, 163, 167, 169, 179, 183, 184, 185, 186, 187, 189, 208
    worship of, 2, 7, 8, 21, 22, 29, 42, 43, 44, 51, 93, 105, 112, 113
Anglican Church, 71, 193
apartheid, 1, 2, 49, 84, 85
    abolition of, 2
Apostolic Papers, 73
approach, dialogical. *See also* Nussbaum, Stan and Weaver, Edwin and Irene, 206
Ashanti, 36, 38
Azusa Street Revival, 72
Azusa movement, 73

Baba, 8, 129, 161, 165
Balia, Daryl M., 68, 69
Bantu, 39, 46, 47, 54, 59, 71, 80

Index

baptism, 3, 63, 64, 67, 72, 75, 97, 99, 134, 170
  spirit, 82
Baptist Church, 3, 193
Barrett, David B., 25, 59, 60, 62, 89, 90
Barth, Karl, 192
Beck, Roger B., 46
Becken, Hans-Jurgen, xi, 17, 25, 26, 150
Bediako, Kwame, xvii, 30
Being, 6, 36, 49, 50, 51, 143
  Supreme, Transcendent, 7, 19, 20, 28, 29, 35, 36, 37, 41, 43, 45, 47, 48, 49, 50, 51, 83, 96, 98, 131, 133, 143, 162, 163, 165, 166, 167, 168, 171, 184, 185, 186
belief system, 106, 169
  religious, xii
beliefs, xv, 17, 22, 27, 29, 34, 35, 49, 57, 58, 77, 79, 82, 89, 100, 113, 126, 139, 151, 156, 175, 182, 183, 190, 208
  and practices, 1, 7, 28, 30, 31, 32, 34, 35, 36, 45, 49, 75, 77, 79, 82, 83, 84, 86, 87, 91, 93, 103, 105, 117, 126, 127, 134, 139, 142, 143, 154, 156, 164, 173, 179, 182, 185, 186, 189, 191, 192, 193, 195, 196, 197, 202, 207, 209, 211
  religious, 2, 34, 78, 86, 179, 185
Berglund, Axel-Ivar, 48, 50
Beyerhaus, Peter, 78, 79
Bible, xix, 13, 14, 17, 49, 63, 67, 89, 90, 91, 92, 96, 97, 99, 120, 148, 149, 150, 151, 153, 161, 162, 165, 167, 174, 192, 193, 194, 195, 196, 200, 202, 204, 205, 206, 207, 209
black messiah, 15, 25, 63, 66, 78, 79, 80, 201
black messianism, 66, 80

Black Theology movement. *See also* theology, black, 67
Boot, Francis, 22, 52
Bosch, David J., 185, 198
Buchler, Johannes, 71, 72
Buhrmann, M. V., 179
Bujo, Benezet, 29

Calverton, V. F., 207, 208
  and cultural compulsives, 207, 208
ceremonies, 28, 40, 48, 55, 107, 110, 116, 178, 179, 182, 208
  healing, 20, 75, 156, 162
chief, 4, 26, 46, 54, 55, 68, 90, 95, 118, 124, 125, 147, 171
Christ. *See* Jesus Christ
Christian
  church, xi, 58, 66, 78, 80, 143, 160, 163, 193, 195, 202, 204, 211
  evangelical, 2, 3, 118
  movement, xi, 4, 62, 63, 64, 194, 197, 203
  non-African, ix
Christian Apostolic Church, 73
Christian Catholic Apostolic Holy Spirit Church of Zion, 73
Christian Catholic Church, 72
Christianity
  African indigenous, xii
  indigenous form of, 3
  orthodox, 2, 3, 98, 188
Christology, ix, xviii, xix, 5, 6, 17, 23, 30, 48, 66, 78, 79, 80, 82, 84, 140, 142, 144, 156, 162, 163, 164, 174, 178, 187, 189, 202, 206, 209
  African, xv, 23
Christward movement, xi, xii, 5, 6, 9, 12, 13, 14, 48, 139, 163, 188, 189, 193, 197, 202, 211
Church of the Lord, 192, 193, 202
civil rights era, 85
communion service. *See* service, communion

244

Index

Cone, James H., 84
Congregational Church, 71, 215
Congregationalists, 70
conversion, 13, 84, 170, 191
Cooper, Archibold H., 72
Council of Chalcedon, 211
Council of Constantinople, 211
Council of Nicaea, 211
cultural compulsives. *See also*
    Calverton, V. F., 207, 208
customs, xx, 4, 34, 55, 113, 183, 185, 195, 204

dance, 48, 65, 105, 116, 120, 146, 150, 179
Daneel, M. L., 1, 27, 41, 59, 60, 61, 62, 64, 65, 66, 71, 78, 81, 82
deity, 7, 43, 201
    Supreme, 47
democracy, 2
Dickson, Kwesi, 41
discipleship, xix, 3, 91, 164, 202, 204, 205, 206, 207, 208, 211
dissension, 1, 7
diviner. *See also isangoma*, 20, 44, 45, 50, 53, 55, 56, 57, 77, 180, 181
divinities, 5, 7, 28, 37, 38, 39, 43, 178
divinity, 15, 17, 36, 45, 50, 134, 136, 187
Donna, Beatrice. *See also* Vita, Kimpa, 67
Dowie, John Alexander, 72
Dube, John, 24
Durban, xv, 1, 6, 91, 101, 103, 120, 138, 146, 147, 154, 208
Dutch Reformed Church, 71, 72, 81, 85
Dwane, James M., 69, 70, 71
Dzobo, Noah, 39, 55

Ebuhleni, xiii, 4, 6, 8, 90, 92, 101, 111, 119, 124, 145, 146, 147, 150, 154, 156, 157, 158, 175, 180, 208
ecclesiology, ix, 87, 106

Ekuphakameni, 4, 9, 24, 87, 118, 120, 130, 131, 151, 153, 154, 155, 166, 175
Ela, Jean-Marc, 43
emic perspective, 32, 205
emsamo, 53, 95, 107, 108, 110, 111
enthronement passage, 15, 201
Ethiopian Church, 26, 64, 68, 69, 70, 71
Ethiopian-type churches, 62, 68
evangelicals, 2, 3, 118, 206
evangelists, 8, 76, 90, 92, 94, 102, 103, 106, 127, 145, 147, 156, 204, 205
exorcism, xi, 1, 82
extrinsic centered set, 12, 13, 191

faith
    Christian, xix, 1, 5, 12, 22, 45, 63, 78, 89, 100, 126, 127, 163, 164, 184, 188, 189, 190, 191, 193, 208
    three tenets of. *See also* Fee, Gordon, 184
faith-healing. *See* practices, faith-healing
fast, 65, 110, 146
Fee, Gordon D., 184
    and three tenets of Christian faith, 184
Firstfruits Celebration, 158
forgiveness, 6, 94, 114, 132, 166, 199
Fortes, M., 51
Free Scottish Presbyterian Church, 73

Geertz, Clifford, 32,
God
    kingdom of, 3, 79, 170
    truine, xviii, 7
Goody, Jack, 4
gospel, xi, xvii, xviii, xix, 30, 58, 64, 77, 78, 85, 100, 197, 198, 200, 202, 204, 205, 206
Greenslade, S. L., 192
Gunner, Elizabeth, 25, 88

Index

Hammond-Tooke, W. D., 54
Hauerwas, Stanley, 176
healing. *See also* ceremony, healing; and service, healing, xi, xvi, 1, 5, 6, 15, 20, 21, 30, 31, 39, 44, 45, 56, 57, 64, 65, 72, 74, 75, 76, 77, 81, 82, 84, 94, 97, 99, 121, 124, 127, 133, 137, 138, 139, 140, 142, 143, 149, 157, 161, 162, 173, 174, 175, 179, 192
Hebraist movement, 196, 202, 203
Heiler, Friedrich, 19, 184
    and primary and secondary prayers, 184
Hiebert, Paul G., 9, 12, 13, 14, 181, 188, 190, 191, 193
Hexham, Irving, xi, 10, 18, 88, 166, 171
Holiness Church, 65
Holy Catholic Apostolic Church, 73
Holy Spirit. *See also* umoya, xviii, xix, 14, 27, 30, 64, 65, 72, 75, 82, 88, 97, 98, 99, 123, 132, 133, 135, 148, 159, 160, 161, 162, 164, 169, 170, 194, 209, 211
    Shembe as, 96, 97, 98, 122, 123, 131, 132, 133, 134, 136, 141, 143, 148, 159, 162, 164, 169, 170, 176, 209
    represented by pillow, 97, 148
Hostetter, Darrel M., 29
hymn, 10, 15, 16, 18, 24, 25, 124, 125, 127, 149, 150, 151, 152, 155, 156, 162, 165, 175, 177, 185, 188
hymnbook. *See also* songbook, 9, 17, 18, 25, 124, 148, 149, 150, 156

idogolo, 146
Idowu, E. Bolaji, 7, 8, 28, 34, 35, 39, 43, 44
ifortini, 8
Igbo, 42, 43

illness, 5, 44, 56, 75, 76, 79, 94, 104, 107, 137, 138, 143, 157, 174, 179, 180, 183
impepho, 52, 95, 108, 109, 110, 111, 146
indigenous autonomous churches, 203, 204
indigenous churches, 57, 60, 86
intercession, xi, 5, 139, 163, 186, 188, 189
intrinsic bounded set, 12, 190
isangoma. See also diviner, 9, 20, 44, 56, 57, 93
isihlabelelo, 9
Isivivane, 145
Israel, xviii, xix, xx, 62, 63, 120, 126, 147, 168, 171, 197, 200
Izihlabelelo ZamaNazaretha, 149, 150, 151, 156, 165

Jackel, Theodor G., 76
January celebration, 145
Jehovah, 50, 125, 130, 131, 150, 151, 155, 162, 165, 166, 167, 168, 198
Jenkins, Philip, 59, 67
Jesus Christ
    and the healing of the blind man, 11, 20, 173, 175
    as Brother-Ancestor, 23, 187
    as healer, xviii, 142, 173
    as intercessor, xi, 5, 139, 163, 186, 188, 189
    ascension, 30, 97, 170, 173, 186
    death, 5, 30, 173, 178, 184, 185, 186, 188, 197, 198, 199
    enthronement, 15, 198, 201
    incarnation, 30, 171, 178
    mediatorial role, xi, 5, 139, 163, 184, 186, 188, 189
    resurrection, 5, 23, 30, 172, 173, 178, 185, 186, 188, 197, 198
    second coming, xi, 5, 72, 163, 170, 171, 188, 189

work of atonement, xi, 5, 163, 188, 189
Jewish laws or teachings, 3, 195, 196, 203
Judaism, 185, 195, 196
July celebrations, 92, 111, 146
justification, 192

Kaiser, Walter, 87
  and antecedent theology. *See also* theology, antecedent, 87
Karenga, Maulana, 8
Kiernan, J. P., 71, 75, 76
Kitshoff, Mike, 24, 25, 89
Kolie, Cece, 5
Koza, M. G., 73
Kraft, Charles H., 182
  and several forms, same meaning, 182
Krige, Eileen, 55
kugadzira, 41
Kuiper, B. K., 178
KwaZulu-Natal, xv, 17, 46, 49, 101, 103, 104, 106, 115, 164, 175

labola or *lobola,* 47, 115, 116
language, xi, 33, 46, 50, 54, 78, 88, 102, 121, 131, 177, 191, 192, 202, 207
Lea, Thomas D., 186
Lekganyane, Engenase (Ignatius) Barnabas, 73, 74, 75, 80, 81, 83
Le Roux, P. L., 71, 72, 73, 85
Leshega, William, 3
Levitical laws, 172, 195, 200
Lewis, Gavin, 2
life force, 55, 183
Lincoln, Andrew T., 201
linguistic drift. *See also* Sapir, Edward, 207, 208
living-dead, 28, 39, 45, 47, 51, 93, 94, 95, 96, 105, 108, 111, 112, 124, 129, 143, 175, 177, 181
Loubser, J. A., 16, 17, 176, 177

theory of orality. *See also* theory, 17
Lukhaimane, E. K., 76
Luthuli, Fred, 73

Mabilitsa, Paulo, 73
Magesa, Laurenti, 36
Mahlange, Elias, 73
Mahon, Edgar, 72
Marsh, John, 21
Mbiti, John, 19, 28, 29, 33, 34, 35, 38, 39, 45, 47, 51, 105, 111, 112, 121, 124
mediation
  asymmetrical, 19, 20
  symmetrical, 19, 20, 165, 166, 184
mediator. *See also mesites*, xviii, xx, 4, 5, 7, 15, 18, 19, 20, 21, 23, 25, 28, 37, 39, 41, 42, 45, 47, 65, 76, 80, 81, 83, 84, 94, 112, 122, 124, 127, 131, 143, 163, 165, 166, 168, 171, 172, 173, 178, 184, 185, 186, 187, 192, 201
mediatorship, 81
  question of, ix
medium, 20, 40, 42
memorial service. *See* service, memorial
mesites. See also mediator, 21
messiah, xviii, xix, 4, 15, 16, 18, 79, 80, 83, 127, 131, 185, 196, 198, 200
messianic-type churches, 64, 80, 84
method, Chronological Bible Story, 206
Methodism, 192
mfundisi, 8
Mindolo
  conference, 77, 80
  consultation, 65, 77
minister, 22, 69, 70, 71, 76, 84, 90, 91, 92, 94, 97, 102, 103, 104, 105, 106, 109, 112, 114, 118, 119, 121, 122, 123, 125, 127, 128, 130, 131, 132, 133, 135,

Index

minister (*continued*)
 136, 140, 141, 145, 147, 148, 149. 154, 157, 158, 159, 164, 168, 173, 181, 195, 204, 205, 208, 209
ministry, xviii, 3, 21, 65, 69, 70, 74, 87, 89, 168, 205
missiology, xii, 78, 189
mission
 Christian, ix, 143
 churches, 26, 59, 60, 61, 67, 68, 70, 71, 202
missionary, xi, 1, 16, 24, 30, 49, 50, 58, 68, 69, 71, 81, 85, 96, 154, 205
Mitchell, Robert C., 25
mkhokheli, 8
Mokone, Mangena, 69, 70
Moria, 74, 75, 81
Morris, Leon, 172, 173
Moses, xix, 120, 126, 138, 168, 171, 172
Motaung, Edward, 74
Mpanza, Mthembeni, xiii, 22, 88, 90, 96, 97, 103, 106, 118, 119, 122, 126, 134, 147, 148, 150, 158, 159, 160, 161, 176, 185, 186, 195, 203, 204
mshumayeli, 8, 90
Msimang, Daniel, 69
Mthethwa, B. N., 150
Muller, Carol, 25, 150
Muzorewa, Gwinyai H., 163
mvangeli, 8
Mwari, 41, 81

Nazarite, xvi, xviii, xx, 3, 4, 89, 104, 119, 127, 129, 133, 141, 143, 148, 185, 193, 195, 196, 199, 203
neo-pagan movement, 63
neo-primal movement, 14, 194, 202
new religious movement, xvi, xx, 13, 14, 16, 59, 61, 62, 160, 193, 202, 203, 204

New Testament, xvii, xix, 6, 14, 77, 143, 151, 176, 185, 192, 193, 194, 195, 196, 197, 198, 199, 200, 203, 204, 206
Nghlangakasi Mountain, 145, 158, 159
Ngubane, J. B., 54
Nguni, 46
Nida, Eugene A., 31, 77, 85
nikela, 93, 94, 95, 104, 110, 114, 115, 117, 120, 127, 129, 132, 136, 139, 149, 156, 162, 177
Nkonyane, Daniel, 73
Nkonyane, Stephen, 73
Nkosi, 90, 166, 167, 168
Nkulunkulu. *See also Unkulunkulu*, 166, 167, 168
 ka Shembe, 18
Nussbaum, Stan, 25, 206
 and the dialogical approach. *See also* Weaver, Edwin and Irene, 206
Nxumalo, Jabulani, 53
Nyamiti, Charles, 4, 5, 23, 84, 186, 187

Old Testament, xvii, xix, 3, 4, 14, 27, 63, 65, 89, 126, 143, 146, 148, 150, 151, 160, 162, 165, 167, 171, 172, 182, 183, 185, 186, 192, 193, 194, 195, 196, 197, 198, 199, 201, 203, 204, 206, 209
Ong, Walter, 17, 91
Oosthuizen, G. C., xi, xiv, 3, 4, 5, 16, 18, 20, 21, 22, 24, 25, 26, 27, 44, 50, 52, 55, 56, 57, 59, 65, 66, 78, 80, 93, 96, 127, 131, 165, 196, 204, 211
Ositelu, Gabriel, 61

Parrinder, Geoffrey, 39, 43, 47
Pentecostal, ix, 65, 72, 82
 Church, 65
 movement, 73

248

Philips, J. G., 73
pilgrimage, 26, 145
Placide Temples, 56
pneumatology, 82, 84, 143, 164, 195, 209
Pobee, John, 28, 29, 40, 48, 51, 61
post-Christian, 4, 59, 66, 78, 197, 203, 204
practices. *See also* beliefs and practices
    ancestral, 106
    cultural, 7, 83, 93, 100
    faith-healing, 72
    Jewish, 182, 186
    religiocultural, 21
    religious, xvi, 34, 55, 63, 67, 93, 121
    sociocultural, 63
    syncretistic, 1, 58
prayer, xv, xvi, 5, 8, 15, 16, 18, 19, 20, 21, 48, 50, 56, 65, 98, 99, 110, 111, 112, 122, 124, 125, 126, 127, 128, 129, 130, 131, 133, 138, 139, 140, 141, 146, 148, 150, 151, 153, 154, 155, 156, 160, 161, 162, 164, 165, 166, 167, 168, 169, 170, 171, 172, 173, 184, 189, 192
    experiential, 19, 166
    formal, 19, 166
    mat, 147, 148
    primary and secondary. *See also* Heiler, Friedrich, 184
    symmetrical, 171
preacher, xi, 8, 69, 70, 89, 90, 91, 92, 94, 102, 103, 106, 111, 127, 145, 147, 151, 153, 156, 176, 177, 204, 205, 206
preaching, 16, 17, 25, 67, 103, 127, 137, 149, 153, 159, 176, 177, 192, 193
Presbyterians, 70
priest, 6, 8, 23, 41, 55, 57, 63, 95, 124, 132

prophet, xv, xvii, xviii, xix, 23, 25, 26, 27, 63, 65, 74, 75, 76, 77, 80, 81, 83, 87, 88, 89, 132, 133, 135, 168, 196, 197
purgatory, 94, 117, 178

Ray, Benjamin, 35, 36, 38
reconciliation, 1, 5, 6, 132
regeneration, 192
religiocultural ethos, 4, 6, 32, 42, 93, 121, 195
religion
    primal, 14
    tribal, 202
Rhodes, Cecil John, 70
rites, 32, 41, 44, 178, 179, 181, 186
ritual, xviii, xix, 3, 28, 31, 32, 35, 41, 45, 51, 52, 55, 56, 63, 85, 89, 94, 95, 100, 107, 108, 115, 143, 175, 179, 181, 183, 184, 186, 208
Roberts, Esther L., 24, 26
Roman Catholic Church, 95, 178
Rynkiewich, Michael A., 4

Sabbatarians, 27, 146, 204
Sabbath. *See also* service, Sabbath
    liturgy or liturgical, 16, 147, 150, 156, 172, 185
    worship. *See also* worship, Sabbath, 97, 103, 147, 177
sacrament service. *See* service, sacrament
sacrifice, 15, 36, 40, 44, 52, 56, 93, 95, 107, 108, 109, 110, 111, 114, 115, 117, 127, 143, 179, 186
salvation, 15, 64, 65, 127, 130, 139, 143, 177, 178, 188, 191, 197,
    basis of, ix
sanctification, 191, 192
Sapir, Edward, 207, 208
    and "linguistic drift," 207, 208
Schlosser, Katesa, 26
Schreiter, Robert J., 204, 205

249

Index

secession, 1, 3, 26, 59, 68, 69, 71, 73
segregation, 2
    abolition of, 2
Senior, Donald, 198
sermon, 16, 17, 25, 64, 81, 87, 92, 98, 103, 145, 148, 149, 151, 152, 153, 156, 162, 175, 176, 177, 185, 193
service
    communion, 199, 208
    funeral, 53, 97, 208
    healing, 16, 22, 23, 156, 157
    liturgical, 16
    memorial, 208
    Sabbath, 15, 17, 18, 48, 90, 92, 124, 125, 126, 130, 137, 145, 146, 150, 151, 153, 154, 156, 162, 169, 175, 180, 200
    sacrament, 199, 208
    worship, 1, 25, 76, 92, 97, 103, 148, 157, 175, 177
Seventh-Day Adventist secession movement, 73
Shembe
    as Holy Spirit. *See also* Holy Spirit, Shembe as, 96, 97, 98, 122, 123, 131, 132, 133, 134, 136, 141, 143, 148, 159, 162, 164, 169, 170, 176, 209
    as intercessor or mediator, xii, xx, 7, 15, 18, 25, 80, 121, 127, 131, 132, 139, 163, 164, 166, 168, 169, 171, 172, 177, 178
    as messiah, 18, 127
    Church, 6, 30, 48, 58, 61, 90, 93, 95, 96, 97, 100, 106, 119, 136, 203
    Movement, ix, xvi, xvii, 160
    role of, xi, xii, 6, 16, 93, 132, 142, 163, 164, 177
Shembe, Amos, 3, 4, 6, 17, 20, 22, 25, 97, 122, 123, 127, 137, 149, 176
    death of, 4, 97, 127
Shembe, Galilee or J. G., 3, 17, 18, 20, 25, 26, 92, 96, 97, 101, 122, 123, 127, 130, 132, 137, 149, 150, 154, 159, 174, 176, 180, 196
    death of, 3, 26, 132
Shembe, Isaiah, xi, xv, xvi, xviii, xix, xx, 3, 4, 6, 7, 16, 17, 18, 20, 22, 24, 25, 26, 27, 30, 55, 57, 58, 61, 87, 88, 89, 91, 92, 95, 96, 97, 98, 118, 119, 122, 123, 127, 128, 131, 132, 133, 134, 135, 136, 137, 138, 142, 145, 146, 147, 148, 149, 150, 151, 153, 156, 159, 162, 165, 166, 167, 168, 169, 170, 171, 172, 174, 175, 176, 180, 181, 185, 193, 196, 201, 203, 204
    birth of, 87, 88, 97
    death of, xi, 3, 24, 26, 127, 168
    deification of, 16, 87, 96, 98, 136
Shembe, Lindewe, 103, 104, 105, 109
Shembe, Londa, 3, 4, 16, 18, 196
    murder of, 4, 18
Shembe, Vimbeni, xi, xii, xiii, 4, 6, 7, 15, 16, 17, 20, 21, 48, 55, 57, 76, 87, 90, 91, 95, 97, 98, 100, 101, 103, 122, 123, 125, 127, 128, 130, 131, 132, 133, 134, 135, 136, 137, 138, 139, 140, 141, 142, 145, 147, 149, 150, 153, 154, 155, 156, 157, 158, 159, 162, 163, 164, 165, 168, 169, 170, 174, 175, 176, 177, 182, 187, 192, 193, 195, 200, 204, 205, 208
    interview with, 21, 103, 145, 157, 158, 159, 160, 161, 162
Shona, 1, 27, 41, 42, 81
    Zion Church, 60, 81
Shooter, Joseph, 49
Shorter, Aylward, 19, 165, 171, 184
    and symmetrical mediation, 20, 165, 166, 171, 184

typology of African prayer, 19, 165, 171, 184
Simpson, E. K., 201
sin, 52, 65, 78, 82, 94, 97, 110, 114, 118, 125, 128, 131, 135, 136, 155, 166, 172, 177, 178, 189, 198, 199
singing, 1, 17, 105, 148
Snyder, Howard A., 170
socioreligious system, 4, 32
Son of God. See also Jesus Christ, 6, 82, 98, 99, 209, 211
songbook, 131
  liturgical, 18, 90, 126, 149, 162
Soshanguve Zionists, 82
Sotho, 46, 74
spirit. See Holy Spirit
spirit baptism. See baptism, spirit
Spirit-type churches, 64, 65
spirits, 4, 5, 20, 28, 30, 31, 35, 36, 39, 42, 44, 45, 47, 50, 51, 52, 53, 56, 69, 76, 121, 180, 194
stories, 35, 87, 88, 89, 91, 92, 96, 97, 98, 99, 101, 102, 103, 104, 105, 106, 109, 110, 111, 118, 119, 120, 128, 129, 131, 136, 137, 138, 151, 153, 161, 174, 176, 177
Sundkler, B. G. M., 24, 25, 26, 58, 59, 62, 64, 68, 72, 73, 78, 79, 80
Swazi, 29, 46
symbols, 8, 32, 35, 42, 43, 51, 55, 75, 85, 109, 134, 146, 148, 149, 182, 183
Synthesist movement, 202, 203

Taryor, Nya Kwaiwon, 59
Taylor, John V., 35, 36
Tembu, 68
  politics, 68
  tribe, 68
  Church, 68, 69
  political protest movement, 68
temple, 8, 75, 90, 92, 94, 96, 97, 111, 125, 133, 138, 147, 148, 149, 153, 154, 156, 158, 162, 201, 208
Ten Commandments, 172
theism
  relative, 19, 20
  strict, 19, 20
theology, xiii, xv, xvi, xvii, xviii, xix, xx, 18, 24, 30, 71, 77, 79, 82, 84, 86, 87, 98, 106, 127, 135, 144, 162, 163, 164, 177, 178, 185, 205
  African Christian, xvii
  antecedent. See also Kaiser, Walter, 87, 145
  black, 67, 84, 95
  Christian, ix, xix, 143, 187
theoretical framework, 9, 189
theory, 13, 16, 17, 18, 20, 22, 25, 97, 165, 190
Thixo, 166, 167
Thorpe, S. A., 52
ticket, release, 94, 149, 177, 178
Tile, Nehemiah Xoxo, 26, 68, 89
tithing, 65
Torah, 204
Trinity, xviii, 97, 98, 123, 143, 164, 165, 169, 187, 203, 209, 211
Tsonga, 46, 74
Turnbull, Colin, 31
Turner, H. W., 13, 14, 25, 26, 27, 59, 60, 61, 62, 63, 64, 65, 70, 78, 188, 192, 193, 194, 195, 196, 197, 202, 203, 204, 207
  four-part classification of new religious movements. See also theory, 13, 14, 27, 188, 194, 202
  revision of, 202, 203

ukubuyisa idloza, 52
uMninimandla, 50
umoya. See also Holy Spirit, 1, 75
uMvelinqangi, 49, 50
Unkulunkulu. See also Nkulunkulu, 1, 49, 50, 51, 131, 133

251

Index

uSomandla, 50
Utikxo, 50
uumbwardo, 40

Vaseline, 149, 156, 161, 173, 174
  and water, 138, 139, 156, 157, 161, 173, 174, 175
Venda, 46, 74
veneration. *See also* worship, 7, 8, 28, 29, 42, 43, 44, 65, 80, 93, 105, 112, 151
visions, 3, 27, 88, 145, 170
Vita, Kimpa. *See also* Donna, Beatrice, 67

Walls, Andrew, 61, 86
Warren, Max, 86
Weaver, Edwin and Irene, 206
  and the dialogical approach. *See also* Nussbaum, Stan, 206
Wendland, Ernst R.
  the centrality of religion in African life, 32
  facets that make up African Religion, 33
  hierarchical structure of the spirit world, 37
Wesley, John
  and the doctrine of Christian perfection, 192
Wesleyan Church, xi, 3, 68, 89, 204
Wesleyan Methodist Church, 68
West, Martin, 52
Westermann, Diedrich, 59
white gown, 104, 105, 109, 120, 153, 154, 180
Whiteman, Darrell L., 181, 202, 207
Wilson, Monica, 52
worldview, 5, 20, 22, 23, 28, 30, 33, 35, 37, 42, 46, 52, 56, 60, 77, 83, 86, 87, 113, 183
worship, xv, xvi, 1, 2, 3, 7, 8, 14, 15, 20, 25, 28, 36, 42, 43, 44, 50, 51, 60, 64, 65, 93, 96, 103, 105, 112, 118, 126, 147, 148, 149, 150, 158, 165, 170, 171, 175, 177, 184, 194, 200
Sabbath. *See also* Sabbath worship, 97, 143, 147, 177, 195, 200
Wright, N. T., 14, 15, 197, 198, 199, 200

Yoruba, 37, 38
Young, Josiah U., 25

Zahniser, A. H. Mathias, 32, 37, 183
Zion Apostolic Church, 73
Zion Apostolic Faith Mission, 73
Zion Christian Church, xii, 71, 73, 74, 75, 76, 77, 82, 86, 90, 110, 195, 207
Zion City Church, 59
Zionism, 76, 80
Zionist Church, 73, 82
Zionist movement, 71, 72, 73, 77, 85
Zulu traditional religion, xii, 30, 31, 34, 50, 57, 95, 118, 183, 195, 196

www.ingramcontent.com/pod-product-compliance
Lightning Source LLC
Chambersburg PA
CBHW050345230426
43663CB00010B/1990